ALFRED NORTH WHITEHEAD
Essays on His Philosophy

Edited and with an Introduction By
George L. Kline

UNIVERSITY
PRESS OF
AMERICA

Copyright © 1989 by

University Press of America,® Inc.

4720 Boston Way
Lanham, MD 20706

© Copyright 1963 by Prentice-Hall, Inc.

Library of Congress Cataloging-in-Publication Data

Alfred North Whitehead : essays on his philosophy / edited, and with an
introduction, by George L. Kline.
p.   cm.
Includes bibliographies and idnex.
1. Whitehead, Alfred North, 1861–1947. I. Kline, George Louis, 1921–
B1674.W354A63   1989   192—dc20   89–33904 CIP

ISBN 0–8191–7283–9 (pbk: alk. paper)

All University Press of America books are produced on acid-free paper.
The paper used in this publication meets the minimum requirements of American
National Standard for Information Sciences—Permanence of Paper for Printed Library
Materials, ANSI Z39.48–1984.   ∞

Preface To The University Press Of America Edition

Although this book has been out of print for some time, in this twenty-fifth anniversary of its original publication (in 1963) it enjoys a modest but steady demand among the growing number of students of process thought generally and of the thought of Alfred North Whitehead in particular. I therefore welcome the reprinting which the University Press of America has agreed to undertake.

The reprint edition differs from the original in several limited but significant respects:

—The list of "Corrigenda for *Process and Reality*" which occupied pp. 200-207 of the 1963 edition has been omitted, since these, as well as numerous other, corrections were incorporated in the Corrected Edition of *Process and Reality*, edited by David Ray Griffin and Donald W. Sherburne (New York: Macmillan/Free Press, 1978).

—The penultimate paragraph of the Preface to the first edition (p. vi), concerning a projected series of volumes to be made up of articles drawn chiefly from the *Journal of Philosophy*, has been omitted, since the plan for such a series was not in fact carried out.

—A number of misprints, inconsistencies, and minor errors, including certain inaccuracies in direct quotations, have been carefully corrected.

—Consideration was given to updating the biographical sketches under the rubric "Contributors," but it was finally decided that this would have been misleading. The authors of the various chapters of this book wrote them either just before or some time before 1963. Thus it seemed most appropriate to leave the accounts of their professional careers as they stood then rather than as updated to 1988. It did, however, seem fitting, and important, to note that in the interim five of the contributors have died. These are: Mason W. Gross (1911-1977), William Ernest Hocking (1873-1966), Nathaniel Lawrence (1917-1986), Victor Lowe (1907-1988), and Daniel D. Williams (1910-1973).

May this new printing of the book to which they contributed so richly stand, in part at least, as a memorial to their life and work.

George L. Kline
December 13, 1988

Preface

The eighteen essays which make up this volume share a common concern with the thought of Alfred North Whitehead; they differ with respect to the date and circumstances of their composition.

The first and largest group (eight papers) consists of articles written for a special Whitehead Centennial Issue of the *Journal of Philosophy* (Vol. 58, No. 19: September 14, 1961). This group includes the papers by V. C. Chappell, Lucio Chiaraviglio, William A. Christian, William Ernest Hocking, Nathaniel Lawrence, Hugues Leblanc, Ivor Leclerc, and Robert M. Palter. Chiaraviglio's paper has been retitled and substantially enlarged. The papers by Lawrence, Leblanc, and Palter have been slightly revised. The remaining papers of this group are reprinted without change.

The second group (five papers) represents a selection from among the many articles on Whitehead published by the *Journal of Philosophy* over the past thirty-odd years. This group, ranging in date of original publication from 1930 to 1959, includes the papers by Mason W. Gross, Everett W. Hall, J. W. Robson, Gregory Vlastos, and Daniel D. Williams. Robson's paper has been slightly abridged; the other papers are reprinted in full. In all cases references to Whitehead's works have been simplified and standardized, using the abbreviations now generally accepted by Whitehead scholars (e.g., SMW for *Science and the Modern World*—see complete listing in "Sources").

The last group (five papers) is made up of articles written for this volume and not previously published. This group includes the papers by Charles Hartshorne, Victor Lowe, Ralph V. Norman, Jr., Richard M. Rorty, and Donald W. Sherburne.

In this volume the papers are arranged not by date of composition or publication, but systematically by topic. They fall into four broad groupings: Part I, "Whitehead as Man and Thinker"; Part II, "Logic, Mathematics, and Methodology"; Part III, "Metaphysics and Cosmology"; and Part IV, "Ethics, Aesthetics, and Philosophical Theology." Within each of these parts, individual papers are arranged alphabetically by author. The place and date of original publication of the reprinted papers, and the extent of revisions (if any), are indicated in footnotes on their respective title pages. The concluding section of the volume (Part V, "Documents and Materials") contains a hitherto unpublished letter from Whitehead to Hartshorne and a list of Corrigenda for *Process and Reality.*

Albert William Levi's paper, "Substance, Process, Being" (*Journal of Philosophy,* 55 [1958], 749-761) was to have been included (in Part III), but unfortunately had to be omitted for reasons of space.

Thanks are due to the publishers mentioned in the "Sources" (below) and in various footnotes for permission to quote from copyrighted materials.

George L. Kline

The Journal of Philosophy was founded by F. J. E. Woodbridge and Wendell T. Bush. Its present editors are John H. Randall, Jr., Robert D. Cumming, George L. Kline, Sidney Morgenbesser, and Leigh S. Cauman.

Sources

Throughout this volume Whitehead's principal works are referred to by means of the following standard abbreviations. For the convenience of students and interested readers, the names of publishers of American paperback editions of Whitehead's works are given in parentheses following the appropriate entries.

AE *The Aims of Education and Other Essays*. New York: The Macmillan Company, 1929. (New American Library.)

AI *Adventures of Ideas*. New York: The Macmillan Company, 1933. (New American Library.)

CN *The Concept of Nature*. Cambridge: At the University Press, 1920. (Ann Arbor Books.)

ESP *Essays in Science and Philosophy*. New York: Philosophical Library, 1948. (Wisdom Library—under the title *Science and Philosophy*.) The edition of 1948, but not that of 1947, contains the important paper, "Uniformity and Contingency."

FR *The Function of Reason*. Princeton University Press, 1929. (Beacon Press.)

MT *Modes of Thought*. New York: The Macmillan Company, 1938. (Capricorn.)

PM *Principia Mathematica* (with Bertrand Russell). Cambridge: At the University Press, 3 vols. (PMI, PMII, PMIII), 1910-1913.

PNK *An Enquiry Concerning the Principles of Natural Knowledge*. Cambridge: At the University Press, 1919; second ed., 1925.

PR *Process and Reality*. New York: The Macmillan Company, 1929. (Harper Torchbooks.)

R *The Principle of Relativity*. Cambridge: At the University Press, 1922.

RM *Religion in the Making*. New York: The Macmillan Company, 1926. (Meridian Books.)

SMW *Science and the Modern World*. New York: The Macmillan Company, 1925. (New American Library.)

Example: 'PR 32' means "page 32 of *Process and Reality*"; the only exception is *An Enquiry Concerning the Principles of Natural Knowledge,* where reference is not to pages but to the continuously numbered sections, e.g., 'PNK 9.5.'

NOTE: A useful one-volume edition of selections from all of Whitehead's major works is *Alfred North Whitehead: An Anthology:* edited by F. S. C. Northrop and Mason W. Gross, New York: The Macmillan Company, 1953. (Macmillan paperback, 1962.)

Contents

ix

Part V. Documents and Materials

Introduction

The studies in this volume have as their aim a clarification, criticism, and theoretical development of some of the central philosophical ideas and insights of Alfred North Whitehead (1861-1947), a thinker recognized even by his intellectual opponents as one of the most sensitive, original, and systematic minds of the first half of this century.

In the decade and a half since his death, Whitehead's thought has been studied with growing interest and seriousness. At least a dozen careful book-length studies of his philosophy have appeared in English (six of them by contributors to the present volume), and more than half a dozen in foreign languages. Chapters or sections of another fifty-odd books—more than thirty of them in languages other than English, including such exotic tongues as Russian and Japanese—have been devoted to Whitehead's thought. The total number of articles on Whitehead in English and American journals probably exceeds a hundred; in addition, there are forty-odd articles in foreign journals, ranging from French and German to Welsh and Slovak.

Whitehead's works have been more extensively translated than those of any other twentieth-century philosopher writing in English, with the possible exception of his one-time pupil and subsequent collaborator, Bertrand Russell. *Science and the Modern World,* Whitehead's best known work, has been published in Dutch, French, German, Italian, Japanese, Korean, and Spanish.[1] In recent years, paperback publication, notably in the United States and the United Kingdom, has made available to a broad reading public an impressive range of Whitehead's philosophical writings, including *The Concept of Nature, Science and the Modern World, Religion in the making, Process and Reality, The Function of Reason, Adventures of Ideas, Modes of Thought,* and *Essays in Science and Philosophy.*

All of the contributors to the present volume would, I think, agree that this strong current interest in Whitehead's philosophy is both justified and desirable. But they would and do differ about the relevance or validity of specific Whiteheadian positions. For example, Whitehead's theory of forms or "eternal objects" is searchingly criticized by Everett W. Hall—in one of the first competent and serious evaluations of *Process and Reality* to appear in print (1930); V. C. Chappell sees basic difficulties in Whitehead's "epochal" theory of becoming, as does Richard

1

M. Rorty with respect to Whitehead's theory of actual entities. The reader
will find in this volume neither uncritical praise nor impatient rejection
of Whitehead's thought. All of the contributors have been at great pains to
understand what Whitehead was trying to say; they have employed to
that end close (if not narrowly "analytic") philosophical analyses, making use of fresh distinctions and, in some cases, novel terminology and
notation.

For example, William A. Christian makes a useful "metatheoretical"
distinction between "presystematic," "systematic," and "postsystematic"
types, or levels, of discourse in Whitehead's writings. He argues that such
speculative systems as Whitehead's are constructed in order to "throw
light on the facts" by making postsystematic statements possible. Postsystematic discourse has a factual or empirical reference; postsystematic
statements are used to interpret the "facts" or "items of experience"
which have been stated and described in presystematic terms. In contrast, systematic statements as such do not refer to items of experience,
but to items—terms and relationships—within the philosopher's systematic scheme.[2]

By means of the distinction between presystematic, systematic, and
postsystematic discourse, many apparent confusions and inconsistencies
in Whitehead's thought can be shown to be verbal and superficial rather
than substantive and systematic.[3] To be sure, such attempts to separate
Whitehead's "logic" from his "poetry" involve risks as well as gains at
the level of understanding and interpretation. (Victor Lowe has been
especially sensitive to the risks.) But when carried out with tact and
restraint, they can—it seems to me—be genuinely illuminating.

Whitehead's relation to his philosophic forebears—a topic which he
himself discussed perceptively and at length—is touched upon in a number of these papers: Nathaniel Lawrence explores the relationship to
Plato; Ivor Leclerc that to Leibniz; Mason Gross and J. W. Robson
that to Hume; Gregory Vlastos that to Hegel. In my own judgment, the
comparison with Hegel needs further exploration. In 1931, at a Harvard
banquet in honor of his seventieth birthday, Whitehead noted, in response to critical comments, that, although he had never read much
Hegel, he had known and been influenced by several of the leading
British Hegelians, including McTaggart, Lord Haldane, and Bradley.
"Lack of first-hand acquaintance," Whitehead modestly added, "is a
very good reason for not endeavoring in print to display any knowledge
of Hegel."[4] This is doubtless the reason why Whitehead so seldom refers
to Hegel in his own writings, even when he is making his most Hegelian
points. For he went on to observe, "It is true that I was influenced by
Hegel."[5] The influence is obvious and pervasive; but the tracing of it
will require philosophic persistence.

Preliminary to any detailed comparison of Hegel and Whitehead
would be a close study of their respective terminologies. Although

Whitehead followed Hegel in stretching certain old terms to embrace new—and, to some readers, confusing—meanings (cf. his use of 'feeling' and Hegel's use of '*Aufhebung*'), Whitehead's terminology is generally un-Hegelian, even anti-Hegelian. Both Whitehead and Hegel use the terms 'abstract' and 'concrete' in systematic ways; but they give the terms very different meanings. The sense in which Hegel uses 'concrete' (which we might identify, a bit awkwardly, as 'concrete$_H$') is equivalent to 'many-sided, adequately-related, complexly-mediated'; the sense in which Whitehead uses 'concrete' ('concrete$_W$') is equivalent to 'experient' or 'self-significant'.[6] Only actualities are concrete$_W$, whereas forms and universals may be concrete$_H$ (cf. Hegel's 'concrete universal').

'Abstract' for Hegel ('abstract$_H$') means 'non-concrete$_H$', that is to say, 'one-sided, inadequately related, unmediated'; 'abstract' for Whitehead ('abstract$_W$') means 'non-concrete$_W$', that is to say, 'non-experient' or 'non-self-significant' (having significance only for another). Thus, though forms and universals are necessarily abstract$_W$, they may—as we have seen—be concrete$_H$. Immediate experience, on the other hand, is concrete$_W$ but abstract$_H$ (cf. Hegel's 'abstract immediacy'). This does not, of course, mean that for Whitehead immediate experience is without form. Rather, it means that an experient actual entity (which is concrete$_W$) actualizes or enacts a form (which is abstract$_W$); and that the resulting unified "actualization-of-a-form," though it includes an abstract$_W$ element, is itself concrete$_W$.

Systematic completeness would require a further distinction: between 'concrete$_W$' in the strict sense as applied to the (non-repeatable) *process* of an actual entity's self-functioning—what Whitehead calls a "concrescence"—and 'concrete$_W$' in a derivative sense as applied to the (repeatable) *product* of such self-functioning—what might be called a "*concretum.*" [7]

Finally, 'concrete$_W$' (but not necessarily 'concrete$_H$') would appear to be an all-or-none predicate, even though 'abstract$_W$' (if not 'abstract$_H$') might possibly be quantifiable as "more-or-less." Yet Whitehead himself often uses expressions like 'more concrete' and 'most concrete'; and many of his commentators and critics have continued this usage. No one, to my knowledge, has yet sifted the texts to determine whether such expressions occur primarily in "systematic" discourse, or whether—as seems to me more likely—they are confined (at least for the most part) to Whitehead's "presystematic" and "postsystematic" utterance.

Whitehead has said that his philosophy is "in the main" a "recurrence to pre-Kantian modes of thought" (PR vi). This remark has generally, and I think correctly, been taken to refer to his realistic epistemology and "monadistic" cosmology. The major pre-Kantian influence in these areas stems from Plato and Leibniz, respectively. But Whitehead also recurs to "pre-Kantian modes of thought" in his ethics, and this recurrence has not been sufficiently noticed. If Kant's epistemology and ethics be taken, as they traditionally have been taken, as points of reference, it might be said that Whitehead recurs to a "pre-epistemological" position in his theory of experience and to a "pre-ethical" position in his theory of value. In any case, Whitehead, like Hegel, wrote no treatise on ethics, although—again like Hegel—he wrote treatises in virtually all of the other traditional fields of philosophy—logic, metaphysics, cosmology, philosophy of mathematics, philosophy of civilization, philosophy of religion, and (what is not quite the same) philosophical theology.

Hegel is a post-Kantian in ethics, Whitehead a pre-Kantian; both are decisively anti-Kantian. Hegel tries to absorb Kant's autonomous moral agent into the self-propelling historical dialectic of a collective *Kultur*. He sees Kantian ethics as unhistorical, bleakly "abstract$_H$", general to the point of vacuity. Whitehead's objection to Kantian ethics is not so much historical as *aesthetic*; he is uncomfortable with Kant's normativism and "rigorism," the stubborn emphasis upon duty and rightness to the exclusion not only of interest and impulse—what Kant called "Sinnlichkeit"—but also of value and the good. Central to Whitehead's theory of value is a blending of aesthetic and moral categories (kept rigidly separate by Kant) into something very close to the classical Greek conception of the "nobly fair"—"τό καλόν."

It is a narrowly Kantian type of ethics that Nathaniel Lawrence has in mind when he writes: "Where mere morality obtains, only the forbidden and the forbidding or else the compulsive and barren sense of duty operate." [8] Professor Donald Meiklejohn reports Whitehead's reaction to Meiklejohn's Harvard dissertation of 1936—an essay in Kantian ethics: "But, Mr. Meiklejohn, don't you have a place for kindly, gentle, or affectionate feelings?" "Yes, Professor Whitehead, but not in ethical theory." [9]

Even the most careful effort to determine precisely what Whitehead meant leaves us with open questions—questions about the internal consistency and coherence of his speculative system, and questions about its relevance and adequacy as an interpretation of pre- and post-philosophical experience. The essays in this volume give no final answers to such questions. The contributors differ among themselves about the value of essential elements of Whitehead's system. As we have seen, some of them—beginning with Everett Hall, and including such distinguished Whitehead scholars as Charles Hartshorne and Victor Lowe, have suggested that Whitehead's metaphysics might profitably be "de-Platonized" by eliminating the category of "eternal objects." Hall and Hartshorne feel that such elimination would leave Whitehead's system substantially intact, but Victor Lowe feels that the resulting system would be only "half-Whiteheadian." (Lucio Chiaraviglio's approach is more formal, though equally anti-Platonic: he attempts to reinterpret eternal objects in terms of sets of actual entities, using the technical resources of contemporary set theory.) Other scholars, including William Christian, have argued that eternal objects, as "pure potentials for definiteness," are not categoreally expendable; that without them neither the novelty nor the individuality of actual occasions, nor their causal interaction, could be systematically accounted for. Obviously, the last word in this dispute is still to be spoken.

Similar remarks are relevant to the "naturalization" of Whitehead's cosmology (eliminating God as the ground of the relationship between actual occasions and eternal objects), a project which has been suggested by Victor Lowe, though not favored by Charles Hartshorne or William Christian. Whitehead's "epochal" theory, which postulates the atomic or discrete (non-continuous) becoming of temporally unextended and indivisible "quanta of process" raises thorny questions. But part of the difficulty uncovered by Chappell's vigorous analysis of the epochal theory of becoming could, I think, be removed by distinguishing between *past* actual entities, which *are,* and *present* actual entities, which are *not,* temporally divisible.

Many other open questions might be mentioned, for example: the "ground" of the "givenness of the past," here explored by William Christian; the justification of induction, debated by Mason Gross and J. W. Robson; the nature of moral obligation and personal responsibility, examined by Donald W. Sherburne and Daniel D. Williams; the role of mathematics in Whitehead's thought, discussed by Ralph V. Norman, Jr. and Robert M. Palter.

It may not be amiss, in conclusion, to add a word about Whitehead's style. The prevailing loose talk about the "obscurity" and "opacity" of Whitehead's philosophic idiom is reduced to proper perspective by two informed and sensible commentators who stand a generation apart: (1) William Wightman remarked in 1961 that "any philosophic work which is both crystal clear and free from internal inconsistencies is so, either because it is merely restating in a clearer form what has already been labored by more creative minds, or because it is dodging the real difficulties." [10] (2) In 1935 Samuel Alexander (in a note that remained unpublished until 1947) declared: "[Whitehead's] books are difficult, but their difficulty arises from their subject and not from his exposition. His writing is never obscure and his technicalities, which were often complained of, though not always happy, were inevitable. . . . He possessed an admirable literary style, vivid and arresting and pregnant." [11]

If the essays in this volume are of help to students of philosophy in their effort to understand Whitehead's "vivid, arresting, and pregnant" —though sometimes difficult—books; if they stir readers, and rereaders, of those books to a fresh examination of Whitehead's problems—most of which are "problems of men," generated by the concerns of art, science, religion, social life, and common sense, and not just "problems of philosophers," generated by rumination on books about books—then this volume will have served its purpose.

Notes

[1] For details see my "Bibliography of Writings by and about Alfred North White-head in Languages Other than English," in a forthcoming *Festschrift* for Charles Hartshorne (edited by William L. Reese and Eugene Freeman), (Lasalle, Illinois: Open Court, 1963).

[2] William A. Christian, "Some Uses of Reason," in Ivor Leclerc, ed., *The Relevance of Whitehead* (London: George Allen and Unwin, Ltd.; New York: The Macmillan Company, 1961), pp. 76-77. Whitehead's systematic scheme includes not only the "categoreal scheme"—set forth in Pt. I, ch. II, of *Process and Reality*—but also its systematic elaboration, including "derivative" as well as "categoreal" notions.

[3] See William A. Christian, *An Interpretation of Whitehead's Metaphysics* (New Haven: Yale University Press, 1959), p. 3.

[4] *Symposium in Honor of the Seventieth Birthday of Alfred North Whitehead* (Cambridge: Harvard University Press, 1932), p. 25. (Reprinted in ESP, p. 88.)

[5] *Loc. cit.*

[6] But since for Whitehead the experient, or self-significant, actual entity is related in a perfectly definite way—through positive and negative prehensions—to every other item in the universe, the meaning of 'concrete$_W$' might be said to include that of 'concrete$_H$', though the converse does not hold. Victor Lowe has pointed out (in a letter to the present editor, December 13, 1962) that Whitehead in effect attempted to do justice "both to the tradition which identifies the concrete with the present drop of immediate experience and to the tradition which identifies it with fullness of relationships."

[7] Cf. "Genetic division is division of the concrescence; coordinate division is division of the concrete [i.e., *'concretum'*]" (PR 433).

[8] Nathaniel Lawrence, "The Vision of Beauty and the Temporality of Deity in Whitehead's Philosophy," this volume, p. 178.

[9] Details of this incident, communicated by Professor Meiklejohn in letters to the editor of December 17 and 26, 1962, are here published with his kind permission. Whitehead's students recall that in private conversation he could be quite vehemently anti-Kantian. "Of course, Kant was a great systematic thinker," he is reliably reported to have said, "but—that *damned* categorical imperative!"

[10] William Wightman, "Whitehead's Empiricism," in *The Relevance of Whitehead*, Leclerc, ed., p. 399. In another context Victor Lowe uses a lively metaphor to make a similar point. "There is in the production of ideas," he writes, "a ferment which interferes with their bottling" (*Understanding Whitehead* [Baltimore: The Johns Hopkins Press, 1962], p. 218. Originally in "The Development of Whitehead's Philosophy," Schilpp, ed., *The Philosophy of Alfred North Whitehead* [New York: Tudor, 1941, Second ed., 1951], p. 88).

[11] Samuel Alexander, "Alfred North Whitehead," *The Manchester Guardian*, December 31, 1947, p. 4.

Part I
Whitehead as Man and Thinker

Whitehead as I Knew Him

by William Ernest Hocking

Those who were teaching at Harvard when Alfred Whitehead joined us in the fall of 1924 knew from the first that we were peculiarly fortunate. We also realized—and had intended—that our new member should be an exception to some of our customary rules—for example, the customary retirement at sixty-five. Whitehead was sixty-three when he came. And since the transplanting of his labors from England to America meant that he had ideas to develop which would require their own leeway, that time limit fell away automatically, with President Lowell in full agreement. He was to be with us for at least five years.

As it turned out, Whitehead continued his active teaching for thirteen years, retiring at seventy-six, and remained with us for ten years more. During most of this time he gave little impression of age: though senior to all of us, he was in all daily doings completely contemporary and a vigorous sharer in the community of thinking that constitutes a "department." One of us said of him, "Whitehead is the youngest man I know!"

Though he came to us with the aura of leadership, he was temperamentally devoid of every gesture or assumption of authority. When he

"Whitehead as I Knew Him." Reprinted from the Whitehead Centennial Issue of the *Journal of Philosophy*, 58 (1961), 505-516.

7

spoke, we heard a voice notably equable and unassertive. But when he
said "I *think* . . ." so and so, we listened to an authentic bit of thinking,
coming from fresh impressions—original in the literal sense of the word,
often with a ready humor and with a frequent resort to the colloquial
quip. As when, in dilating on his theme of process, he remarked,

> Reality is becoming; it is passing before one—a remark too obvious to make.
> . . . You can't catch a moment by the scruff of the neck—*it's gone,* you
> know.

Or when, in swiftly disposing of the mystery of how we know minds
other than our own, he declared,

> Hang it all! *Here we are.* We don't go behind that; we begin with it.

He was at home in the vernacular. And in part, on principle. For while
it was at once apparent that Whitehead was doing the necessarily lonely
work of formulating a new vision of the universe, it was also evident
that he was working not from one foundation, but from two: the highly
technical thought of advanced analysis, and the immediate experience of
common humanity. In one of his early lectures he asserted, "I am a very
naïve individual"; fully aware that the purely naïve don't know it, still
less say it! In any case, he carefully preserved his bonds of kinship with
the man of the street.

And this bond, by the way, was of the greatest use in retaining, as he
did, his hold upon undergraduate students, whom he unsparingly led
into rugged paths, and in a terminology already strewn with coins of his
own mintage. For his speculative structure, which came to fruition during his American years, was already well advanced in its main outlines.
Had this not been the case, he would have lacked the compelling motive
to cross the ocean. Any impression that he began his mature philosophical
work in America is far from the fact.

What was the motive for this grave decision on his part? For it was
a grave decision, even though he remained within the British tradition
and in a sense never left Great Britain, whether in affection or in political
belonging: "in spite of all temptations . . . he remained an English-
man." It is also true that he was as little a captive of space as of time:
he seemed almost as one insulated from locality. It remains true that the
step was, for him and his family, momentous, and not least so on account
of the growing scope of his philosophical audience on the Continent as
well as in England; Bergson had given his opinion that Whitehead was
the most significant philosopher writing in English. I agree with his
son, North Whitehead, who has kindly answered an inquiry of mine on
this point, that we seldom know the full reason for any important decision, and that my suggestion of the "wider field of philosophical re-

flection" open to him at Harvard as a defined topic of teaching, while to the point, was probably not the whole motive. But from my own conversations with Whitehead I have a further clue, substantiated by certain facts in the history of Harvard which had laid the foundation for his decision.

In Sir Charles Snow's Rede Lecture of 1959 on "The Two Cultures and the Scientific Revolution" there is pictured a cleavage in a typical British university—a cleavage in understanding between the traditional human-ists and the oncoming scientific wave. Allowing for a degree of exag-geration in this picture, it is true that the Cambridge in which Whitehead was first a student and then a don was inclined to sharp specialization. As a student there, Alfred Whitehead attended lectures on mathematics and *nothing else!* When I first heard him make this statement I was in-credulous; for if I had to name a man of exemplary breadth of culture, I should think first of Whitehead. "There must have been something else," I said. "Yes," he admitted, "there was something else, but it was not by way of the academic routine. It was largely 'The Apostles.' " [1]

In the American Cambridge of the same period a quite different spirit was at work: science and the "genteel tradition" were finding common ground. William James had come into philosophy from medicine and biology, having opened a psychological laboratory in Dane Hall (per-haps the first in the land), outfitted with calves' brains, scalpels, micro-scopes—to the scandal, it must be confessed, of certain colleagues. But it was Josiah Royce who most effectively welded the disciplines of science into the work of philosophy and made this welding a part of the Harvard temper.

It was Royce who introduced into his lectures on metaphysics inquiries into the mathematics of infinite collections. It was he who first offered courses in symbolic logic, and began technical inquiries into scientific method. His interest in these topics was stirred by conversations with Charles Peirce and guided by unpublished lectures of that restless and fecund spirit, for whom he, with James, had solicitous regard and respect. Royce gathered around him a number of colleagues—astronomers, biolo-gists, physicists, mathematicians—meeting usually on Sunday evenings for supper and discussion. I recall one evening when Royce opened the de-bate with a paper on statistical methods, later printed in *Science*. After Royce's death in 1916, this group carried on as "The Royce Club." Pro-fessor E. B. Wilson tells me that in the 1920's there were twenty-six mem-bers.

It now transpires that members of this Royce Club played a decisive part in paving the way for Whitehead's coming to Harvard.

Already in 1920 the Department of Philosophy had become interested in this possibility. Professor Woods, then chairman, had written in March to President Lowell in that interest, but there were financial problems that could not then be solved. It was not until 1923 that the issue was revived. It seems that Lawrence Henderson, biologist and Royce Club member—probably during a summer visit to England—had learned of Whitehead's impending retirement from the University of London. A bit later, when he, with Professors Wheeler and Wilson (also Royce Club members), was a week-end guest of Henry Osborn Taylor, he mentioned the matter; and there was common agreement that Whitehead's work was far from finished and that the possibility of his coming to America should be actively explored. From that resolve to the actual invitation, there were steps involving university policy and finance—steps in which Taylor's practical intervention was decisive.

By January of 1924, Whitehead had been informed through a friend and fellow scientist, Mark Barr, that there was "a chance at Harvard." On January 13, Whitehead wrote to this intermediary:

> . . . If the post should be offered to me, I should find the idea of going to Harvard for five years very attractive. The post might give me a welcome opportunity of developing in systematic form my ideas on Logic, the Philosophy of Science, Metaphysics, and some more general questions, half philosophical and half practical, such as Education. . . . I do not feel inclined to undertake the systematic training of students in the critical study of other philosophers. . . . If however I should be working with colleagues who would undertake this side of the work, I should greatly value the opportunity of expressing in lectures and in less formal manner the philosophical ideas which have accumulated in my mind.[2]

On February 4, President Lowell sent by way of Taylor a formal offer to Whitehead, with the appended remark:

> If you cable, you can add that the professors in the Department of Philosophy are delighted with the prospect of his coming.[3]

On February 24, Whitehead accepted the post for five years, effective September, 1924.[4] I am told that when the proposal came and was first mentioned by Whitehead to his family as a concrete possibility requiring joint decision, it was with the remark, "I have long wanted to teach philosophy." Fortunately, Mrs. Whitehead was by temperament disposed to adventure.

In this tenuous chain of events, there is a large element of accident; there is also a substantial element of mutual fitness—let us say an unplanned convergence. Harvard had laid a foundation peculiarly favorable to Whitehead's constructive genius by developing a collegiate atmosphere in which the mutual insulation of Sir Charles Snow's "two cultures" was simply nonexistent. The two cultures were there in full vigor, definitely not alien, but duly fused and seeking joint philosophical expression. The cleavage characteristic of the "modernity" stemming from Descartes, and imperfectly mended by a series of great unifiers from

Spinoza and Leibniz to our own day, was here rejected in practice and moving toward philosophical solution. To this extent, it is fair to say that we owe Whitehead's presence to this group of colleagues, and ultimately to Royce.

Whitehead himself was, of course, unaware of this connection. He came, indeed, to hold in high regard the "great period" of Royce and others, having the essential merit of "a group of adventure, of speculation, of search for new ideas" (MT 237). But he was immediately influenced by what he already knew of the general spirit of America and its higher education. He had once visited this country. He lectured at Bryn Mawr, April 18, 1922, on "Some Principles of Physical Science." There, as his son, North Whitehead, puts it, he "fell in love with America" as realizing some of the ideals for which he had been laboring in England— a wider access of the people to the universities and especially an ample provision for the higher education of women. He knew something of what he could anticipate; and I feel confident that he continued to approve his step. In North Whitehead's words, "My father not only did not regret crossing the Atlantic. He thought it one of the best things he ever did; he genuinely loved this country and believed in it." [5]

No doubt, a part of its promise, in his eyes, lay in our own unfinishedness and our faith in directed change: it was this which attracted him to the work of William James and John Dewey. For in his view, "The use of philosophy is to maintain an active novelty of fundamental ideas illuminating the social system" (MT 237), an expression which by itself seems to involve a definite waiver of finality. In this sense, America could impress him as holding a greater promise, for explorative thought, than the Old World; and indeed, in a late letter to Professor Charles Hartshorne,[6] he indicated his impression that the (next) future of philosophy was to be in America, Europe being hopelessly entangled in traditional modes of thought.

This is in accord with his thoroughly individual attitude toward the history of philosophy. No one has touched that history with more masterly assurance throughout its western extent from Plato to Weierstrass, Einstein, Niels Bohr; yet Whitehead showed equally masterful selectivity —for there were considerable stretches not relevant to his work, which he could regard (with Samuel Crothers) as "honorable points of ignorance." He felt here a definite release from the Anglo-European pressure on details of that history: "At home I should have been constantly reminded," he remarked, "that I know too little of Hegel—a man whom I have found writing such nonsense about mathematics that I am not tempted to pursue his thought in depth." He was prone in lecturing to wave a playful disclaimer of historical lore: "But you know far more about these things than I do!" Yet the play covered a serious conviction, which so far as I recall he had not formulated, but which may be stated thus: The history of philosophy is never "learned" nor learnable; for it, too, grows with that "active novelty of fundamental ideas" and has to be restated with every radical advance. In this sense, Whitehead frequently knew the history of thought far better than that history (via its exponents) knew itself.

It belonged to the situation that his topics were his own; and it turned out that during his first year with us, while the university catalogue for 1924-1925 mentioned three courses over his name—one full course for undergraduates, two "seminary" courses for graduates, each a half-year program—there was just one topic for them all: "The Philosophical Presuppositions of Science"!

Of personal recollection there is far more to relate than I can possibly compress into this note. Let me simply mention three facets of this rare experience: our joint seminar in metaphysics; Whitehead's way with students, more especially his mode of conveying criticism; the paradox in his ultimate aim.

The joint seminars.   Long ago—about 1910—when I was teaching in Yale, I brought to President Hadley a rather audacious proposal: that in topics open to discussion, it is too easy for an instructor to refute a doctrine he disagrees with in the absence of its proponent. *The proponent should be there.* The students should enjoy the benefit of the living debate. Hadley agreed. But he noted the practical difficulty, for a university needing to widen its offering, of expending the energy of *two* teachers for *one* exercise.

This difficulty prevented my realizing the idea until I could find colleagues so overflowing in their own resources that they could contribute an extra hour or two per week without undue exertion. At Harvard I had the rare good fortune to find two such colleagues: Roscoe Pound in philosophy of law, Alfred Whitehead in metaphysics.

For the spring term of 1933-1934—Whitehead was then finishing his tenth year with us—we planned (for graduate students, and for ourselves) a two-headed exploration of topics of mutual interest and difficulty. The title of this experiment was "Seminary in Metaphysics" (Philosophy 20h), meeting Friday afternoons from 3:30 to 5:30. We were counting on the advantages of binocular vision.

The topics were, naturally, chosen from matters in which there was a divergence of views as between AW and EH; but the interest was in the inquiry—the conflict was incidental, representative of a major human problem. We were to take turns in presenting our analyses, and open the matter for discussion by the students.

The general theme was "Necessity and Contingency": what features of the world we live in are what they necessarily have to be? what features are pure matter of fact, accident, or chance? For example, are space and time, mass and energy, life and the lifeless, necessary features of every possible world? or are they factual conditions that might be otherwise?

If they are necessary, it becomes the task of metaphysics to "deduce the categories" from some necessary first principle, the ideal of a rationalist philosophy. If they are contingent, we must proceed empirically, reporting what we find as traits of the existing world epoch, subject perhaps to slow change; metaphysics then becomes a problem of description, in terms adequate and consistent, the aim of Whitehead's *Process and Reality*. I was far from being a "rationalist," but held that there were elements of necessity in our world and that the search for necessity was—for metaphysics—a necessary search.

The success of this joint enterprise obviously depended on complete frankness on both sides, and on the part of the students as well. Whitehead was most insistent on this point: in the nature of any new point of view there is required "a certain measure of ferocity." When a student modestly suggested that his point of criticism "may be superficial," Whitehead's swift word was, "Don't be polite to me." After accusing me on one occasion of having spoken from a Hegelian standpoint, he added, "Don't be afraid of exposing my ignorance before the class—say anything you like—I speak in complete ignorance of Hegel."

He was consistently unsparing in characterizing *my* views, which he condemned as "too orthodox," assuming naturally, but a bit hastily, that I stood squarely in the Bradley-Royce tradition. In one of our preparatory sessions (we used to meet for lunch on Thursday to outline the next day's discussion) he said, "You are always using words that are awfully suspect. I am always in doubt whether I ought not to burn you." On a suggestion of mine that we mean by "the Real" the *source* of things-and-events, that which *explains* what is and what occurs, he commented,

> You are too intellectual and dialectical; you have too much trust in linguistic discussion. The Real does not explain; it is the Doctrine that explains. Like the drunk who meandered from one lamppost to another, and when he had successively embraced and explored three of them, said "O, I shee, zis is a damned proshession"—everything explained, but hardly by that Real of yours. . . . The simplest notion of the Real . . . is History. And what is the prime character of History? Compulsion—symbolized by the traffic cop—No, this is still too intellectual—*being tackled at Rugby, there is the Real*. Nobody who hasn't been knocked down has the slightest notion of what the Real is. . . . I used to play in the middle of the scrum. They used to hack at your shins to make you surrender the ball, a compulsory element—but the question was *How you took it*—your own self-creation. Freedom lies in summoning up a mentality which transforms the situation, as against letting organic reactions take their course.

In point of fact, I was in considerable agreement with this view of proximate Reality, thinking that the will to win in Rugby or elsewhere had more than a little explanatory power. And Whitehead was equally

ready to welcome a convergence of views. When I brought out the "will
to power" as central in the instinctive life of man, he asserted "enthusi-
astic agreement: before this, I have been off and on with you." And this
spirit of frank divergence as a way to better-founded convergence was
typical of the experience of the seminary. The debate was real.

And the results were tangible. Each of us was ready to acknowledge
certain changes of mind. At one of our March meetings Whitehead said
to the Seminary,

> I am conscious of having started with a decided antagonism to the Royce-
> Bradley tradition, and of having in the course of time approached to it. . . .
> Its success lies in the wealth of intuitions expressed. But there is the great
> difficulty in verbalizing them, and making them consistent with one another.
> That is the task of this century.

As to the necessity of the system of categories, he remained dubious of
the ideal, but said "I reserve the right to change my mind at any time,
regarding that as a privilege of the seminary." As for me, I noted in the
record, "I have been led to a revision of the place of consciousness
within mentality." And I doubt not that my growing sense of the inductive element in metaphysics, involving the judgment that the "a
priori," constantly sought, is likely to be the last thing we arrive at, is in
part a product of this experience.

The next year, we offered a second seminary on the same plan with
the topic, "What do you mean when you appeal to experience?" Later
we planned a third, which was set aside by a call of the Gifford Lectures
in Scotland. These experiences with Whitehead were among the richest
in my life as a teacher; I feel confident that they were helpful to students.
They remain a treasury of informal dialogue with a mind of unique
charm and resource.

Whitehead's way with students.   In spite of the reputed difficulty of
his discourse, his student audience continued to grow. His attitude was
encouraging but never condescending. Collectively he credited his students with an advancement well beyond their actual attainment; no one
got everything, but almost all responded to the spur. He sat there inviting
us to follow his argument and helping us over hard spots with a rhetorical
"You see . . . you see"—usually an assumption contrary to fact.

He sometimes had notes, but, as I recall, seldom stuck to them; he gave
the impression of a mind not repeating former results but winning anew
the insights he had to convey—it was water from a living spring, not
from a faucet. It was at times as if he were speaking to himself, wrapped
in the movement of the thought and almost unaware of the group before
him, they straining to hear the words which became less audible as his
own wrestling became intense. One of his Radcliffe students tells me that

on one occasion, as his voice drifted away toward soliloquy, he abruptly recovered himself with the words, "Excuse me, ladies; I forgot that you were there!"

In his criticism of their work, there was a generous interpretation of effort, but also an unsparing rigor in dealing with defects in his own line of fire. He was capable of a uniquely adroit union of friendly spirit with deadly analysis. One such occasion holds its own in my memory with almost verbal insistence:

It was toward the end of October, 1924. An able graduate student in Whitehead's first "seminary" had just returned from a year in Europe under a highly technical philosopher. He had read a lengthy paper, using much of that philosopher's terminology. I looked at Whitehead, who appeared studiously attentive, wondering how much he was absorbing. At the end, he addressed three accurately pointed questions to the reader, and then summed up his judgment:

> This careful paper reminds me of something. (An inquiring pause.) Oh yes! It is a passage in Tolstoy's *War and Peace,* dealing with the evening before the battle of Austerlitz. The joint Austrian and Russian staffs had met to prepare for the impending attack by Napoleon. The Austrian chief-of-staff was reading the dispositions for the next day; everything was provided for, to the last detail; it was a masterly affair. And Kutuzov, the old Russian general, *went fast asleep.* On the next day Napoleon appeared, but in an entirely different quarter than had been anticipated in the admirable dispositions, which therefore *went for nothing!*
>
> Now, for our purposes, *Napoleon may represent reality!* When I hear a paper as intricate as this, I find myself very much in the position of the old Russian general. I say to myself, reality cannot be half so complicated! (This last, with the gentlest quietude.)

As I recall the event, this shaft, carried by the kindly humor of the analogy, went home with full force, just for that reason. The members sat for a moment in silence, partly in recognition of the aptitude of the comment, partly in sympathy with the reader (who received it with firm equanimity), and partly—in at least one hearer's mind—with an inquiring sense whether the implied criterion of a relatively uncomplicated reality is universal.

On this point, Whitehead had his own comments, as in an early lecture (Nov. 8, 1924), when he said:

> The dilemma of metaphysics is that either you are clear, and leave much out, or else you are adequate—and muddled. . . . You come to a point where clearness is impossible. . . .

For example (from a later lecture, Nov. 24):

> To meet the difficulty of secondary qualities . . . you can't say they are there in the object; you don't like to say they are in your head; and so you

say they are in the mind! If so, you make Hume inevitable, and Kant. To avoid this you must recognize that the description of the given fact has been too simple. . . .

   Mind is inside its images, not its images inside the mind. . . . I am immersed in the topic, not the reverse. . . . We are actors in scenes—you and I in this scene—not the scene inside us. . . . This is not a horrid paradox, but a plain man on top of a bus. . . . (Nov. 11).

No one has described the impact of Whitehead's teaching on the students more eloquently than one of those students, an editor of *The Crimson*, who wrote of him (Nov. 20, 1936):

   He teaches no dogma . . . [but achieves] an ignition between mind and mind . . . [such that] the torch lives on . . . as indestructible as philosophy itself.

The paradox of Whitehead's ultimate aim. It seems to me particularly important for our confused era to recognize that Whitehead himself was in some sense a union of opposites. No one could have used more scrupulous care to set up a system of categories, consistent and adequate to the full breadth of experience. No one has used more vigorous language in condemning not only the assumption but the hope of finality. If we ask whether any set of categories is a necessary set, we seem to have in him two answers: a firm yes, and an equally firm no.

   His achievement is undoubtedly a *system*, a complex of categoreal principles, each of which is demanded for an adequate description of human experience in its most universal scope. Of the concept of God, primordial and consequent, he said to me:

   I should never have included it, if it had not been strictly required for descriptive completeness. You must set all your essentials into the foundation. It's no use putting up a set of terms, and then remarking, "Oh, by the by, I believe there's a God."

It is precisely the *necessity to which one feels him obedient* as he moves from point to point that constitutes the power of Whitehead's thought, lifting the entire level of contemporary speculation and felt constantly by all who were near him.

   Yet it is Whitehead who repeatedly declares common conviction the final authority in metaphysics, and who in the final section of his last public lecture at Harvard[7]—four years after his retirement—twice uses the term "fake" to describe the claims of "logic" and "exact statements" to serve as "adequate analysis of the advance of thought." "The exactness is a fake": these were his last public words to us.

   One consequence of this striking coexistent contrast was, I think, the permanent companionableness of Whitehead, always meeting new questions with an unfeigned interest—a modesty in achievement which was entirely sincere. As a profound interpreter of the era of relativity, whether in physics or in morals, he was a living rebuke to the assumption that relativity implies an absence of ground to stand on and, therefore, a relaxation of all effort toward foundations. The impression, "There is no firm ground," comes near to being the dominating malaise of our time. Whitehead draws the opposite conclusion: the acceptance of non-finality means not a letdown but a heightened task. The failure of formulated absolutes leaves the absolute requirement to think again toward that uncaptured reality which contains and guides the total meaning of existence.

With little concern for the philosophical mystics of past eras, he comes to a restatement of the aims of philosophy:

> If you like to phrase it so, philosophy is mystical. For mysticism is direct insight into depths as yet unspoken. But the purpose of philosophy is to rationalize mysticism . . . (MT 237).

His life and his felt dedication were a summons to the eternal discontent in which even mental despair confesses itself the mother of creativity— the unexplained first principle.

NOTES

[1] A group of fellow students limited to twelve at any one time, said to trace its origins to Tennyson and Hallam. Its proceedings and membership were strictly secret. It met on Saturday evenings at ten in the room of some member. An appointed member read a paper on some theme which concerned him. The remaining members drew lots, and in order of their numbers must stand each with his back to the fireplace and state without reserve precisely what he thought of the paper. "The revelations were often extraordinary. Themes were developed that remained permanent interests."

[2] Quoted from official records with the kind permission of the President and Fellows of Harvard College.

[3] *Loc. cit.*

[4] *Loc. cit.*

[5] Letter of January 19, 1961.

[6] Included in the present volume, pp. 196-199.

[7] The Ingersoll Lecture, April 22, 1941 (ESP 74).

Whitehead's Novel Intuition

by Charles Hartshorne

It may seem that Whitehead's system is not particularly new. Thus he is a theist, an epistemological realist, a pluralist, an indeterminist, a metaphysical idealist or psychicalist—in the sense of denying any mere matter ("vacuous actuality") irreducible to mind or experience as such—and have there not been many theists, realists, pluralists, indeterminists, psychicalists? Even this combination of doctrines is not altogether new. For instance, Fechner, Varisco, James Ward, and Bergson approximated it. To be sure, Whitehead qualifies his pluralism by the recognition of a profound organic unity of reality, but so did the philosophers just mentioned, and also Royce, Lotze, and still others. Again, the "philosophy of organism" holds that past events are immortal as constituents in subsequent process, but did not Bergson say as much? Finally, Whitehead stands for a seemingly neoplatonic version of eternal forms as integral to the divine reason, an old doctrine indeed! Is, then, his system merely a somewhat new combination of old factors, an eclectic contrivance, as Pepper once suggested?

According to Bergson, a great system is the elucidation of a single novel intuition. Is there such an intuition in Whitehead?

I believe that intellectual affairs are too complex for Bergson's contention to be wholly sound. Probably no philosophy, not even Bergson's, is limited to the elucidation of an organic insight. Eclectic elements, I suspect, always enter in.

However, I also think that Whitehead is a strongly intuitive as well as highly original philosopher. And he wrote one phrase which comes as close as any to capturing the novel insight which his philosophy expresses: "The many become one and are increased by one" (PR 32). Since this assertion is used to elucidate "the category of the ultimate," we have Whitehead's own word for its central position. Let us see how various aspects of his philosophy are implicated in this supreme category.

18

Pluralism is indicated by "the many." There are numerous realities, not just one, or a mystical reality beyond number. So far the doctrine is simply pluralism. But what pluralist had ever clearly stated that it is the destiny of the many to enter into a novel unity, an additional reality, which, since we are dealing with a principle, not a mere fact, must in its turn be united with the others in a further unity, and so on without end? We have here an admission not merely of emergence, but of emergent or creative *synthesis* as the very principle of process and reality. This is brought out in another phrase, defining the "Principle of Relativity": "To be is to be a potential for every [subsequent] becoming" (cf. PR 33). Each item of reality has the destiny of forming material for endlessly compounded and recompounded acts of synthesis—producing new and more complex realities.

This "pluralism" is original in so many ways at once that I scarcely know in what order to take them. The many *are* not one, they *become* one. This is not the usual "Organicism." First an item is, on its own, through its own unification of its presupposed items; then it is included in, possessed by, subsequent items. In other terms, relationships to prior entities are internal to the given entity, but not conversely. Thus we have both internal and external relations. Bradley and Hume (or Russell) are alike left behind, with all the paradoxes of their two extreme positions.

Again, the "many" are not existing individuals or substances, in the usual sense, but "actual occasions" or unit-events. "Actual" is opposed to "potential," and in any individual thing or person there are always both the actual individual past and the potential individual future. In an occasion, however, there is only actuality, so far as that unit of reality is concerned. It is indeed a "potential" for subsequent becoming; but the actualization of *this* potentiality can never be a possession of the occasion itself, but only of later occasions. The occasion *is,* it does not have, the potentiality, and it is contradictory for a potentiality to be or have its own actualization.

In other language, it is not the items of actuality which change; change is merely their successive becoming. Here Whitehead takes a step beyond Leibniz, who interpreted spatial multiplicity in terms of many reals (not in terms of mere parts of reals), but did not so interpret temporal multiplicity, succession. Whitehead takes this additional step. Succession, he holds, never concerns merely a single-unit reality. Thus process is individualized in time as well as in space. The final "individual" is a spatiotemporal unit, an event, which becomes as a single entity. (Bergson seems to deny any definite units.) Of course there is a radical difference between time and space, for in temporal multiplicity we have the creation of new unities out of the previous ones. Still the units are least terms of actual succession, as well as of coexistence in space. (Vere Chappell's critical remarks,[1] the validity of which I do not wish here to deny or affirm, concerning Whitehead's epochal theory of becoming, seem to be neither intended nor adapted to upset the main point of Whitehead's doctrine of spatiotemporal unit-actualities.)

Whitehead's indeterminism is implicit in what has been said. If the new unity were deducible from the old, it would logically be no addition at all, and the degree of multiplicity would not be "increased." Any causal laws used for the deduction must be viewed as mere abstract aspects of the previous multiplicity; and in any case, how can a law prescribe just how a set of items is to be embraced in a new equally unitary item?

What of the Whiteheadian denial of mere matter (or "vacuous actuality")—that is, the rejection of dualism as well as of materialism? Whitehead's epistemology comes in here: we must always look to experience for our model of reality. An experience is precisely a synthesis emergent upon, and not deducible from, its data. The category of the ultimate tells us that all process, and so, in this philosophy of process, all concrete reality, must at least in this respect be analogous to experience. Moreover, Whitehead sees no way to distinguish between cases of emergent synthesis, or creativity, which are experiences of some sort (however different from the human) and cases which are just not experiences of any kind. For one thing, how would the latter sort be given or known? When given, an entity is taken into the unity of one or more experiences, and this unity is a case of "feeling of feeling," not a case of the subject's feeling the merely insentient as such. How *could* one feel this? We can sense or feel how various already-actualized occasions sensed or felt; we cannot sense or feel that they simply did not sense or feel at all. A dualism of experiences and non-experiences would at best be a grave obscurity in the theory of process as creative synthesis.

Two doctrines of Whitehead seem not to be covered by our account, his view of God and eternal objects. I believe that the latter doctrine, so far as I grasp it at all (and I may misconceive it), is to some extent a genuinely eclectic affair, not wholly pertinent to the central insight. I shall not argue this here, but simply say that I think a somewhat more nominalistic version would improve the coherence of the system.

How does God come in? There are many ways (I shall mention but two of them) in which creative synthesis requires a divine level of synthesizing. In the ordinary case most of the items entering into an experience are but ineffectively present in it. They are "negatively prehended," which seems to amount, for most purposes, to not being prehended at all. Only a divine prehension could effectively and positively unify its data. And is not the intelligibility of "negative prehension" dependent upon the reality of some positive prehension of the same items? What makes it *true* that an item is *not* effectively prehended, if this is the whole story? Whitehead himself says that the truth itself is but the way in which "all things are together in the Consequent Nature of God." Only in contrast with His definitive and positive prehension of an item can it make sense to speak of the deficiency of *our* prehension of it.

In another way, God is needed because the order of process is unintelligible without His influence. Each unit of process is a partly free act, somewhat transcending its conditions and any mere causal regularities or laws. But sets of data cannot be synthesized at all unless there is a sufficient degree of order in them. Process would come to an end if limits were not imposed upon the development of incompatible lines of process. The comprehensive order of the world is enjoyed, but not determined or created, by ordinary actual entities. Since the particular order is logically arbitrary, it must be either a blind fact wholly opaque to explanation or the result of a synthesis which deliberately selected it. The only alternative to such selection is the chance agreement of the multitude of acts of synthesis. The theistic explanation meets the difficulty head on. A divine prehension can use its freedom to create, and for a suitable period maintain, a particular world order. This selection then becomes a "lure," an irresistible datum, for all ordinary acts of synthesis.

Is this the traditional theistic view? It seems not. For (1) it conceives even God as endlessly enriched by new data, and (2) it conceives the divine creativity as the supreme, but not the sole, case of creative decision. The old problem of Job cannot then arise in its customary form. If all-mighty means "having power unilaterally to decide the details of the world process," then for Whitehead's philosophy the term is meaningless, or contradictory. God's power may in some sense be perfect, but it is not "absolute," for power in its very definition is relative, power to deal with antecedent decisions as data and to influence all subsequent decisions; and thus a monopoly of decision-making exercised in a single act or by a single agent is nonsense. How, nevertheless, power may in God be ideally great or "perfect" is a point which is not explicitly elucidated by Whitehead, but which I believe can quite well be rendered in terms of his basic conceptions.

Thus the category of the ultimate really does express the central intuition of Whitehead's philosophy, with some qualification as to eternal objects.

It is my personal view that a metaphysics can also be integrated by taking as intuitive starting point, not creativity or the category of the ultimate, but deity, defined in Anselm's words as a reality such that none greater (meaning better) can be conceived—provided we understand this to connote, not unsurpassability in every sense, but only unsurpassability *by another*. It can then, I hold, be shown that divine self-surpassing will not only not be ruled out, but will be implied. Also that the self-surpassing, otherwise unsurpassable, deity exists necessarily and eternally, and in addition, that non-divine creativity must also have actual instances. One will in this way have derived the equivalent of "the category of the ultimate" from the religious idea alone. For self-surpassing deity must be creative. In other words, the theistic intuition, properly understood and expressed, without distortions due to neoplatonic prejudices about the absolute superiority of being over becoming, or of the absolute or infinite over the relative or finite, will yield the essence of the Whiteheadian metaphysics. The foregoing is but a hint or two. Certain parts, at least, of the reasoning involved are set forth elsewhere.

William Christian's beautifully argued but to me unconvincing version of Whitehead's account of pastness[2] I take to be destructive of one of the most important elements in the system. This account puts emphasis upon one side of the puzzle of negative prehending and misses the equally essential aspect that even the negatively prehended is present in the "subjective form." Also he has, I think, mistaken the meaning of 'past' or 'perished.' 'Past' is a relative term, and cannot describe a quality of the actual entity, taken in itself. 'Perished' seems to describe such a quality, implying that the entity is dead, lacking in subjective activity. For this reason I think that the metaphor was an unfortunate one. On the contrary, the principle of process means that the entity *is* its activity, and to say that it lacks this activity is to say that the entity is not what it is. Nor does it help to say that it "no longer is what it was." For this "no longer" takes one outside the entity within which the "was" is meaningless. The conclusion is that the pastness of an entity is the *same* as its being objectified by successors. It is not first past and then objectified; rather it first completes its process of becoming, and then it is objectified. There is nothing between, unless you want to say that its readiness for becoming past, that is, for becoming objectified, is between. The pastness itself is only potential until objectification has taken place. When we are told that the indeterminacy of the actuality's self-creative process has "evaporated" with the achieving of a determinate satisfaction, this only means, I take it, that the particular resolution of the indeterminacy is henceforth definitive; i.e., the "decision" cannot be made over again or otherwise. But the process of deciding is not done away with, since it *is* the actual entity, and this, we are expressly told, can never change. "Perishing," as a sort of drying up of subjective immediacy, would be a change, or nothing that I can imagine. We should remember too that the very "being" of an entity is its availability for objectification (principle of relativity). Hence how can it "be" unavailable? And indeed, if being past is relative, meaning that some new present has the entity as its past, then there can be no legitimate puzzle as to how what is past and gone can be yet now had. For what else is its pastness than this being now had as past? The only "loss" through perishing is due to negative prehensions in an entity's successors, and I cannot concede that these are attributable to God as prehending the creatures (or in any other way). Apparently contrary texts in Whitehead I have dealt with elsewhere.[3] Nor do I concede that nothing is past to the divine prehensions. Nothing is past to God; but only because of His previous prehensions, whose data, however, did not include the entity in question, but only its antecedent conditions. Thus I hold that Christian's solution of his problem leads to a vicious regress. There is only one form of concrete prehension, "inheritance," and to be inherited and to be past for the prehending experience are one and the same.

Perhaps this view is indeed "too simple." But if so, I do not know what complication would really help. The view is rather less simple than Christian's, so far as God is concerned, for it makes Him a society of actual entities, not a single entity. I take Whitehead to have been rather seriously confused in those remarks in which he seems to imply such singularity. If the many in becoming prehended into a novel unity is thereby "increased by one," then in the case of God there is a new entity with each of His unified prehensive acts. To say that there is only one such act is to say either that God never does attain subjective unity or satisfaction at all, or else that His actuality is the *totum simul* of Boëthius, surveying all time once for all.

Neither alternative seems to have any place in the Whiteheadian philosophy.

On one point Christian and I agree: Whitehead did not always say unambiguously what he meant, and, therefore, to achieve clarity and consistency we must resolve certain ambiguities at our own risk. But Christian's risks seem excessive. True, he can take Whitehead's "God is an actual entity" literally, and I cannot. But with some other passages it is my account, not his, which can accept the literal meaning. And Whitehead told me himself that he felt his account of deity to be "very vague," and he went on to suggest that certain other features of his philosophy were more adequately defined in his writings.

It should, I think, be added that there is none the less a good deal of admirable clarity in the Whiteheadian discussion of deity. Thus it is perfectly clear that God is viewed as perceiving or prehending the evolving world and thereby endlessly acquiring new content and enhancing the aesthetic richness of His own experience; also that the strictly eternal, infinite, or non-derivative aspect of deity is "abstract" or "deficiently actual," by itself, while only the aspect which is derivative ("consequent"), "in flux," and "in a sense temporal," is concrete or fully actual; further, that this aspect not only perceives, but consciously perceives, the world in all its aspects and thus forms "the unification of all things" whereby they achieve immortality. Thus the divine form of creativity is a perpetual and ideal summing up of *all* anterior products of creativity, and so, in the penetrating though simple colloquial phrase, things always "add up to something," for God never fails to perform the addition.

In essence this doctrine is not new. Intuitively it was, I believe, always present in religious thought. And as early as the Socinian catechism it became, in some respects, lucidly explicit. In vain—for Europe had other things to do, even with respect to Socinianism, than to read this part of the catechism intelligently. Later, Fechner, Lequier, W. P. Montague, and many others gave fairly clear anticipations of the Whiteheadian doctrine. I myself first acquired such a view from my teacher W. E. Hocking. I cannot believe that any theism which fails to include an equivalent of the features mentioned in the preceding paragraph can do justice to the intellectual situation which has resulted from the realization that the medieval or neoplatonic form of theism is not only a doctrine riddled with antinomies but one which never did have a genuine warrant from religious experience, or from the idea of worship, but was rather the result of certain philosophical biases introduced into European thought by Parmenides and Plato. We have, in fact, become aware that to worship Being—or the infinite, immutable, absolute or independent— may be to worship not God, but an idol. Perhaps deity is eminent becoming as much as eminent being. Is not divinity in the "eminence," rather than in an identity with one category as opposed to the other? In supposing that pure being would be the same as eminence, what did we do if not worship a category instead of God? Eminence may not consist in being on one side of ultimate polarities, such as infinite-finite, nonrelative-relative, eternal-temporal. Eminence may overflow these simple and easy dichotomies, and be in its own unrivaled fashion on both sides of them. Thus the *way* in which God's concreteness is "consequent" upon the world is radically and in principle superior to the way in which we are consequent upon it. And nothing less than deity *could* be consequent upon *all* other things, by means of prehensions positively inclusive of them in all their aspects.

Yet the neoplatonists (including Aquinas under this designation) were still, from the Whiteheadian standpoint, correct in an important point. God, to be sure, is not exclusively eternal, infinite, absolute; but yet He and He alone has even an aspect of His individuality (the Primordial nature) which is these things. He and He alone is the finite-infinite, the relative-absolute, the consequent-primordial form of creativity; other forms are exclusively finite, relative, consequent. Thus Whiteheadian theism essentially embraces classical theism, but not conversely (though the doctrines of the Trinity and of the Incarnation point, in some respects, toward a Consequent Nature). Here is the crucial problem in religious metaphysics, the decision between God as supreme Being, and God as supreme Becoming or process, inclusive of an abstract element of eternal Being.

It is my conviction that in Whitehead western metaphysics moved appreciably closer than ever before to a technical language capable of formulating without inconsistency the content of the ancient saying, "God is love." This could not be accomplished so long as the magnificent achievements of the Greeks blinded men to the grave limitations and defects of the platonic (or perhaps pseudoplatonic) exaltation of the

fixed and impassible. The "many become one" only because the new
unity is one of "feeling of feeling," sympathetically appropriating the
feeling-content of the previous entities. Experience is never merely of
some insentient "object," but is always experience of others' experience.
But what is the root idea of love but this, participation by one subject
in the life of others? This is the very process of realization, in Whitehead's system. Obviously no immutable form can engage in such participation. Nor can the Aristotelian "thinking of thinking," unless Aristotle
failed badly in explaining his meaning.

Almost the whole of Greek ethics is based upon the notion of substances which never overlap in their being. In one way or another the
attempt is made to derive love from self-interest, for instance as a means
of remedying deficiency by comparison with the absolute model of
beauty. But if value is essentially found in participating, in living the
life of another, then supreme value must be the supreme form of such
integration of the many into one, and then there cannot be an absolute
case, for the novel unity becomes a potential item for a further act of
synthesis, and there can be no final stage. There can only be an inexhaustible progress of the divine life as summing up ever anew the *de
facto* actualities. 'Divine love' means "divine relativity" in the concrete
or consequent aspect of deity, and absoluteness only in the abstract
eternal form of perfection common to all possible stages of the divine
creativity. Perhaps Plato had glimpses of such an idea, but certainly
Greek thought never clearly elucidated it.

Apart from his eternal objects, Whitehead's mode of thought is, to a
remarkable extent, reminiscent of ancient Buddhism, the venerable tradition which most adequately rights the balance against certain exag-
gerations in the Greek tradition. The Buddhists renounce the effort to
explain love by self-interest; indeed, they deny the ultimacy of the idea
of self as capable of an identical interest through the vicissitudes of time.
Whitehead once remarked, with a quizzical smile, "I sometimes think
that all modern immorality is due to the Aristotelian notion of individual substances." A Buddhist would understand this remark without
difficulty. But would those immersed in the platonic tradition understand it?

However, Whitehead is deeply original even when taken as a neo-
Buddhist. He sees the synthetic nature of the momentary realities or
actual entities (which Buddhism alone of the great traditions realized
were the concrete units of reality) and he understands—as the Buddhists
seem not to have done—the fashion in which each such entity pre-
hensively sums up its predecessors (but *not* its successors). This *asym-
metrical* organicity was made into a formal, clearly-stated category for
the first time (so far as I know) in *Process and Reality*. Here is the key
to a philosophy of process according to which, so far from its being the
case that "all things change," no concrete reality changes at all, though

every concrete reality becomes by its act of self-creation. (Even God is self-created, with the difference that there can never have been a first and can never be a last divine becoming.) Thus the fear of transition, influential in Buddhism as well as in Greek thought, is overcome without either the futile attempt to explain becoming as a special and inferior case of being or the renunciation of rational explanation altogether. Becoming is no longer the enemy of permanence, but its everlasting foundation. The many are not lost in the new unity, but preserved in it with all their concrete distinctiveness. Values seemingly lost (through negative prehensions) on lower levels of emergent synthesis abide "evermore," thanks to the operations of the highest level. And thus one of Whitehead's principal aims, to give "importance" to the passing moment, is fulfilled, and fulfilled upon the rational plane. It is an old aim, but when and where was it achieved before with so much clarity and coherence?

Of course there are aspects of Whiteheadian originality not covered in the foregoing account, such as the distinctive theory of relativity in physics, the theory of extensive abstraction, and some aspects of the logic of *Principia Mathematica*. But the central intuitive novelty seems to be in the idea of synthetic psychical creativity, which feeds on its own previous products, and (except, perhaps, for eternal objects) on nothing else whatever.

NOTES

[1] "Whitehead's Theory of Becoming," this volume, pp. 70-80.

[2] *An Interpretation of Whitehead's Metaphysics* (New Haven: Yale University Press, 1959), chs. 6-8. In his essay in the present volume (pp. 93-101) Professor Christian indicates that on this issue his mind is less closed than it once was.

[3] "The Immortality of the Past," *Review of Metaphysics,* 7 (1953), 98-112.

Part II
Logic, Mathematics, and Methodology

The Algebra of Logic and
the Theory of Deduction
by Hugues Leblanc

Whitehead's earliest love was algebra, and it may be by way of algebra, the so-called *algebra of logic* in particular, that he came to logic. It is thus surprising to find *Principia Mathematica* so reticent on the twinship between the algebra of logic and the theory of deduction, or, as we might put it today, the (Boolean) class calculus and the propositional calculus. Whitehead and Russell note that "the properties of negation, addition, multiplication and inclusion [for classes] . . . are, with certain exceptions, analogous to the properties of negation, addition, multiplication and implication for propositions" (PMI 89). This, however, is about as far as they carry the matter. I should accordingly like, in this volume devoted to Whitehead, to study two ways of converting postulates for the (Boolean) class calculus (CC, for short) into full-fledged postulates for the propositional calculus (PC, for short) and thus elaborate somewhat on the above-quoted remark.

"The Algebra of Logic and the Theory of Deduction." Reprinted, with minor revisions, from the Whitehead Centennial Issue of the *Journal of Philosophy*, 58 (1961), 553-558.

That the properties of negation, addition, multiplication, and inclusion for classes are *analogous* to the properties of negation, addition, multiplication, and implication for propositions can be dramatically enough illustrated. Let the primitive signs of CC be a list of variables, the negation (or, better, complement) sign '−', the addition (or, better, union) sign '∪', the identity predicate '=', and the two parentheses '(' and ')'; let the metaaxioms of CC be as in Huntington's 1933 paper:[1]

CC1: $(\alpha \cup \beta) = (\beta \cup \alpha)$,
CC2: $((\alpha \cup \beta) \cup \gamma) = (\alpha \cup (\beta \cup \gamma))$,
CC3: $(- (- \alpha \cup - \beta) \cup - (- \alpha \cup \beta)) = \alpha$,
CC4: $\alpha = \alpha$;

and let the rules of inference of CC be:

CC5: From $\alpha = \beta$ to infer $\beta = \alpha$,
CC6: From $\alpha = \beta$ and $\beta = \gamma$ to infer $\alpha = \gamma$,
CC7: From $\alpha = \alpha'$ to infer $\beta = \beta'$, where β' is like β except for containing occurrences of α' at one or more places where β contains occurrences of α.

The results (call them PC1-PC4) of substituting '∼' for '−', '∨' for '∪', and '≡' for '=' in CC1-CC4 will all be tautologies and, hence, be fit to appear among the axioms or theorems of PC; the results (call them PC5-PC7) of performing the same substitutions in CC5-CC7 will, on the other hand, preserve tautologies and, hence, be fit to appear among the primitive or derived rules of inference of PC.

That the properties of negation, addition, multiplication, and inclusion for classes are, *with certain exceptions*, analogous to the properties of negation, addition, multiplication, and implication for propositions can likewise be dramatically illustrated. Whereas CC1-CC7 yield as theorems all the valid formulas of CC, PC1-PC7 (in which, by the way, '∼' and '∨' may be treated as primitive connectives and '≡' as a defined one[2]) yield as theorems only such tautologies as are of the form $\alpha \equiv \beta$.

Whitehead and Russell nowhere suggest what to add, by way of metaaxiom or rule of inference, to the propositional rewrites of postulates for CC if all tautologies are to be forthcoming as theorems. The problem, to my knowledge, was first tackled by C. I. Lewis in *A Survey of Symbolic Logic*[3] and in *Symbolic Logic*.[4] In the first passage Lewis suggests that a further axiom, or, as I would have it here, metaaxiom, be enlisted, namely: $\alpha = (\alpha = 1)$, where '=' must clearly be understood as '≡' and '1' as a propositional rewrite of the constant '1' of CC if the formulas collectively referred to by means of $\alpha = (\alpha = 1)$ are to be formulas of PC. The suggestion, however, is idle, since the formulas in question are already provable as theorems of PC by means of PC1-PC7. In the second passage Lewis makes a similar and equally idle suggestion, $(\alpha = 0) \equiv \sim \alpha$ doing duty this time for $\alpha = (\alpha = 1)$. Before laying down this new meta-axiom, Lewis notes, however, that $\alpha = 0$ and $\sim \alpha$, on the one hand, and $\alpha = 1$ and α, on the other, are henceforth to be interchangeable. This offhand remark of his constitutes a first solution to the problem, for PC1-PC7 plus the following rule of inference:

PC8: From $\alpha \equiv (\alpha \equiv \alpha)$ to infer α,

yield all tautologies as theorems.[5] A second solution to the problem is offered in another paper of mine,[6] where PC1-PC7 plus the following rule of inference:

PC9: From α and $\alpha \equiv \beta$ to infer β,

are also shown to yield all tautologies as theorems. Other rules of inference likewise fill the bill:

PC10: From $\alpha \equiv (\beta \equiv \beta)$, where β is any formula of PC, to infer α,
PC11: From $\alpha \equiv \beta$, where β is any one of PC1-PC4, to infer α,
PC12: From $\alpha \equiv (\alpha \,\&\, \beta)$ to infer $\alpha \supset \beta$,
PC13: From $\beta \equiv (\beta \vee \alpha)$ to infer $\alpha \supset \beta$,

the first two of which were suggested to me by Jean Porte.

That PC1-PC7 and PC8 yield all tautologies as theorems can be demonstrated as follows. Let α be any tautology and let α^* be the formula of CC of which α is the propositional rewrite. Since CC1-CC7 yield as theorems all the valid formulas of CC, they yield as a theorem the following valid formula of CC:

$$\alpha^* = -(-(-\alpha^* \cup \alpha^*) \cup -(-\alpha^* \cup \alpha^*)).$$

Hence PC1-PC7 yield as a theorem the following tautology:

$$\alpha \equiv \sim (\sim (\sim \alpha \vee \alpha) \vee \sim (\sim \alpha \vee \alpha)),$$

or, for short, $\alpha \equiv (\alpha \equiv \alpha)$. Hence, by virtue of PC8, α is a theorem of PC.[7] That PC1-PC7 and PC9 also yield all tautologies as theorems can be demonstrated as follows. If $\alpha \equiv \alpha$ and $(\alpha \equiv \alpha) \equiv \alpha$ are theorems of PC, then, by virtue of PC9, so is α. But, by virtue of PC4, $\alpha \equiv \alpha$ is a theorem of PC. Hence, if $(\alpha \equiv \alpha) \equiv \alpha$ is a theorem of PC, then so is α. Hence, by about the same reasoning as before, if α is a tautology, then α is a theorem of PC.[8]

II

Of the two extra rules just considered, the first might have appealed to Whitehead less than the second. When PC8 rather than PC9 is thrown in with PC1-PC7, *modus ponens,* the one rule of inference for PC officially acknowledged in *Principia Mathematica,* holds indeed in only one of its two guises. The same sort of thing happens with a good many sets of metaaxioms and rules of inference for PC recently offered in the literature and hence may be worth reviewing in detail.[9]

A finite sequence of formulas of PC is said to be a proof in PC if each formula in the sequence is an axiom of PC or follows from previous formulas in the sequence by application of a (primitive) rule of inference of PC; a formula of PC is next said to be provable in PC or to be a theorem of PC if it is the last formula of a proof in PC; a finite sequence of formulas of PC is next said to be a derivation in PC with n ($n \geq 0$) formulas α_1, α_2, . . . , and α_n of PC as assumption formulas if each formula in the sequence is one of α_1, α_2, . . . , and α_n, or is an axiom of PC, or follows from previous formulas in the sequence by application of a (primitive) rule of inference of PC; a formula of PC is finally said to be derivable in PC from n ($n \geq 0$) formulas α_1, α_2, . . . , and α_n of PC as assumption formulas if it is the last formula of a derivation in PC with α_1, α_2, . . . , and α_n as assumption formulas.

Writing 'α_1, α_2, . . . , $\alpha_n \vdash \beta$,' where $n \geq 0$, for 'β is derivable in PC from α_1, α_2, . . . , and α_n as assumption formulas' and '$\vdash \alpha$' for 'α is a theorem of PC,' we are accordingly led to distinguish[10] between two versions of *modus ponens:* the so-called *provability* version, which reads

$$\text{If } \vdash \alpha \text{ and } \vdash \alpha \supset \beta, \text{ then } \vdash \beta$$

and is to be referred to here as MP1, and the so-called *derivability* version, which reads

$$\alpha, \alpha \supset \beta \vdash \beta$$

and is to be referred to here as MP2.

Whether both versions of *modus ponens* are forthcoming as rules of inference of PC depends on the metaaxioms and rules of inference PC is fitted with, as the following should show. To simplify matters I shall presume that the metaaxioms and rules of inference in question are such that

(a) If α is a theorem of PC, then α is a tautology,

and

(b) If α is a tautology, then α can effectively be shown to be a theorem of PC—that is, instructions can be supplied for constructing a finite sequence of formulas of PC of which α is the last formula.

Conditions (a) and (b) are met by PC1-PC7 and PC8, by PC1-PC7 and PC9, by Whitehead and Russell's own metaaxioms and rules of inference for PC, and by the recent sets of metaaxioms and rules of inference alluded to at the opening of II.

(1) When, as is the case with *Principia Mathematica,* a rule reading: "From α and $\alpha \supset \beta$ to infer β," appears among the (primitive) rules of inference of PC, both versions of *modus ponens* are of course forthcoming as rules of inference of PC.

(2) In all other cases MP1 is provable as follows as a metatheorem of PC: If two formulas α and $\alpha \supset \beta$ of PC are theorems of PC, then, by condition (a) above, α and $\alpha \supset \beta$ are tautologies; hence, by the definition of a tautology and the truth table for '$\supset$,' β is a tautology; and hence, by condition (b) above, β can effectively be shown to be a theorem of PC. The foregoing proof of MP1 is effective.

(3) In the same cases as under (2), MP2 sometimes fails for some pairs of formulas α and β of PC and hence is sometimes not provable, whether effectively or not, as a metatheorem of PC.

(4) MP1 and MP2 qualify as derived rules of inference of PC, that is, as licenses for passing (in the course either of a proof of PC or of a derivation of PC) from two formulas α and $\alpha \supset \beta$ of PC to β itself, when and only when effectively provable as metatheorems of PC. In the same cases as under (2), therefore, MP1 is always forthcoming as a derived rule of inference of PC; MP2, on the other hand, is not always so forthcoming.

It comes as a surprise that PC may be fitted with such metaaxioms and rules of inference that MP2 is not forthcoming as a derived rule of inference of PC. PC1-PC7 and PC8, however, are a case in point, as Jean Porte recently pointed out to me. Consider the two formulas 'p' and '$p \supset q$' of PC, where 'p' and 'q' are two propositional variables of PC. If any formula of PC, 'q,' for example, is to be obtained from one or two other formulas of PC by application of PC5, PC6, PC7, or PC8, the one or two other formulas in question must be biconditionals. 'p' and '$p \supset q$,' however, are not biconditionals. Hence 'q' cannot be obtained from 'p' and '$p \supset q$' by application of PC5, PC6, PC7, or PC8. MP2 is therefore not provable as a metatheorem of PC when PC1-PC7 and PC8 are elected to serve as metaaxioms and rules of inference for PC.[11]

The situation, however, changes drastically when PC1-PC7 and PC9 are elected to serve in that capacity: MP2 is then effectively provable as a metatheorem of PC, and hence both MP1 and MP2 are forthcoming as derived rules of inference of PC. Proof of MP2 is as follows. $\alpha \equiv (\alpha \equiv (\alpha \equiv \alpha))$ is effectively provable as a theorem of PC by means of PC1-PC7. Hence, by means of PC9, $\alpha \equiv (\alpha \equiv \alpha)$ is derivable in PC from α and $\alpha \supset \beta$ as assumption formulas. But $(\alpha \supset \beta) \equiv (\alpha \equiv (\alpha \,\&\, \beta))$ is effectively provable as a theorem of PC by means of PC1-PC7. Hence, by means of PC9, $\alpha \equiv (\alpha \,\&\, \beta)$; hence, by means of PC9 again, $\alpha \,\&\, \beta$; and hence, by means of PC7, $(\alpha \equiv \alpha) \,\&\, \beta$, are successively derivable in PC from α and $\alpha \supset \beta$ as assumption formulas. But $((\alpha \equiv \alpha) \,\&\, \beta) \equiv \beta$ is effectively provable as a theorem of PC by means of PC1-PC9. Hence, by means of PC9, β is derivable in PC from α and $\alpha \supset \beta$ as assumption formulas. The foregoing proof of MP2 is effective.[12]

In view of the results just arrived at, Whitehead might have preferred PC9 over PC8 as a way of converting postulates for CC into full-fledged postulates for PC.

NOTES

[1] See *Transactions of the American Mathematical Society*, 35 (1933), 274-304. CC1-CC3 appear in the paper as Postulates 4.3, 4.4, and 4.6 on page 280, CC4-CC7 as Postulates A, B, C, and D on the same page.

[2] To be more explicit, $\alpha \supset \beta$ may—as in *Principia Mathematica*—be short for

$$\sim \alpha \vee \beta, \alpha \,\&\, \beta$$

short for $\sim (\sim \alpha \vee \sim \beta)$, and $\alpha \equiv \beta$ short for

$$(\alpha \supset \beta) \,\&\, (\beta \supset \alpha) \text{ or } \sim(\sim(\sim \alpha \vee \beta) \vee \sim(\sim \beta \vee \alpha)).$$

[3] (Berkeley: University of California Press, 1918), pp. 222-224.

[4] Lewis and Langford (New York: Century Company, 1923), pp. 80-83.

[5] This result, as Jean Porte informs me, is a corollary of a theorem mentioned by Tarski in the course of his Paris lectures of 1955.

[6] See "Boolean Algebra and the Propositional Calculus," *Mind*, 71 (1962), 383-386.

[7] The argument offered in the text is a simplification of one due to Jean Porte.

[8] For another proof that PC1-PC7 and PC9 yield all tautologies as theorems, see the paper mentioned in footnote 6.

[9] See, for example, H. Hiż, *The Journal of Symbolic Logic*, 24 (1959), 193-202; A. R. Anderson and N. D. Belnap, Jr., *ibid.*, 301-302; and J. Porte, *Comptes rendus des séances de l'Académie des Sciences*, 251 (1960), 188-189.

[10] The same distinction is drawn and studied by Jean Porte in the paper listed in footnote 9.

[11] The same result holds true with PC10 or PC11 in place of PC8.

[12] The same result holds true with PC12 or PC13 in place of PC9.

Whitehead and "Mathematicism"

by Ralph V. Norman, Jr.

Is there a single appropriate philosophical posture—that is, one and only one allowable mode of construing the shape and function of inquiry? Whitehead would not have said so, but he did maintain that some postures can be more fruitful and illuminating than others. He recognized that the look which investigation takes is a function of the way in which its base and direction is conceived, of what is expected from it. There is a *model* commonly implicit in these expectations, expressing our fundamental decision and orientation with respect to experience. This model informs the theory of evidences; it determines procedure; it influences criteria of success or failure.

There runs through Whitehead's writing an arresting ambivalence toward one such model, the *mathematical*. To explore his reflections upon mathematical method in philosophy is perhaps to win the most fascinating lesson in the Whiteheadian legacy. A close reading of his remarks upon the subject suggests that he found two uses of mathematics —the one abortive and barren, the other rich and indispensable. We shall call these the *skeptical* and the *aesthetic* use, respectively.

If we define "mathematicism" in philosophy as the project of moving out exclusively from strict and certain premises to correspondingly strict and certain consequences, of piling theorems and proofs upon axioms or securities first accepted, of disallowing what is not so accredited, we define a model for inquiry which is mathematics in its *skeptical* philosophical use. Skepticism is the mathematical method executed honestly and consistently. It holds fast to the despair generated by that method, to the disparity therein arising between what can be thus certified and what men have wanted and claimed certified. Behold, says the skeptic, the claim, and now the bankruptcy of the claim; behold and beware, lest you hand out certificates to impostors. Of course Whitehead could behold

An earlier version of this paper was read before the Ohio Philosophical Association at Antioch College on April 7, 1962.

as well as the next man, and he knew the value of wariness. But he simply was not convinced that the primary vocation of the philosopher is to hand out certificates to promising candidates. Sterilize your primary concepts, remove the smudge and complication from them, and you have got rid of them altogether.

Nevertheless Whitehead remained fascinated by the mathematical method, not in its function of building upon certainties but in its characteristically modern function of discovering and exhibiting types and modes of coherence. This is mathematics in its *aesthetic* philosophical use—i.e., in its use as the search for infinitely rich and diverse patterns of order, in its confidence that the conception and enjoyment of such coherence is an open-ended enterprise, that in fact the mind deployed has as its destiny whatever expansion of its initial systems may be required in the large encounter of looking and finding. This use may be termed *aesthetic*, because Whitehead's primary definition of order is an aesthetic definition. " 'Order' is a mere generic term; there can only be some specific definite 'order,' not merely order in the vague" (PR 128). That is, order has its primary significance in the complex unity of definite moments of experience, not in any given set of a priori, preliminary, or obvious abstractions. Every subjective unity enjoys and manifests its own peculiar aesthetic harmony, and it is this primal enjoyment which is definitive of all order whatever. The most fruitful clue to the conception both of order and of value is "that section of value-theory which we term aesthetics" (ESP 98). Why aesthetics? Because the complex individual, or the complex constellations defined by individuals, have in structure an intensity and richness from which all the more manageable and familiar types of coherence which we can put together in systematic conception are high abstractions. Hence the most appropriate generic term for coherence at the higher reaches and in the being of God is 'Beauty.' By this we may understand that whatever order the world may be found to exhibit will be only analogously construed in terms of the lesser coherences characteristic of any given familiar department or dimension.

Beauty as such a regulative concept affords a working recognition of the constant necessity for the recasting of available categories and systems. It is Whitehead's equivalent to the Thomist apparatus of "analogy of being," in that it provides a built-in corrective to the unfortunate but perennial proclivity of man to freeze up coherence at some preliminary stage and to relegate what cannot now be organized in terms of available categories to final or irrevocable incoherence. The "logic of discovery" as Whitehead understands it is what he calls "the Greek secret"—"how to be bounded by method even in its transcendence" (FR 52). In this mood the aim of inquiry is not certification of candidates but expansion of insight. Mathematics as the science of order furnishes a philosophical model not because it can deck out its inferences with deductive or seriatim certainty but because it can reason toward and display a whole variety of meaningful systems in terms of which experience might be organized. It is in this sense that Whitehead's audacious claim for mathematics must be understood:

> Mathematics is the most powerful technique for the understanding of pattern, and for the analysis of the relationship of patterns. . . . Having regard to the immensity of its subject-matter mathematics, even modern mathematics, is a science in its babyhood. If science continues to advance, in the next two thousand years the overwhelming novelty in human thought will be the dominance of mathematical understanding (ESP 84).

This from the philosopher whose most characteristic objection to Descartes is precisely the mathematicism of Cartesian method, whose concern was consistently to deplore the notion that proper philosophical method is "dogmatically to indicate premises which are severally clear, distinct, and certain; and to erect upon those premises a deductive system of thought" (PR 11-12)!

In the course of a letter to Bourdin, Descartes has provided us with an image that quite nicely expresses the temper and direction of the skeptical possibility. He tells us that the aim of his whole enterprise is the separation of good apples from bad apples. The philosoher starts with a basketful of assorted odds and ends—notions, opinions, facts and fancies, myths and prejudices:

> Supposing he had a basket of apples and, fearing that some of them were rotten, wanted to take those out lest they might make the rest go wrong, how could he do that? Would he not first turn the whole of the apples out of the basket and look them over one by one, and then having selected those which he saw not to be rotten, place them again in the basket and leave out the others? [1]

The primary assumption of this passage is that conscious experience is, in Whitehead's phrase, "a clear-cut knowledge of clear-cut items with clear-cut connections with each other"—a "trim, tidy, finite experience uniformly illuminated" (FR 62). Each item will be inspected "singly and in order," and only those judged indubitable will remain.[2] Whatever quarrel Locke and Hume may have had with Descartes, neither will disagree with the view that good apples must be separated from the bad; and neither will question the possibility of a productive inquiry fashioned in such a manner. In this respect Cartesian rationalism and British empiricism agree in accepting the skeptical variety of mathematicism. They see the following as the appropriate posture of inquiry:

1. To assume that because being hides rather than presents itself, doubt is safer and more appropriate than is belief.

2. To assume that genuine cognitive possession of being must therefore be marked by absolute certainty.

3. To seek this certainty by moving out from initial clarity and self-
evidence, adding bits and pieces of certainty to the foundation.

4. To define and to organize everything in terms of the certainties with
which we began, and so to reject at the outset any expansion or redefini-
tion of these certainties.

5. To divorce permanently whatever disparities or contrasts appear
in present experience, and so to make suspect any dissolution of them
in synthesis.

An alternative Whiteheadian posture might be thus indicated:

1. Confidence is more fundamental in inquiry than is doubt. Doubt
presupposes reliance upon implicit beliefs.

2. Knowledge is achieved only through gradual emergence into clarity.
The mind moves toward its distinctions out of an initial vague confusion. But we *know*, even confusedly. The progress of knowledge is not
to ascertain whether initial certainties are immutable but to trace the
character and implications of what we know. There is no single model
for cognition and no one set of data to which all appeal must be made.

3. It is impossible to organize everything from the point of view of a
single item or aspect of present experience. Such an attempt always
results in the reduction of one thing to another and so in the denial of
the genuine "reality" of the former. Of course differential principles
taken from limited or selected aspects of experience are necessary and
crucial; this is one thing Whitehead means by the use of imaginative
generalizations. But we distrust the simplicity thereby achieved. The
organizing principles are at best mere analogies of the pattern which
we seek but do not yet possess. Recognition of this tentativeness of first
principles must be written into our method of entertaining them. Just
this possibility is excluded by the skeptical attempt to move out from
some one central item.

Thus, for Hume, all ideas must be derived from some impression of
the passive intellect. What is problematic on Hume's terms is not the
segmentation of experience into any such series of percepts but just the
opposite—the achievement of any connection of separate impressions
one with the other. The association, not the achievement, of discrete
ideas is questionable. If we desire at any given intersection of discourse
to know what is *meant*, we seek immediate acquaintance with discrete
items. On this level of immediacy we can only "observe this diversity
and, by an obvious reflection, pronounce one thing not to be another." [3]
To abstract is, for Hume, to move away from, not toward, the diversity
of percepts.

This vision of things cleaves to a sense of the primary and irreducible
disparity between particular items or modes of experience. If all initial
distinctions are irrevocable, it is not surprising to find that every effort

to organize the totality of experience from such abstract points will fail. Logic, deductively conceived, works admirably in that realm where everything is itself and only itself but breaks apart on the shoals of existing things which by participating in each other yield rather more ambiguous testimony. Consequently, if logic so conceived as to catch only particularity represents exhaustively the full range of possible coherence or order, we must find that all coherence is merely ideal and all existence incoherent.

On such a view every synoptic thrust is an illegitimate wedding of elements that do not belong together. The skeptical possibility is thus born of disenchantment with synthesis, where synthesis must be carried out from the point of view of one of the elements to be organized. When such projects prove clumsy, one counsel of the skeptic is to tend our gardens and let the anomaly be. This, Whitehead says, is the positivist option; and it has a certain attractiveness, since "it is always possible to work oneself into a state of complete contentment with an ultimate irrationality" (MT 202-203). The positivist, too modest to go searching for connections that have not appeared, simply states what he sees and only what he sees. But there is arrogance in such modesty; its rigid assumption is that we know already what system is. What our systems cannot organize, nothing can organize.

An alternative counsel when such synthesis has failed is to accept this wooden estimate of our categories, abandon the use of method altogether, and rely upon random intuitions of the nature of things, hoping that we have chosen a profitable set of prejudices. "Philosophers boast that they uphold no system. They are then a prey to the delusive clarities of detached expressions which it is the very purpose of their science to surmount" (AI 287).

A third counsel—Whitehead's counsel—is to conceive a logic of discovery so as to utilize available order and method and yet stand ready to transcend it in the face of the inevitable anomalies. Explicit attention is given to this "third handling of anomaly" in *The Function of Reason,* which defines speculative reason as the mutual reinforcement of system and imagination. Whitehead does not directly relate this discussion to the remarks on Beauty in *Adventures of Ideas,* but the relevance is great. What he has done is to deny that *mystery* and *coherence* are mutually exclusive. Significant mystery always testifies to the impingement upon our segmented commonplaces of a kind of order which the familiar coherences imperfectly but perhaps analogously reflect. The hallmark of order, being aesthetically defined, *is* the pattern in things. Our specific systems, whether logical, moral, or aesthetic, are echoes and diminutives. If one of the echoes be taken as the criterion of order, mystery is then genuinely dispelled and the natural frame of meaning twisted out of proportion. The so-called mystery which springs into view is but another name for irrationality, and can be said to exclude reason only because a truncated notion of reason is here in use. There is a rationalism of another sort, which Whitehead holds to be the ultimate premise of all philosophy, all science, all religion—"trust that the ultimate natures of things lie together in a harmony which excludes mere arbitrariness" (SMW 27).

Now rationalism has a number of possible meanings. It may imply, whether as faith, postulate, or dogma, that the world is a single, unified, logical, internally related and structured whole, such that the proverbial omniscient mind ranging over its vastness might intuit in a moment the sheer harmony of it. Following from this first meaning, rationalism may also imply that the supposed irrationalities are mere appearance. Where things appear irrational, they are only imperfectly understood.

Rationalism may mean that the proper mode of access to this ultimate structure of unity is a method grounded upon strict deduction. In this sense rationalism is a procedure as well as a content.

It is not apparent that Whitehead is a rationalist in any of these senses. The metaphysical scheme does not offer one logical, internally related whole; such unity is precluded by the ontological principle. "The notions of 'sporadic occurrences' and of 'mutual irrelevance' have a real application to the nature of things" (AI 255). Time is not transcended, even by God; so that there is no one intuitive vision of the whole. Again, Whitehead is no simple methodological rationalist. Philosophy operates best by recourse to a combination of fundamental intuitions clarified by but always themselves modifying and redirecting tentative systems of thought, which systems derive heavily from an imaginative sensitivity to nuances not caught by strictly deductive procedures.

Of what sort, then, is Whitehead's rationalism? What, beyond mere arbitrary mystery, might we expect to find once we have posited the many actual entities as the only real agents (and in that sense, the only "reasons")? Rationalism is "the belief that clarity can only be reached by pushing explanation to its utmost limits" (PR 232). Its hope is "[t]hat we fail to find in experience any elements intrinsically incapable of exhibition as examples of general theory" (PR 67). It is an abiding dissatisfaction with incoherence. Incoherence is a more general notion than mere logical disorder. Things might be in logical disarray and yet exhibit coherence to which discursive categories do not seem adequate. The requirement of coherence in philosophical construction ("everything of which we are conscious, as enjoyed, perceived, willed, or thought, shall have the character of a particular instance of the general scheme") does not mean that you can define one ultimate notion in terms of another. (Cf. PR 4.) Nor does it mean that you can necessarily deduce the one notion from the other, in the skeptical mode. It means instead that no one notion can be considered "in abstraction"—that is, neglecting the reciprocal relevance in which it stands to other basic notions. Otherwise there is the "arbitrary disconnection of first principles" (PR 9). The

Cartesian division between *res extensa* and *res cogitans* and the Humean divorce between pure reflection and the practice of life typify such disconnection. Hume's irrationalism lies in his neglect of the principle that " 'explanation' is the analysis of coördination" (PR 232). To understand is to bring into intelligible relationship, but where the items under consideration are intrinsically so diverse that they can be abstracted completely each from the other, understanding must inevitably fail.

Whitehead's demand that beliefs based upon practice be brought into coordination with (understood in relation to) the sources of knowledge is a function of his more basic view that the cognitive relation is only one aspect of our becoming as active subjects. Knowing is constructive, not simply repetitive. Therefore the ultimate notions of *knowing* and *acting* must not be divorced.

The discussion of order and law both in *Process and Reality* (127-147; 151-167) and in *Adventures of Ideas* (131-204) hinges upon the repudiation of arbitrary disconnections, especially at the initiation of inquiry. The doctrine of "imposed law," as Whitehead understands it, holds that order may be supposed to characterize a grouping of entities none of which requires just that order to be what it is. (Cf. AI 144-147.) Most forms of atomism posit such law at the core of things. What makes the critique of rationalism so devastating on these terms is the fact that nature does not really exhibit any rigidly defined patterns. There are patterns of massive generality and endurance; but interwoven with them are gaps, jolts, and jumps—the disorderly and chaotic. Since the items organized by imposed law can be had without the law, law will inevitably be suspect.

In contrast, a doctrine of "immanent law" holds that "the order of nature expresses the characters of the real things which jointly compose the existences to be found in nature" (AI 142). On this account, laws of nature express uniquely the many unique things, so that when and as the many things change, the laws expressing their being in relation change too. C. F. von Weizsäcker's term, 'the history of nature,' is then appropriate; for the order in things, in process of becoming, has a history.[4] Whether the talk is of persons or of cosmic occurrences, this principle will hold. To understand such a world is to undergo a steady expansion of simpler, earlier forms so as to get at the complex and everdeveloping structures there before us.

> Thus understanding has two modes of advance, the gathering of detail within assigned pattern, and the discovery of novel pattern with its emphasis on novel detail. The intelligence of mankind has been halted by dogmatism as to patterns of connexion (MT 80).

The wealth of possible modes of order is seldom profitably acknowledged outside the disciplines of logic and mathematics. Here and there, most notably in the artistic sensibility, one finds some recognition that this wealth is significant for the understanding of inquiry. To use, as Whitehead has done, the notion of Beauty to cover the many ranges of order is to reinforce and articulate this awareness. For where is there such a variety of logics, so undeniable and impelling a set of enhancements of order as in the always improbable disclosures of the aesthetic? I will grant you quickly the necessities which issue from the laws of excluded middle, of identity, and noncontradiction, but you must grant me in return the unending surprises of order that are there on the canvas, in the poem, and on the stage. To sense these expansions and enhancements of coherence, produced in the white heat of man's imagination, or perhaps simply to have the elusive feel of coherences less deliberate that are closer at hand, is to know with Whitehead that understanding can but profit from mathematical exploration in the aesthetic, if not the skeptical, mode.

NOTES

[1] *Philosophical Works of Descartes*, II, trans. Elizabeth Haldane and G. R. T. Ross (New York: Dover Publications, 1955), p. 282.

[2] *Loc. cit.*

[3] David Hume, *An Enquiry Concerning Human Understanding* (Chicago: Open Court, 1900), p. 19.

[4] *The History of Nature* (Chicago: University of Chicago Press, 1949).

The Place of Mathematics in Whitehead's Philosophy

by Robert M. Palter

Like his master, Plato, Whitehead views mathematics as fundamental to philosophy.[1] Indeed, both philosophers have been criticized for an alleged tendency to model philosophy after, if not to identify it with, mathematics. Mere reading should dispel this last misunderstanding. After all, the third level of the divided line is different from the fourth, and Whitehead does explicitly repudiate the method of mathematics in philosophy. Still, even Whitehead's aesthetic-psychological theory of prehension (see PR pt. III)—which seems about as nonmathematical as a philosophical theory could well be—may be viewed in Whitehead's own terms as a temporary makeshift to serve only until symbolic logic has progressed to the point where it can serve as an adequate tool for aesthetics. What, then, is the relation between Whitehead's philosophy of organism (of which the theory of prehension is one part) and mathematics? One way of approaching an answer to this and similar questions about the place of mathematics in Whitehead's philosophy is to consider Whitehead's conception of the role of pure mathematics in the history of thought. In discussing this question in *Science and the Modern World* (ch. II), Whitehead compares the development of mathematics to the development of language with respect to the degree of analysis of the concepts represented and concludes that the intellectual function of pure mathematics consists in its "resolute attempt to go the whole way in the direction of complete analysis, so as to separate the elements of mere matter of fact from the purely abstract conditions which they exemplify" (SMW 37). The value of such mathematical analysis, as a general habit of thought, is threefold: (1) it focuses attention, by isolating it, on the *direct aesthetic appreciation of the mere matter-of-factness* of any given occasion of experience; (2) it encourages the *abstraction of the particular*

"The Place of Mathematics in Whitehead's Philosophy." Reprinted, with minor revisions, from the Whitehead Centennial Issue of the *Journal of Philosophy*, 58 (1961), 565-576.

entities (e.g., colors, physical objects, physical magnitudes) involved in any given occasion of experience; and (3) it makes possible the *apprehension of the absolutely general conditions* satisfied by the particular entities involved in any given occasion of experience.

Systematic studies of the abstractions mentioned in (2) and (3), respectively, are, it seems clear, precisely what Whitehead means by natural science (founded on sense perception) and pure mathematics (founded on logic). The direct aesthetic appreciation of experience, moreover, requires for its satisfactory completion a movement away from sheer absorption in the experience itself to a reflective discrimination of details,[2] and this movement, I would suggest, then leads quite naturally to the development of aesthetics (in the sense of systematic analysis of the general character of any occasion of experience).[3] The latter discipline seems to be what Whitehead means by "cosmology" (sometimes, "philosophy" or "metaphysics"). Cosmology, as thus understood, would presumably embrace at least one set of explicitly mathematical theories—namely, the canons of proportion which have figured so prominently in the history of architecture, sculpture, painting, and music.[4] In fact, as we shall find below, cosmology in the strict sense includes much, though not all, of pure mathematics, while all pure mathematical propositions have cosmological significance in a somewhat loosened sense. (Cosmology also includes a kind of aesthetic-psychological analysis, mentioned above, which cannot be easily identified with anything that currently passes for mathematics.) For the purpose of subsequent discussion, therefore, I assume that "mathematics" has three senses in Whitehead's philosophy: mathematics as "logic"; mathematics as "natural knowledge"; and mathematics as "cosmology." I illustrate with the example of the proposition: "One and one makes two."

Now, first of all, this proposition (or, better, its symbolic equivalent, "$1 + 1 = 2$") is proved in PM (II *110.643). This means that the proposition is deduced according to a few fixed rules of inference (e.g., *modus ponens* and the rule of substitution for variables) from a small number of (hopefully) purely logical axioms.[5] Like the latter, then, "$1 + 1 = 2$" is a purely logical, or necessary, truth. Such truths are about pure abstractions; more precisely, they contain no individual constants, but only individual variables, and, hence, are incapable of referring to specific, concrete entities. (This would, of course, become apparent in the case of the proposition "$1 + 1 = 2$" if one were to substitute for '1,' '2', '+,' and '=' their meanings as defined in PM.)

When we turn to the physical application of the proposition "one and one make two," the quality of necessity disappears; applied arithmetic is an empirical science:

> . . . it is only by experience that we can know that any definite process of counting will give the true cardinal number of some class of entities. It is

perfectly possible to imagine a universe in which any act of counting by a being in it annihilated some members of the class counted during the time and only during the time of its continuance. . . . The most we can do is to assert that a universe in which such things are liable to happen on a large scale is unfitted for the practical application of the theory of cardinal numbers.[6]

Thus, one and one might *not* always make two if two similar entities, during the process of being counted, coalesced into a single entity indistinguishable from the original two. It is evident that Whitehead is here envisaging a sequence of physical processes including the initial grouping of a set of physical objects (e.g., by bringing them into sufficiently close proximity) into a suitable spatial configuration and subsequent acts of identification, memory, and manipulation by the agent who is counting. Each or all of these acts might conceivably influence the physical objects being counted in such a manner as to reduce or augment their original number.

This influence would presumably be physical in character, hence in principle subject to physical laws that would enable one to predict the results of counting in any given case. Two points should be noted, however. (1) The fact that the counting agent himself would be essentially involved in the statement of such physical laws would not necessarily constitute a violation of Whitehead's dictum that natural science excludes all reference to knowing minds, since we may assume that only the counting agent's body would be significant during the counting processes in question. (2) This influence would be in an important sense *external* to the physical objects being counted, since these objects could be said to exhibit their bizarre[7] arithmetical behavior only while subjected to the influence of a counting agent.

According to Whitehead, the passage from natural science to metaphysics involves (among other things) (1) the introduction of knowing minds, and (2) the investigation of the ontological status of the entities of natural science. Furthermore, any genuinely metaphysical proposition must satisfy three criteria.[8] The proposition must (a) be meaningful for any *actual occasion*[9] entertaining it, (b) be "general" in the sense that its predicate potentially relates any and every set of actual occasions providing the suitable number of subjects for the predicate, and (c) have a "uniform" truth value in the sense that its truth value is the same as that of each of the singular propositions derivable from it by specification of a definite set of logical subjects. In order for the proposition "one and one make two" to be accepted as a genuinely metaphysical proposition, the above criteria imply, first of all, that the entities referred to in the proposition must be actual occasions (rather than, say, physical objects) and that the proposition "one actual occasion and another actual occasion make two actual occasions" must be meaningful for any actual

occasion capable of entertaining it. Next, of course, one must ask about
the truth value of the proposition and of its singular substitution instances. Within the context of Whitehead's metaphysical scheme it is
difficult to imagine an exception to the truth of the above arithmetical
proposition, since every actual occasion possesses a unique self-identity
(a "real, internal constitution" in Locke's phrase, which Whitehead is
fond of quoting), and an actual occasion is a changeless entity fixed for
all time once it has come into existence. Accordingly, Whitehead suggests
that the most obviously metaphysical propositions are the arithmetical
theorems.

It is important, however, to realize that, with a different—but, from
Whitehead's point of view, inadequate—choice of ultimate metaphysical
categories, the proposition "one and one make two" might not turn out
to be uniformly true in all instances. If, for example, "enduring objects"
(in Whitehead's special sense—see PR 51) were chosen as ultimate ontological entities, then it might very well be possible for two enduring objects that are ordinarily distinct literally to coincide at a particular instant
and then resume their independent existence thereafter. This possibility—
which would lead to the falsity of the proposition "one and one make
two" at the instant in question—depends on the fact that Whitehead's
enduring objects are abstractions and hence two distinct (noncontrary)
enduring objects are capable of qualifying a single actual occasion (see
PR 302). Since the entities of primary significance in both natural science
and everyday affairs are generally *not* actual occasions, there could be a
world in which arithmetic was metaphysically valid and yet practically
useless. Hence Whitehead's conclusion that

> There is no difficulty in imagining a world—i.e. a cosmic epoch—in which
> arithmetic would be an interesting fanciful topic for dreamers, but useless
> for practical people engrossed in the business of life (PR 303).

Such a world might be one in which the fluid state of matter pre-
dominated, so that, for example, whenever discrete drops of liquid approached one another they would tend to fuse into a single drop, while
under other conditions a single drop would tend to shatter into many
smaller drops. Thus, arithmetic might be of little avail in describing the
behavior of matter in this world. In general, the applicability of
arithmetic to a given species of entities requires that some principle of
individuation for these entities remain undisturbed during the aggregative processes characteristic of the species (see MT 124-125). Incidentally,
the central role of *process* in interpreting arithmetic carries over, according to Whitehead, to all other branches of mathematics (see below, p. 48).

Before proceeding to further mathematical examples, I shall attempt
to characterize schematically and in general terms the place of mathematics in Whitehead's philosophy.

	Mathematics as Logic	Mathematics as Natural Knowledge	Mathematics as Cosmology
Subject matter.......	Pure abstractions [eternal objects]	Physical objects [corpuscular societies]	Ultimate onto-logical entities [actual occasions]
Kind of truth........	Necessary	Empirical	Metaphysical
Method of validation.	Deduction	Sense perception	Descriptive generalization

Several things should be noted about the above table. The point of view from which it is constructed is that of Whitehead's metaphysics, the philosophy of organism. This is made explicit by the bracketed entries in the "Subject matter" row: *eternal objects* and *actual occasions* are the two ontologically fundamental types of entities in the universe; *corpuscular societies* represent an ontologically derivative type of entity of particular importance in our own cosmic epoch. Also, each actual occasion is analyzable into components called *prehensions* (or feelings) whose data may be either eternal objects (conceptual prehensions) or other actual occasions (physical prehensions). The ontological status of each of the three kinds of mathematics may now be briefly characterized as follows. The concepts and propositions of pure mathematics have the kind of existence associated with all eternal objects; namely, they participate in the primordial nature of God, which means that God perpetually conceives (or conceptually prehends) each eternal object both in its individual uniqueness and in its interrelations with all other eternal objects. The study of the interrelatedness of mathematical eternal objects[10] is precisely that "intellectual analysis of types of pattern" (ESP 83) governed by "the necessity of abstract logic" (SMW 39) which Whitehead often alludes to in his discussion of the nature of mathematics. It follows that all pure mathematics has metaphysical significance insofar as it discloses part of the primordial nature of God.

Mathematical eternal objects may be conceptually prehended by finite actual occasions either as consciously entertained ideas (e.g., by individual human minds) or as structures exemplified in some actual occasion or some *nexus*[11] of actual occasions (e.g., the cardinal number or the geometrical form of the nexus). Insofar as the propositions of pure mathematics are truly exemplified by *any* actual occasion or *any* logically appropriate nexus of actual occasions, to that extent pure mathematics becomes amenable to metaphysical interpretation and hence belongs to the part of cosmology concerned with the general theory of actual occasions and of nexūs. Furthermore, when we realize that human mathematicians have finite minds and therefore require specially devised symbols to aid them in discovering the implications of the propositions they choose to entertain, then we also realize that the study of mathematical symbolism and of the general character of propositions as such might themselves be considered promising topics for mathematical investigation. And, indeed, Whitehead's *Universal Algebra* is concerned with both these topics, the theme of the book being the comparative study of various algebraic systems—one of them the algebra of symbolic logic—as a means of gaining insights into the general theory of symbolic reasoning and into algebraic symbolism in particular. The subject matter of universal algebra, therefore, belongs to those parts of cosmology which treat of propositions and of symbolism. In his metaphysical writings (e.g., PR and *Symbolism*), Whitehead tends deliberately to ignore mathematical symbolism and the mathematical analysis of propositions, and concentrates instead on developing a set of principles and a terminology, largely aesthetic-psychological in character, capable of dealing with symbolism and with propositions[12] in their broadest senses, so that the emphasis is on nonverbal symbols and on propositional properties other than truth value.

Up to this point we have encountered five of Whitehead's eight basic ontological categories: actual occasions, eternal objects, prehensions, nexūs, and propositions. Now, the datum of a prehension (or the content of a feeling) is prehended in a particular way called its *subjective form*—another of the basic ontological categories. Also, there are indefinitely many modes of synthesis of the other types of entities in a single prehension; each such mode is called a *contrast*.[13] An important example of a contrast can occur when a conceptual prehension of an eternal object, derived from a physical prehension whose datum is dominated by that eternal object, has the subjective form of an *adversion;* then, if the two prehensions are integrated (the result being called a *physical purpose*), there will be a strong tendency for the original physical prehension to be reproduced in later actual occasions (see PR 420-422). The constancy of physical purposes accounts for the persistence of the order of nature, including the relative stability of ordinary physical objects. Thus, physical purposes furnish the ontological foundation for physical laws; in fact, one might even say that a physical purpose whose dominating eternal objects belong to the objective species *is* a physical law. Since, however, the transmission of a physical purpose may be distorted or even stopped by an unfavorable environment, it is to be anticipated that physical laws may alter with time. And, indeed, this is the basis of Whitehead's concept of successive cosmic epochs, each of them characterized by some dominant set of natural laws. Within a particular cosmic epoch (such as our own) the regnant natural laws will appear as contingent truths about the universe, but in a broader and longer cosmological perspective these laws may be seen to represent basic metaphysical necessities.[14] This is perhaps the meaning of the following remarks by Whitehead:

> The physical field expresses the unessential uniformities regulating the contingency of appearance. In a fuller consideration of experience they may exhibit themselves as essential; but if we limit ourselves to nature there is no essential reason for the particular nexus of appearance (R 8).

No attempt will be made here to discuss the concepts of necessary, empirical, and metaphysical truth as Whitehead uses them; the first two involve many difficult technical problems which demand—and in recent years have received—much attention from specialists, while the crucial problem of metaphysical truth is perhaps simply how to relate it to each of the other two kinds of truth.[15] Whitehead treats this last problem by means of examples: he defines metaphysical propositions (see above, p. 43) and offers many instances of such propositions in his metaphysical writings (although the clearest instances of metaphysical propositions, it will be recalled, are said to be arithmetical theorems). Another approach to the problem of metaphysical truth—an approach, incidentally, used with considerable success in the philosophical analysis of necessary and empirical truth—is to study the method of validating metaphysical truths. In the opening chapter of *Process and Reality* Whitehead denotes this method as "descriptive (or imaginative or philosophic) generalization" and characterizes it as "the utilization of specific notions, applying to a restricted group of facts, for the divination of the generic notions which apply to all facts" (PR 8).

If each of the three mathematical disciplines—pure mathematics, applied mathematics, and cosmological mathematics—has its own distinctive subject matter and method, there are, of course, also important interrelations among them. The relation between pure mathematics and physics is evident; e.g., Whitehead points out that the birth of modern physics would have been impossible without the prior elaboration by mathematicians of the various abstract ideas associated with the notion of periodicity (SMW 47). The relation between metaphysics and pure mathematics is more subtle. On the one hand, pure mathematics must recognize some metaphysical limits to its degree of generality: "The generality of mathematics is the most complete generality consistent with the community of occasions which constitutes our metaphysical situation" (SMW 38). That is, if we attempt to imagine actual occasions *totally* different from any known to us, then we cannot legitimately assert even that any pure mathematical proposition holds for such actual occasions: "If anything out of relationship, then complete ignorance as to it" (SMW 38). But what, then, of logical truths (such as the axioms of PM)? Are not these necessarily valid even for totally unknown—or unknowable—entities? Whitehead's answer seems to be that pure mathematics and logic in this regard have exactly the same status;[16] that both are bounded in their scope by our metaphysical horizons; that the validity of both—which is the validity of deductive reasoning—rests ultimately on a single principle, namely, that "every thing must be just its own individual self, with its own individual way of differing from everything else" (SMW 39); and that this principle is the most general aesthetic, or metaphysical, truth involved in the mere fact of interrelated existence disclosed in every actual occasion.[17]

Although pure mathematics is, in the sense just explained, grounded in a metaphysical principle, it does not follow that pure mathematics is not, in general, an independent and autonomous discipline. It is only when one attempts to understand the ontological status of pure mathematical entities or the relationship of pure mathematics to other kinds of knowledge that one is forced back on metaphysical considerations. In general, the pure mathematician need not be—perhaps had better not be—a metaphysician. Thus, to return to arithmetic for a moment: the attempt in *Principia Mathematica* to exhibit arithmetical truths as logical truths is unsuccessful, Whitehead holds, because it requires essential reference both to the metaphysical notion of types and to the particularities of (natural) history.[18] Hence Whitehead's later attempt to base arithmetic on what he calls "purely logical constructions"[19] (this being, of course, only one of numerous recent attempts to improve on the Frege-Russell, or "logistic," interpretation of mathematics). Nevertheless, the view that arithmetical theorems are merely more or less disguised tautologies—the usual accompaniment of the logistic interpretation of mathematics—is not ultimately satisfactory, since it fails to account for the relevance of arithmetical theorems to the actual world, which, as Whitehead conceives it, is a world of ceaseless process. Now, in order to avoid postulating the existence of numbers in the sense of a realm of eternal abstract static entities only accidentally and sporadically related to the actual world, Whitehead holds that arithmetic (and indeed, all mathematics) is essentially concerned with certain "forms of process (or transition)" (see MT 112, 126). Specifically, "The very notion of number refers to the process from the individual units to the compound group" (MT 127). Arithmetical theorems, then, refer to alternative forms of this aggregative process issuing in the same resultant (e.g., "$2 \times 3 = 2 + 4$"). Even a proposition like "$6 = 6$" Whitehead proposes to interpret as more than a bare assertion of identity. Not all mathematical eternal objects, of course, need be forms of *actual* processes (e.g., the ideas of an abstract geometrical system may remain physically unrealized), but every such eternal object—in fact, *all* eternal objects—must be envisaged as "apt for realization" (SMW 229) in the actual occasions whose totality constitutes the world-process. Finally, nothing that has been said is intended to deny the utility or, indeed, the correctness—up to a point—of treating mathematics in abstraction from the world-process:

> It is true that nothing is finally understood until its reference to process has been made evident. And yet, there is the understanding of ideal relationships in abstraction from reference to the passage of brute fact. In the notion of such relationships there is no transition.
>
> For example, throughout mathematics, in one sense, transition does not enter. The interconnections are displayed in their timeless eternity (MT 64).

As a further illustration of the place of mathematics in Whitehead's philosophy, consider now geometry.[20] In the first place, there is the abstract, usually axiomatic, treatment of: Euclidean geometry, the two main types of non-Euclidean gometry (hyperbolic and elliptic), generalized metrical (or Riemannian) geometry, projective geometry, and topology. Whitehead himself wrote at some length about each of these with the exception of the last, which was in the very process of being created as a discipline in its own right during the years when Whitehead was gradually abandoning his work in pure mathematics (roughly, after 1913). Secondly, there is the four-dimensional physical geometry of space-time (whether classical or relativistic), whose elucidation occupied Whitehead from at least 1906 onward, especially in his *Principles of Natural Knowledge, The Concept of Nature,* and *The Principle of Relativity.* In these three books, Whitehead argues on the basis of the general character of sense perception that space-time must be uniform. He then chooses Euclidean (more precisely, pseudo-Euclidean) geometry as the framework in which to formulate current (c. 1920) knowledge of the physical world, while admitting that uniformly elliptic or uniformly hyperbolic geometry would be equally possible, if more complicated, choices.[21] Furthermore, Whitehead attempts to derive all geometrical entities (e.g., points, lines, planes, etc.) by his *method of extensive abstraction* from the fundamental data of sense perception, namely, *events* and extensive relations between events. Finally, there is Whitehead's *theory of extension* which attempts to discover the most general "extensional" properties of the universe. These properties—which Whitehead characterizes as "ultimate metaphysical necessities" (PR 441)—are expressed in terms of certain formally defined relations among *regions,* which are themselves interpretable in terms of the basic categories of the philosophy of organism. Study of the formal assumptions about regions suggests that they are topological entities, and this is in accord with Whitehead's view that the ultimate extensional properties of the universe probably include indefinite divisibility and unbounded extension, but not dimensionality, straightness, measurability, shape, or the distinction between space and time. Thus each actual occasion and each nexus of actual occasions must conform in its extensive properties to the general conditions imposed by what Whitehead calls the *extensive continuum* of regions, but not necessarily to any more specialized (e.g., metrical) conditions.

One other mathematical illustration may be briefly mentioned here— namely, the principle of least action. An interesting fact about this principle from the pure mathematical point of view is that it can be formulated in differential form as the Euler-Lagrange equations and that the latter are mathematically equivalent, for a large class of mechanically important cases, to the differential equations expressing Newton's second law of motion. Whitehead makes use of this fact in developing his theory of relativity, which consists of relativistic laws of gravitation and electromagnetism as well as a law of motion of the least-action type (see R ch. IV). Finally, the prevalence of least-action principles in physics can be given a metaphysical explanation within the context of the philosophy of organism (see SMW 155).

NOTES

[1] See, e.g., the last sentences of Whitehead's last book: "Philosophy is akin to poetry. . . . In each case there is reference to form beyond the direct meanings of words. Poetry allies itself to metre, philosophy to mathematic pattern" (MT 237-238).

[2] See, e.g., MT 85-86: "The movement of aesthetic enjoyment is in the opposite direction [to that of logic]. We are overwhelmed by the beauty of the building, by the delight of the picture, by the exquisite balance of the sentence. The whole precedes the details.

"We then pass to discrimination. As in a moment, the details force themselves upon us as the reasons for the totality of the effect. In aesthetics, there is a totality disclosing its component parts."

[3] But how can analysis—which deals in abstractions—ever capture the *concreteness* of an occasion of experience? We encounter here the ultimate paradox of philosophy, whose precise task is, in Whitehead's words, "to exhibit the fusion of analysis with actuality" ("Mathematics and the Good," ESP 86). This paradox is bound up with the concept of philosophical, or metaphysical, truth, which is supposed somehow to be completely universal and yet descriptive of reality, necessary but not reducible to tautologies.

[4] Cf. PR 483: "The canons of art are merely the expression, in specialized forms, of the requisites for depth of experience. The principles of morality are allied to the canons of art, in that they also express, in another connection, the same requisites." Such canons must, of course, never be employed as mere formulas for producing art works—that way lies sterile academicism. One purpose of formulating canons of art is perhaps to help draw attention to the subtle differences that may exist among the various art works embodying a given canon.

[5] The precise characterization of "purely logical" propositions is, of course, a difficult problem, and Whitehead's criterion—a proposition "true *in virtue of its form*" ("Indication, Classes, Numbers, Validation," *Mind*, 43 (1934), 296)—amounts to little more than a suggestive hint of a solution to the problem. In any case, Whitehead's *ultimate* criterion of what constitutes a logical truth is "self-evidence of pattern" (MT 71); so proofs become simply "tools for the extension of our imperfect self-evidence" (MT 69). Notice the qualifying 'imperfect': self-evidence, for Whitehead, is *never* final or incorrigible.

⁶ "Mathematics," ESP 202-203.

⁷ Bizarre, that is, relative to the standard laws of pure cardinal arithmetic. It is assumed throughout that physical objects conform to these standard arithmetical laws except when they are perturbed by being counted. This assumption is analogous to the assumption of general relativity that empty physical space is Euclidean except in the presence of gravitational fields.

⁸ Slightly paraphrased from PR 300.

⁹ Actual occasions—the ultimately real ontological entities in Whitehead's metaphysics—are "drops of experience, complex and interdependent" (PR 28).

¹⁰ These are the eternal objects of the "objective" species; there are also eternal objects of the "subjective" species, which include sensa, emotions, and in general what are sometimes classified as subjective psychological states. Now, of course, eternal objects of the subjective species will also be interrelated in various ways (some of which are studied in part III of PR, "The Theory of Prehension"), and one may well ask whether the analysis of such patterns—Whitehead likes to call them "aesthetic" patterns—of interrelations is also to be construed as mathematics. The answer would appear to be that the analysis of aesthetic patterns is not *now* mathematical in character (i.e., it is not a "symbolic examination of pattern with the use of real variables"—see "Analysis of Meaning," ESP 99), but that it may well become so in the future.

It should be noted that Whitehead also sometimes uses "aesthetics" in a still broader sense, as when he says that "all order is . . . aesthetic order" (RM 105). Following this usage, one would have to say that all existing mathematics is simply a branch of the one universal and fundamental discipline—"aesthetics"—which has achieved a high degree of perfection in the analysis of space, quantity, order, and related ideas but whose extension to the realm of subjective psychological states remains an urgent desideratum.

¹¹ A nexus is a grouping of actual occasions whose unity consists in their prehensions of one another.

¹² It is worth remarking that, for Whitehead, *propositions* constitute a new ontological category, different from either eternal objects or actual occasions, a kind of hybrid between the two (see PR 282 ff.).

¹³ The eighth ontological category, *multiplicities,* is of no special interest here.

¹⁴ Not that the universe can be ultimately fathomed as rationally determined throughout. Whitehead asserts that his metaphysical scheme requires a "principle of concretion (or limitation)" not discoverable by abstract reason alone but responsible for the arbitrary, inexplicable features of reality. This principle is God.

¹⁵ It should be noted, for example, that Whitehead refers to *metaphysical* necessity as well as to logical necessity, as in the following passage: "The interrelations of the specific multiplicities of groups of individual things constitute the clearest example of metaphysical necessity issuing in meaningful relations amid the accidents of history. . . . Now necessity permits no alternatives. A century ago, arithmetic as then understood seemed to exclude alternatives. Today, the enunciation of ultimate arithmetical principles is beset with perplexities, and is the favorite occupation of opposing groups of dogmatists. We have not yet arrived at that understanding of arithmetical principles which exhibits them as devoid of alternatives" ("Analysis of Meaning," ESP 94-95).

¹⁶ ". . . logic presupposes metaphysics" (MT 146).

¹⁷ The principle appears as "The Category of Objective Identity" in Whitehead's metaphysical system. See PR 39: "This category expresses that each element has one self-consistent function, however complex. Logic is the general analysis of self-consistency." Cf. MT 82-83, where Whitehead says that "there are two types of inconsistency . . . the logical type and the aesthetic type." Here aesthetics is opposed to logic. A few pages later, however, the previous usage—according to which logic is subordinated to aesthetics—reappears in the remark that "when the topic of aesthetics has been sufficiently explored, it is doubtful whether there will be anything left over for discussion" (MT 86). See also footnote 10 above.

[18] A cardinal number is defined as a complete class of equinumerous classes (of objects); hence every change in the number of physical objects (Whitehead's example is the birth of a litter of pigs) will alter the meaning of each cardinal number.

[19] "Indication, Classes, Numbers, Validation," *Mind*, 43 (1934), 281-297; "Corrigenda," *ibid.*, p. 543. The article *without* the corrections is reprinted in ESP.

[20] For a much fuller discussion of Whitehead's treatment of geometry, see my *Whitehead's Philosophy of Science* (Chicago: University of Chicago Press, 1960), chs. V and VI.

[21] See, for example, R preface and chs. II and IV.

Part III
Metaphysics and Cosmology

Whitehead's Answer to Hume

by J. W. Robson

Whitehead, in developing his philosophy of organism, has frequently been concerned with the problem of finding some rational basis for induction. Our practical life and our sciences depend in large measure upon inductive inferences; and the philosopher, seeking to discover the role of reason in these affairs, must try to determine whether their common inductive procedure can be rationally justified. If one is content to base induction upon "our vague instinct that of course it is all right" (SMW 64), he is no philosopher.

The problem in its most general form might be put in this way: How are we to justify any inference from something observed to something unobserved? Here the conclusion of the inference might be a general law, or it might refer to a particular situation in the past, the present, or the future. But Whitehead holds that induction is "in its essence . . . the derivation of some characteristics of a particular future from the known characteristics of a particular past" (PR 310); and it is induction in this sense of inference to a particular future, which he would try to

"Whitehead's Answer to Hume." Reprinted, with slight abridgments, from the *Journal of Philosophy*, **38** (1941), 85-95.

justify. Let us then confine ourselves to induction in this sense. Also, since it appears that inference to a particular future can never be quite certain, and is often by any standard utterly mistaken, we may assume that what is wanted is only a rational basis for probability in some cases. Whitehead, if I understand him correctly, maintains that sometimes when we infer that a particular future probably has certain specified characteristics, our belief can be rationally justified; and he attempts to show how this is possible. Now I will try to sketch his argument for the rationality of induction, and then venture a few words of criticism.

His argument starts from an analysis of our immediate experience. Like Hume and the positivists who have inherited Hume's principles, he looks for the key to inductive procedure in immediate experience as we find it. But the facts intuitively observed when we examine our concrete psychological field compel us, he thinks, to reject the Humean view that experience reveals nothing more than a succession of loose events. *If* Hume's story of loose perceptions (each of which requires nothing beyond itself in order to be just what it is) were an adequate report of the general nature of experience, *then,* even allowing memory, all we could say would be that certain things have happened in experience—and induction would be mere "bluff" (PR 253). But Whitehead denies that Hume's story is adequate. He says that taking our immediate experience in its concrete fullness, surely what we find is process, activity, with each occasion of experience growing out of a past, and preparing a future, and bearing an inherent reference to our environment. Actually nothing in experience appears loose or self-contained; everything suggests organic interdependence. And in order to justify induction, we must first understand this general character of our experience.

According to Whitehead, Hume and his followers have failed to understand the true nature of immediate experience because they have concentrated on only one mode of perception, namely, that which projects the clear and distinct data of sensation—shades of color, noises, etc., displayed in spatiotemporal relationships. Whitehead protests that this is not the primary mode of perception.[1] It is evident that our sense-perception is wholly dependent on how the body is functioning; for instance, if we close our eyes, visual experience vanishes. Our sense-data abstracted from the more primitive bodily experience with which sense-perception is fused and from which it derives, are indifferent to emotion, purposes, action. Also our customary interpretations of sense-data depend entirely on evidence drawn from the wide background of nonsensuous perception. The primary mode of direct experience, he argues, is emotional and causal. In this mode we are aware of a vague mass of feelings as derived from the past, enjoyed in the present, and conditioning the future; we are aware of our own personal unity, and remember our own past; we are aware of a controlling world about us and of our effective reaction to it; we are conscious that our purposes direct our actions.

Although this type of experience is mostly vague, it enables us to differentiate between our own animal body, where there is peculiar intimacy of feeling and expression, and the rest of nature continuous with it, the vast surrounding region where intense and intimate feeling does not penetrate. But the functioning of the animal body exhibits for us aspects of the surrounding environment, some details of which flash into the useful prominence of sense-data.

Whitehead argues that Hume, by neglecting the causal mode of perception, missed the essential relatedness of things and, by missing the essential relatedness of things, landed in skepticism. Hume could admit no official knowledge of the world, beyond impressions and ideas, barely presented. Temporal order he had to treat as a mere succession of impressions and ideas, instead of recognizing it as an abstraction from the concrete process known to us, wherein present events derive from a "settled" past to which they must conform, and in turn prepare a future which, however novel, must conform to them. Actually our impressions depend on causal relations; but Hume had to invert this relationship, making causal relations depend on the recurrence of impressions. Then when he came to the problem of rational justification for our inferences to the future, he could only note that certain recurrences have been observed in the past, and add that we expect something similar in the future.

Whitehead, however, contends that a reason can be given for our putting a limited trust in induction, provided we use the evidence which immediate experience, including experience in the causal mode, makes available to us. The main line of his argument, proceeding from the analysis of our immediate experience, may, I think, be summarized as follows. (Cf. PR 303-316.) In the first place, we know something of the general pattern of our environment, and of the way in which things happen in it. Secondly, we know that what happens depends on the character of the environment, and also has a share in changing that character. Thus it seems evident that any specific kind of event requires an environment adapted to it; and also that the general character of any environment will be determined by the dominant kinds of events involved. In the third place, we have reason to believe that the general pattern of our environment, as discerned in experience, will be carried forward into the future. For our immediate experience discloses events inheriting their characters from the past and bestowing them on the future in such a way as to carry on the general pattern of process. Hence we may reasonably look forward to a similar environment in the future. In the fourth place, we can use this presupposition of a continuing type of environment as a basis for making judgments about future events analogous to events within the range of our experience. Every inductive argument is concerned with what will happen in some specified situation or in relation with some specified complex of events analogous to an experienced situation or complex of events. But events require an environment, and an environment adapted to the occurrence of events of that specified sort. Hence there is in every inductive argument a presupposition as to the general character of the environment. We presuppose that the general character of the environment which sustains the experienced situation or complex of events will be continued, and will, when the historical process reaches the anticipated situation or complex, govern the happenings in that particular future. In inductive reasoning there is always an analogy between events observed and events anticipated, and consequently a presupposition as to the general course of nature in so far as it governs the realization of such events. For example, suppose I am about to drink a glass of water, and I predict, on the basis of things I now know, that my thirst will be quenched. The inference here concerns what will happen in a certain specified situation in the near future, a situation which includes my drinking the water and allows some psychological reaction; and I infer that in this anticipated situation the psychological reaction will be of the familiar sort called quenching thirst. Also this anticipated situation is conceived as analogous to remembered situations in which I have drunk water, and thus quenched my thirst. But to specify a future situation containing the behavior of my body and the water, is to presuppose all in the way of environment that is required to sustain my body and the water until that situation, with some reaction or other, is completed. And since it takes a considerable fuss for nature to keep a human organism and a quantity of water going, a great deal is thus presupposed as to the general course of nature. Finally, Whitehead tells us how, according to the philosophy of organism, inductive reasoning gets its validity. It gets its validity, he says, by virtue of "a suppressed premise." This "suppressed premise" is that the particular future involved will contain events analogous to events directly experienced, and will be derived from the present in such a way that the general order of the present environment will be maintained. And only with this presupposition of analogous events and a continuing type of environment, do we have a rational basis for induction.

Moreover, Whitehead asserts that our knowledge of the world is, in part, of the numerical sort required by a statistical theory of probability. He doubts, though, whether a statistical theory can cover all cases where the notion of more or less probability is commonly applied—for instance, where we consider some scientific guess as to the internal constitution of the stars, or some conjecture as to the condition of mankind after some unprecedented upheaval.

He also aims to provide for nonstatistical probability judgments by a theory of "the graded relevance," to an environment, of the different characteristics which might be exhibited in it. Thus he would provide for probable predictions of novelty in cases where we see that the appropriate or suitable outcome from a presupposed situation would be novel.

Now I have tried to present fairly what seem to me the chief points in Whitehead's argument for the rationality of induction. Next I should like to suggest some reasons for doubt as to the strength and success of that argument. I do not wish to question the criticism that Hume slighted the relational character of what we directly observe, nor the contention that the primary mode of perceptual experience is emotional and causal. My comments will be concerned with Whitehead's presupposition about the general course of nature.

To begin with, a few words are needed as to the general character of probability situations wherein someone makes an inference to a particular future. Any such situation will include some evidence and a prediction considered in relation to that evidence. When such a probability situation is expressed in words, at least two propositions will be involved: (1) the prediction, which is supposed to be inductively established, and (2) the proposition which states the relationship believed to hold between the evidence and the prediction. The second proposition may be put in hypothetical form with a statement of the evidence as hypothesis, and it may state the degree of probability which that evidence is believed to confer on the prediction. The second proposition, or rather the assertion of it, may be called "a hypothetical probability judgment." Then we need to distinguish between, on the one hand, making a hypothetical probability judgment—that is, asserting that *if* certain conditions obtain, *then* probably a certain event will occur—and on the other hand asserting that these conditions do in fact obtain, and that hence the prediction is genuinely probable. The latter we may call "a genuine probability judgment." (This distinction is analogous to the familiar distinction in elementary logic, between asserting that "if p, then q," and asserting that "p" and therefore that "q.")

Now when Whitehead discusses the way in which inductive reasoning gains validity, some of the things he says suggest a very modest proposal. Some of the things he says suggest that he is merely proposing that we recognize in the hypothesis of hypothetical probability judgments, an assumption about analogous events and a continuing type of environment. He speaks of this assumption as "a suppressed premise," and he says that an inductive argument always includes it as "an hypothesis." But when we do recognize as part of the hypothesis of hypothetical probability judgments, this assumption of analogous events and a continuing type of environment, we do not thereby assert that this assumption is true. We only assert that *if* it is true and other conditions are fulfilled, *then* the proposition about the particular future is rendered probable. And the net effect of explicitly including a general assumption about the course of nature, it seems to me, would just be to make clear that the analogy upon which our judgment of probability is based is really much wider than we tend to suppose it is when this assumption is merely tacit. For instance, to express the hypothetical probability judgment of our earlier example, I could say: "If drinking water has quenched my thirst in the past and if I now drink this, then probably my thirst will be quenched." But to emphasize the width of the analogy, I could say: "If drinking water has quenched my thirst in the past and if I now drink this and *if the general environment required for the continuance of my body and the water, is maintained till and through the future time in question,* then probably my thirst will be quenched."

Since Hume's day it has often been thought that to justify induction we must make some assumption about the general order of nature. Hume, it may be recalled, distinguished between the general uniformity of nature (the principle that unobserved cases resemble observed cases, and especially that the future will be like the past) and specific uniformities (such as the conjunction of snow and cold, or fire and heat). Specific uniformities, he held, are extended imaginatively into the future when the appropriate habits have been built up. He noted that we tend to justify our expectation of the continuance of those uniformities not only by reference to experienced cases but also by resorting to our confidence in general uniformity. Then he showed that general uniformity could not as an independent assumption be rationally justified. Our confidence in it, as well as in specific uniformities, results from habit or custom. We use the principle that the future will resemble the past as a basis for all our arguments from past experience, and hence cannot argue for it, from past experience, without begging the question. The assumption of general uniformity must remain something we hope is true but cannot verify by any appeal to experience.

However, the question which Hume raised with regard to his uniformity principle might be raised with regard to Whitehead's more limited presupposition of a continuing type of environment—namely, what reason do we have in experience for believing this hypothesis to be true? Unless we can find a positive answer to this question, we have not really done much for induction. We have at most found something which would, *if we had any good reason to believe it,* give us a basis for rational prediction. And Whitehead does, I think, mean to deal with this question. For many of the things he says indicate that his position is that we do have some reason in experience for *accepting* this hypothesis of a continuing type of environment, and hence some justification for making genuine probability judgments.

He relies, it seems, upon the notion that in the present, as actually experienced, there is something which can be known to necessitate a future of a certain sort. He speaks of the future as "immanent" in the present, and when emphasizing our dependence on references to the future, he even goes so far as to talk of "our direct observation" of the future, though he makes it a "short-range intuition" (AI 246-247). He says that "the future . . . lives actively in its antecedent world"; that it has "objective existence" in the present; and that the constitution of each present occasion of experience "necessitates that there be a future" (AI 247-250). But when all is said, it turns out that any specified future is "immanent" in the present "according to the mode of anticipation," and the future has "objective existence" in the present in the sense that what hasn't happened yet may be an object anticipated or expected now (AI 250-254). "The present contains the utmost verge of . . . realized individuality" (AI 247). Whitehead's language, however, sometimes suggests the view that there already is something which hasn't yet happened but which is expected to happen—there is something which isn't yet. We must admit it is very difficult to describe adequately without self-contradiction the deliverances of our actual experience in this matter. But we must also admit, I think, that when such expressions as "the future" and "future occasions" are used, there is nothing *now* which is described by them, except what is now happening. We can, of course, speak of events that are now occurring, as "future" relative to events which preceded them. Also we can fashion descriptions which we expect or hope or fear will describe something later, even though, when we fashion them, there is nothing at all described by them. As Whitehead says, we habitually think and act in anticipation of some specific future. But does this fact warrant the further assertion, "Cut away the future, and the present collapses, emptied of its proper content" (AI 246)? Should we not rather say, "Cut away our *anticipations* of the future—our present anticipations—and the present collapses, emptied of its proper content"? So far as I can see, there is nothing in the mode of anticipation except our familiar psychological bent toward the future. That is, we frequently have anticipations, expectations, purposes, etc., which may or may not later be fulfilled; and what happens later, may, when it happens, be related to these psychological events in such a way as to constitute fulfillment.

Anticipation could not do the trick for induction, so far as I can see, unless anticipation consisted in an intuition of internal relational properties involving future events. It seems clear that any evidence we have for believing in the continuation of our environment must be evidence discoverable by observation of some kind at the time we have this belief. What happens after a belief has occurred cannot possibly provide us with a reason at the time of believing for believing as we do. But if we could by inspecting present events discover that their being what they are requires relations to future events of a sort which would carry on the general pattern of the present partially observed process, then we should have a reason now for believing that the general type of environment will be continued. That we do have such a reason is suggested by some of Whitehead's statements. He says that the very "constitution" of the experiencing subject "involves that its own activity in *self*-formation passes into its activity of *other*-formation. It is by reason of the constitution of the present subject that the future will embody the present subject and will re-enact its patterns of activity" (AI 248). And he declares that "the present bears in its own essence the relationships which it will have to the future. . . . The future is there in the present, as a general fact. . . . It is also there with such general determinations as it lies in the nature of the particular present to impose on the particular future which must succeed it" (AI 250). Such passages might perhaps be interpreted to mean that internal relational properties requiring future events as constituents belong to present events when they occur. Also it might be assumed that we can at least dimly observe such relational properties.

This suggestion that in anticipating the future we are aware of internal relational properties involving future events must, I think, be rejected. My own experience, at least, seems not to provide any verification of it. But, further, there seems to be grave difficulty in supposing that internal properties involving the future are even so much as possible. An internal relational property arises when something is related to other things by an internal relation. An internal relation is a relation which so connects things that one or more of them could not be what they are, were it not for the other things related to them. It is conceivable that an internal dyadic relation should be internal either with respect to both of its terms, or with respect to only one of its terms. It has sometimes been said, for example, that the relation of whole to part is internal so far as the whole is concerned, but not with respect to the part; in order to have the whole we must have the part, but the part might have been just what it is without the whole. Now let us consider temporal relations —more specifically the relation of causation or derivation, which according to Whitehead is a more concrete feature of the world than mere temporal succession. Suppose there occur two events, a and b, which (1) do not overlap, and (2) occur in the temporal order a, b, and (3) are so connected as to make b the effect of a or derivative from a. Whitehead sometimes seems to imply that this relation would be internal with respect to both a and b. I would suggest, however, that this relation, though it may be internal with respect to b, cannot be internal with respect to a. At least it is difficult to see how the relation can be internal with respect to a. The occurrence of b, apparently, cannot make any difference to a, since a, by hypothesis, is complete before b occurs. I am inclined to believe that we may say quite generally that no event can be internally related, so far as it is concerned, to what follows it and does not overlap it, for the simple reason that it must be completed before any subsequent non-overlapping events occur. If this is so, if no event can be internally related, so far as *it* is concerned, to subsequent events, then any terms which we apply to it, such as 'cause' or 'antecedent,' to express our judgment of its relation to succeeding events, must be applied either merely in anticipation, or in retrospect when the succeeding events have occurred. And only in retrospect can we have knowledge of such relational properties as are thus attributed to it. If this view is correct, we have to deny that the present can provide us with any information about the future in the form of relational properties having future events as constituents. This is not to deny, of course, that we may have very definite expectations regarding future developments, that we may now look upon what is happening as an early or intermediate stage in a total process yet to be completed. Experience of similar continuing processes in the past has led us to expect with the greatest confidence similar outcomes in the future. Thus we drink water, plant potatoes, build battleships, and announce forthcoming eclipses.

It might be objected that, after all, we are not completely ignorant of the future; for we know at least that what will happen will be derived from the present and will be subject to those limitations which the present sets for the future. I am not sure that we do know this much. But even if we do, we are not thereby in a position to say anything about the character of the future beyond the bare information that it will be derived from and conditioned by the present, with whatever nature that fact will require. Only further experience will suffice to show us what is thus required. As Hume said, "to consider the matter *a priori,* anything may produce anything." [2] The actual situation then seems to me to be this: by experience we have learned that certain complex processes similar to that, a stage of which is now observed, were continued and completed in a certain way; hence we expect the future to complete this process in a similar way.

Can we, then, using the evidence available in our present experience, give a good reason for believing in a general presupposition about the future course of events—either Hume's presupposition or Whitehead's? It seems to me that no such presupposition can be justified by our present experience. For as Hume pointed out, we cannot argue inductively for any such principle without begging the question. The only other possibility of establishing it empirically would appear to be the one suggested by Whitehead—resting it on our insight into the relational character of experienced events and their environmental connections. But any presupposition regarding the future transcends what is now given in experience, unless present events have internal relational properties connecting them with the future in a way which seems impossible. Hence I think that our present experience affords no intellectually satisfactory ground for presupposing that the general pattern of our environment will be maintained in the future. If this presupposition cannot be justified by present experience and we need it to make induction valid, plainly induction cannot be thus justified by experience. My conclusion is that, although Whitehead gives an account of our immediate experience and inductive procedure in some respects far more adequate than Hume's account, he fails to show how we can ever *reasonably* infer that a particular future probably will have specified characteristics.

Hume's "very curious discovery" seems to me still unshaken: " 'Tis not, therefore, reason, which is the guide of life, but custom. That alone determines the mind, in all instances, to suppose the future conformable to the past. However easy this step may seem, reason would never, to all eternity, be able to make it." [3]

NOTES

[1] On Hume and perception, see especially *Symbolism,* ch. ii; PR Pt. II, chs. v and viii; AI ch. xi; and MT 98-101, 152-154.

[2] *Treatise,* Book I, Part IV, Section V, Selby-Bigge, p. 247.

[3] *An Abstract of a Treatise of Human Nature,* p. 16.

Whitehead's Answer to Hume: A Reply
by Mason W. Gross

Dr. Robson's paper indicates quite clearly that Whitehead's answer to Hume consists of at least two parts. Whitehead not merely attempts to demonstrate that there can be a rational basis for inductive inference; his whole philosophy is concerned with the attempt to provide a more adequate analysis of our experience than is provided by Hume's philosophy. But the two parts of this answer are by no means wholly distinct. In terms of the basic analysis of experience adopted by Hume the problem of induction is completely insoluble. If our experience is properly reducible to a complex of impressions, each of which "requires nothing but itself in order to exist," then Hume's argument concerning induction is irrefutable. Thus to answer Hume on induction it is first necessary to suggest a fundamentally different analysis of experience. Hume himself does not argue that his initial analysis is adequate; in fact, the whole of his critical philosophy can be considered as a demonstration of its inadequacy. The cosmological principles which justify the statements on the first page of the *Treatise* can be traced back to Descartes and are fundamental to the whole rationalistic-empiricistic tradition of the seventeenth and eighteenth centuries. It is this traditional cosmology, of which Hume's philosophy presents only one example, which Whitehead is concerned to attack, and the problem of induction is only one of the problems which this inadequate cosmology has bequeathed to us. We may list a variety of others: the general epistemological problem, the mind-body problem, the problem of internal versus external relations, the problem of final causes, of causality in general, of personal identity, and a host of others. Whitehead claims, and Hume seems to substantiate the claim, that none of these problems can be solved, in terms of the Cartesian cosmology, in such a way as to satisfy those persistent intuitions which are the ultimate criterion of the adequacy of any philosophical interpretation. Thus Whitehead's whole purpose is to provide a more adequate cosmology from which satisfactory solutions to these problems can be derived.

The term 'rational' must be understood in this way. From the Cartesian cosmology, which lies back of and determines Hume's basic analysis of experience, no satisfactory account of the ground of inductive inference

"Whitehead's Answer to Hume: A Reply." Reprinted from the *Journal of Philosophy*, **38** (1941), 95-102.

can be derived, and thus with respect to that cosmology inductive inference is irrational. If, on the other hand, the ground for inductive inference can be derived from Whitehead's general cosmology, then it is rational with respect to that cosmology. But we can go further. The Cartesian cosmology does not satisfy us because it cannot provide an adequate interpretation of so many fundamental aspects of our experience. If Whitehead's cosmology can give us greater satisfaction on all these points, then his cosmology, and with it the derivative account of the ground of induction, can claim to be not merely rational, but "reasonable."

Dr. Robson quotes at length from two passages in Whitehead's books, a chapter in *Process and Reality* where Whitehead is discussing inductive inference, and a chapter in *Adventures of Ideas,* the title of which is "Past, Present, Future." I believe that Dr. Robson somewhat distorts the meaning of both passages by treating the latter as if it were intended to provide the evidence necessary for the support of the arguments given in the former. The connection between the two is, I believe, much less direct. In the former Whitehead claims to show that the ground for inductive inference, which is required to make sense of the statistical theory of probability, can be derived directly from his general cosmology and in particular from his theory of cosmic epochs, which in turn is a consequence of his conception of the nature of an actual entity. The argument is essentially formal. Even if the whole cosmology should turn out to be a fairy tale, Whitehead could still claim that this argument was valid. The second chapter, on the other hand, claims to show the applicability of the category of actual entities to our immediate experience, with the implication that it provides a more adequate interpretation than Descartes' category of clear and distinct ideas or Hume's impressions. Thus these two chapters correspond to the two parts of Whitehead's answer to Hume, and although the connection between them is vitally important, it will be misunderstood if the first chapter is thought to require the second to complete its own particular argument, or if the second is viewed as having been designed primarily to support the argument in the first. The actual connection between the two is mediated by Whitehead's whole cosmological theory, which contains many other formal consequences and appeals to many other types of evidence.

Let us turn our attention first to the passage in *Process and Reality* where Whitehead claims to derive a justification for inductive reasoning from his general cosmological theory. Dr. Robson has presented the argument clearly, but he has failed, I think, to stress sufficiently the difference between Hume's conception of the uniformity of nature and Whitehead's principle of the maintenance of the general order of the environment. These two conceptions stem from two very different theories as to the nature of the actual things which make up the universe as revealed in our experience. Hume is dominated by the Cartesian notion of a substance as "that which requires nothing but itself in order to exist." He applies this definition explicitly to each impression, and thus can find nothing but external relations between the constituents of experience. Thus from the point of view of any one such constituent, whatever may happen to any other is completely irrelevant, and the uniformity of nature is quite accidental. It is theoretically possible that any one item such as this sheet of paper might survive with all its defining properties, although every other item in the universe should perish or be replaced by a totally different set. To be sure, we have a very strong propensity to believe that this will not happen, but that, according to Hume, is merely a belief and is not supported by reason.

Whitehead, throughout his philosophy, is concerned to repudiate this conception of substance and to replace it by his doctrine of actual entities. Each actual entity is essentially "social." That is to say, each actual entity has a very definite relation to every other actual entity in the universe, and it is in virtue of these relations that it has the definite character which it does in fact have. This is a doctrine of internal relations and, more than that, it is a doctrine of a dynamic internal relations, for in the course of the passage of nature an actual entity becomes what it is to be by means of its internal relations to, or prehensions of, its own immediate past and its environment. Societies of actual entities, which is Whitehead's term for the macroscopic things in our experience, physical bodies, organisms, and so on, are similarly dependent upon their environment for their very existence, and if a society of a certain type is to survive, the environment must continue to provide that type of order which makes its existence possible. Should it fail to do so, the type of society would simply disappear. And since the laws of nature dominant at any period actually express the character of the internal relations which constitute the dominant types of societies at that period, should the laws of nature change, the types of societies would change, and vice versa.

Thus Whitehead's principle of the maintenance of order and Hume's principle of the uniformity of nature are metaphysically quite different. The one is a doctrine of internal relations, the other a doctrine of external relations. In the former, if the environment is altered to any extent, the entity within that environment is correspondingly altered. In the latter this connection does not necessarily follow. Whitehead's principle follows from his account of the nature of an actual entity; Hume's principle, on the other hand, has no essential or "rational" connection with his cosmological presuppositions.

Now the problem of induction centers on the question of the validity of using past and present events as a basis for making a prediction, of some degree of probability, concerning a future event. Is the fact that the sun has risen every morning in the past any basis for inferring that it will rise tomorrow morning? Both Whitehead and Hume admit that if we knew that the present laws of nature would be in force tomorrow morning, we should employ the frequency theory to determine the probability of a sunrise, for in that case the future event would be known to belong to the class of events in terms of which the statistical probability of sunrises is reckoned. Thus, according to Hume, if we had any reason to believe that the laws of nature would be the same, our probability inference about the sunrise would be valid, but unfortunately we have no reason to believe in this principle.

Whitehead's answer to this depends upon his analysis of a proposition. Every proposition ultimately designates some actual entity or entities, which are identified by certain properties. A proposition about the sun designates as its logical subject a definite society of actual entities, identified as belonging to a specific type by means of such properties as "spherical," "fiery," "gleaming," "in the sky," etc. This society is the subject of the prediction, which goes on to affirm that tomorrow morning at a specified time this society will stand in certain specified relations to the earth. Every prediction thus definitely indicates its logical subject and then makes an affirmation concerning it.

In terms of this analysis, we may state Whitehead's answer to the problem of induction as follows: Either there is a definite rational justification for our assigning some degree of probability to such a prediction, or else the prediction is completely devoid of meaning. For there seem to be only two alternatives on Whitehead's general theory. Either it will be possible, tomorrow morning, to identify the logical subject of the prediction, or it will not. If we suppose now that it will not be possible, then the prediction is meaningless, for a proposition which fails to identify its logical subject must be strictly meaningless. If, however, we suppose that it will be possible to identify the logical subject, then, in virtue of the social character of all actual entities, we automatically presuppose certain important features of its environment. If we suppose that we can identify an entity analogous to the sun which is recognizable in our present environment, then we *ipso facto* presuppose an environment analogous to this present environment, dominated by analogous laws of nature. This being the case, the event which is the subject matter of the prediction is, by the very fact of the prediction itself, presupposed as belonging to the class of events in terms of which the probability can be reckoned.

Note that this presupposition follows from the theory of the social character of an actual entity and does not follow from Hume's theory. For it is quite possible, on Hume's theory, that the logical subject of the prediction, the sun, can survive through tomorrow morning although every natural law describing the relations of the sun to other elements in the present environment should fail to survive. Note also that both Whitehead and Hume, in discussing predictions, assume that the logical subject will be identifiable on the future occasion and agree that the problem is whether we have any reason for assuming also that the laws of nature, which would enable us to make additional affirmations concerning that subject, will also survive until the future. For Hume that assumption is unwarranted; for Whitehead it is an inevitable consequence of the assumption of the identifiability of the logical subject. Thus it is not merely "something which would, if we had any good reason to believe it, give us a basis for a rational prediction," to borrow Dr. Robson's phrase. Whitehead is not appealing to us here to believe this principle, nor is he insisting with Hume on our very strong propensity to belief in it. He is insisting rather that if we assume that our prediction has meaning, we assume that the logical subject will be identifiable, and that if the logical subject is assumed to be identifiable, we thereby also assume that the laws of nature which make its survival possible will themselves survive.

Thus the different answers which Whitehead and **Hume** give to the problem of induction follow directly from differences in their general analyses of experience. Granting the identifiability of the subject of a prediction, on Hume's theory of external relations we can claim no further knowledge about its relations to other things, and inductive inference remains irrational, while on Whitehead's theory of internal relations we automatically assume such further knowledge and have a rational basis for further predictions. If, on the other hand, it is assumed that the logical subject is unidentifiable, then for both men the problem of induction would not arise, for the so-called prediction would be confessedly meaningless. In Whitehead's words, "the question as to what will happen to an unspecified entity in an unspecified environment has no answer" (PR 312).

The only appeal to experience which Whitehead has made directly in connection with this argument has been an appeal to us to examine the logical structure of a specific prediction. The rest of the argument rests ultimately on his account of the nature of an actual entity. But even here he requires only that the actual entities shall be related internally and dynamically to their own immediate past and their own environ- ment; their internal relations with future occasions do not enter into the argument at all. Thus those features of Whitehead's general answer to Hume which Dr. Robson seems to find acceptable are the important ones for this argument, while those which he finds unacceptable are here irrelevant. But they are not irrelevant to the nonstatistical judgments of probability which are also mentioned. It is not my intention here to discuss this second type of judgment or to present a defence of White- head's cosmology, but I shall consider briefly two objections which Dr. Robson has raised, one of which is logical and one empirical.

According to Dr. Robson, Whitehead's theory involves an internal relationship between an event *a* and a subsequent, non-overlapping event *b.* Here Dr. Robson finds a logical difficulty. The relationship between *a* and *b* can conceivably be internal with respect to *b*, but not with respect to *a*, "for the simple reason that it [*a*] must be completed before any subsequent non-overlapping events occur." This is clearly a logical objection, but I do not find it so very simple, because the meaning of the word 'completed' is left so very vague. If the objection is logical, then there must be some principle in the philosophy of Whitehead which this doctrine of internal relations contradicts, but I can find no such principle. But the main difficulty is that a thing can be complete by one standard and incomplete by another. If, for example, we adopt with Whitehead the Platonic dictum that "the definition of being is simply power," we can easily demonstrate the ambiguity. Consider Whitehead's own example. The utterance of the word 'united' is obviously a complete event by one standard. The dictionary records it as a complete word, and the utterance of it would answer an appropriate question. But if the word is followed in utterance by the word "states," its power as a causal force is clearly altered. If, on the other hand, it is followed by "fruit company" or "mine-workers" or "states of Brazil," in each case its causal force would be different. This seems to be a clear illustration of an internal relation, if we adopt the usual notion of an internal relation as relating two terms in such a way that if one be altered, there is a corresponding alteration in the other. To be sure, not all the properties of the second need be altered. In our example, the utterance of the subsequent words does not alter the sound of the first word, or the amount of breadth expended, or the number of syllables in the word, but it does affect the causal force to the extent that if the subsequent words were altered or omitted, the effect of the original word would be historically quite different. Thus we cannot allow Dr. Robson's objection on the ground of completeness simply because it seems to have no connection with Whitehead's cosmology.

Dr. Robson's other objection is empirical, in that he claims that his own experience provides no verification for "this suggestion that in anticipating the future we are aware of internal relational properties involving future events." We must, I think, agree with this whole section of Dr. Robson's argument to the extent that if we adopt a certain attitude toward our experience, we will find no internal relations to the future. Both Descartes and Hume succeeded in adopting this attitude, the formula for which is provided by Dr. Robson. The essential element in it is that we must reduce the immanence of the future in the present to "nothing . . . except our familiar psychological bent toward the future." That is to say, we must bifurcate our experience into two divisions and dismiss one of them as cosmologically irrelevant. My point is that we can adopt such an attitude, that it will lead us directly to Hume's skeptical conclusions, and that there isn't the slightest reason in the world for adopting it.

According to Whitehead, the actual entities of the universe are acts or occasions of experience. Within each occasion different elements are discriminable and can be labeled past, present, and future in respect of the nature of their causal relations to one another. The causal energy, which is the creative process of the universe, is transmitted from the past to the future, and the present is occupied with the decisions determining how the energy from that particular past can be molded so as to produce that particular future. To say that the future is immanent in the present as a general fact is to point to that aspect of our experience which constantly warns us that we must make our own definite decisions, "or else. . . ." To say that a particular future is immanent is to point to the fact that it is our envisagement of that particular future which determines our actions now, gives them their significance and affects their force as causal agents. Of course, our particular anticipations are not always fulfilled, but we allow for that here and now in the constant realization that other forces will be active in the future, which must be reckoned with now, for those forces are likewise now in preparation in the contemporary world. In this lies the justification for our instinctive belief in the importance of scientific knowledge.

This point could be elaborated endlessly, and its main object is not proof but persuasion. We are confronted with two types of cosmological analysis, each one of which claims to be an illuminating interpretation of our experience. Each should be examined exclusively in its own terms, without prejudgment as to what is "complete" or what is merely "psychological." But what seems to be still more interesting is that if we adopt Whitehead's cosmology, we can, by appropriate limitations, derive the Cartesian cosmology from it, although the converse is not true. Further, if we limit ourselves within this cosmology to internal relations with the immediate past and the environment, we can derive a satisfactory answer to the problem of induction. Whitehead's appeal is directed to our intuitions, but to intuitions which have not been predetermined by Descartes and Hume. To respond to this appeal may require an initial leap of the imagination, but that should not be beyond the power of philosophers.

Whitehead's Theory of
Becoming

by V. C. Chappell

My purpose in this paper is mainly critical: I want to show that one of the positions that Whitehead defends in his later philosophical writings is untenable. My criticism will be twofold. I shall claim, first, that the position in question itself is unintelligible and, second, that the argument on which Whitehead rests this position is invalid. My aim is not wholly critical, however, for I shall make some positive suggestions, in the light of my critical conclusions, regarding Whitehead's conception and practice of philosophy. Whitehead says that his method, in his later works, is that of "speculative philosophy," and he devotes some space to explaining what this is and to defending his conviction that it is "a method productive of important knowledge." But I think it is not altogether clear, from either Whitehead's statements or his practice, just what speculative philosophy is. And since I think that a good deal of the contemporary disregard, if not outright disdain, of Whitehead's later philosophical work is founded on an ignorance or misunderstanding of the business that Whitehead has set himself to do, I think it is worthwhile to try to make this plain. I think more contemporary philosophers might read Whitehead and appreciate his genius if they knew better how he conceived the philosophical enterprise. Of course, there are some who will say that the task of speculative philosophy, as Whitehead understood it, is not one that ought to be or needs to be or even can be done and, hence, that Whitehead's later work is beside any properly philosophical point. I think it would be wrong to say this and that philosophers who do or would say it have too narrow a conception of philosophy themselves, that they arbitrarily limit the scope and power of philosophy. But I shall not here undertake to defend this point; I shall not try to defend Whitehead's claim that speculative philosophy is a method productive of important knowledge. I shall confine

"Whitehead's Theory of Becoming." Reprinted from the Whitehead Centennial Issue of the *Journal of Philosophy*, 58 (1961), 516-528.

myself rather to the task of making clear, at least in part, what speculative philosophy is for Whitehead.

I

The Whiteheadian position that I want to criticize is the "epochal theory of time," or, as Whitehead might better have called it, of becoming (SMW 183-186; PR 105). According to this theory, time (or becoming) "is not another continuous process [but] is an atomic succession" (SMW 185). This means that particular processes, particular stretches of time or becoming, cannot always be divided into divisible processes, for at some point the division will reach the atomic units of these processes, the units whose succession constitutes these processes. But now Whitehead holds that these atomic units of process are themselves processes, though of a quite different kind. The composite sort of process Whitehead calls "macroscopic," or the "process of transition"; the unit sort he calls "microscopic," or the "process of concrescence" (PR 320 ff.). Hence the epochal theory can be more accurately stated as follows: A process of transition is a succession of processes of concrescence; the former process is discontinuous, because division of it will eventually yield its component processes of concrescence, and these component processes are themselves indivisible. The process of transition is divisible, but not *in infinitum;* it is not endlessly divisible into sections that are themselves divisible processes of transition. But the process of concrescence is not divisible at all and, hence, is neither continuous nor discontinuous; this contrast has no application to this sort of process.[1]

According to Whitehead, the process of concrescence is the process by which an actual occasion comes into being; it is the act of becoming that constitutes the actual occasion, that is its "real internal constitution." Hence a process of transition is a succession of actual occasions. Now it is clear that the discontinuous character of the succession is owing to the atomic or indivisible character of the occasions, not the other way around. Hence the fundamental fact to which the epochal theory alludes is the indivisibility of actual occasions, i.e., the indivisibility of the processes or acts of becoming of which actual occasions are constituted. Whitehead sometimes expresses this point by saying that the act of becoming that constitutes an actual occasion "is not extensive" (PR 107), i.e., is not temporally extended. He even says that the act "is not in physical time" (PR 434).

But now, although the becoming of an actual occasion is indivisible and not extensive, according to Whitehead, the occasion that becomes, the completed entity, is temporally extended and so is divisible. The same holds for the completed succession of actual entities that is the creature of a process of transition; it too is divisible, and divisible *in infinitum.* Thus there is a contrast for Whitehead between the *product* and the *process* of becoming, whether microscopic or macroscopic. The former is extensive and continuous for both sorts of becoming; the latter is discontinuous (in the case of macroscopic becoming) or not extensive (in the case of microscopic becoming). Or as Whitehead also puts it, "there is a becoming of continuity, but no continuity of becoming" (PR 53). The same contrast is expressed in Whitehead's double use of the word 'time.' Sometimes he uses it to refer to the *product* of a process of (macroscopic) becoming (so, e.g., in SMW 183), sometimes to the *process* itself (so, e.g., in PR 95, 434).[2]

The conclusions that constitute the epochal theory of time, Whitehead says, "are required by the consideration of [certain philosophical] arguments" (PR 105; cf. SMW 186), in particular of one of the celebrated motion paradoxes of Zeno. Zeno's arguments are not all valid in Whitehead's view, but there is one of them which is; Whitehead refers to this as the "Arrow in Its Flight," but it is actually the Dichotomy that he has in mind, as his discussion of it makes clear. As Aristotle states it, Zeno's argument is "that in traversing any distance we must first traverse the half of it, that these subdivisions are infinite, and that it is impossible to pass through an infinite number of distances [*sc.* in a finite time]."[3] But Aristotle's statement is ambiguous; he fails to make clear whether the "infinite number of distances" to be traversed by any moving object were meant by Zeno to form the series ". . . , ⅛, ¼, ½," i.e., a *regression,* or the series "½, ¼, ⅛, . . . ," i.e., a *progression.* Aristotle himself supposed the latter and hence was able to say that Zeno's Dichotomy argument "is essentially the same as" the so-called Achilles (*Physics* Z, 9, 239b18-19). But Simplicius and numerous commentators after him chose the former alternative.[4] For them the difficulty that Zeno's argument uncovers is not that the motion of a moving body cannot be *completed,* but rather that it cannot *start,* that no body can *begin* to move. For—so the argument runs—a body cannot move without traversing some distance; but before any distance can be traversed there is always another distance, *viz.,* the half of the original distance, which must be traversed first; and since there is therefore no distance that can be said to be *the* first, there is also no movement that can be said to be *the* first, which means that motion cannot begin. On this interpretation the Dichotomy is not the same as the Achilles.

It is clear that Whitehead interprets Zeno's argument as Simplicius did and not as Aristotle did; hence he stresses the difference between it and the Achilles (PR 107). But Whitehead also changes the argument, so interpreted, in at least two ways. First, he generalizes it; he makes the argument apply not just to motion but to becoming generally, which is to say to all forms of change and process and even to mere persistence through time, since on Whitehead's view persistence is simply a succession of distinct becomings.[5] Second, Whitehead adds a premise to Zeno's argument. As it stands, the argument assumes that any process of motion (or, in its generalized form, of becoming) is divisible into parts that are themselves divisible processes of motion (or becoming). But Zeno's conclusion does not follow, Whitehead says, unless it is also assumed that "in a becoming something (*res vera*) becomes" (PR 106)—and indeed, as a later passage makes clear, a "something with temporal extension" (PR 107).[6] So generalized and supplemented, Zeno's argument is valid, according to Whitehead; it "elicits a contradiction" from the two assumptions mentioned. That is, it follows from the argument *either* that in a process of becoming nothing (having temporal extension) becomes *or* that the becoming is not always divisible into parts that are themselves (divisible) becomings (PR 106). And this means that one of these two assumptions must be given up. Whitehead might have given up the first, as Bergson did; he might have regarded the cosmos as something that, in Plato's phrase, "is always in the process of becoming . . . and never really is." But this goes against Whitehead's fundamental rationalism; for a world without real individuals, each with a distinct identity and a definite character, is not a world that can be rationally understood—which of course is just Bergson's point. In any case, Whitehead did respond to Zeno's argument by giving up the second of the two assumptions noted above. The argument is valid, Whitehead holds, and something (with temporal extension) does become in a process of becoming; hence we are forced, in his view, to deny that every process of becoming can be divided into parts that are themselves (divisible) becomings. Zeno's argument *shows* that some becomings are indivisible, according to Whitehead; better, it shows that macroscopic becomings are discontinuous and, more fundamentally, that microscopic becomings are not extensive. And this, as we have seen, is just the epochal theory.

II

I turn now to my criticism of this theory. I shall first argue (1) that the theory itself is unintelligible, and then try to show (2) that the Zenonian argument on which the theory is founded, even in its amended, Whiteheadian version, is invalid.

(1) The epochal theory stands or falls with the notion of a becoming that is not extensive. For the act of becoming that constitutes an actual occasion is indivisible because it is not extensive, and the process of transition whereby each actual occasion gives way to its successor is discontinuous because its component concrescences are indivisible. But the notion of a becoming that is not extensive is an odd notion at best. Becoming is ordinarily thought of as a process that takes a certain time to occur and that extends, therefore, through a certain period of time. To say that a certain act or process of becoming is not extensive, however,

would seem to imply that the becoming does not take any time to occur, that it is an act or process that extends through no time. The becoming may still occur at a time, i.e., at a certain instant, but only at that instant; hence it will be an instantaneous becoming. And it may be wondered how any act or process could be instantaneous, how it could (logically) take no time to occur. Whitehead indeed seems to be aware of this difficulty, for he seems to be pulled in two opposite directions in speaking about the process of concrescence. On the one hand he says things about it that seem clearly to imply its temporal extendedness. It can be "analyzed genetically into a series of subordinate phases which presuppose their antecedents" (PR 234); these phases are "successive" (PR 249); they are "real genetic phases" which together effect "the growth from the real to the actual," the growth "proceeding from phase to phase, each phase being the real basis from which its successor proceeds toward the completion of the [actual entity] in question" (PR 327). On the other hand, Whitehead says things that imply that the process of concrescence is not temporally extended, things over and above the original statement that it is not extensive. He says, e.g., that this process "is not in physical time" and that it "is not the temporal succession" (PR 434).

But even if this difficulty could be met and a sense found or provided for the notion of an instantaneous becoming or of an act or process that takes no time, there is another difficulty to be faced. Concrescences, or acts of microscopic becoming, *take* no time in Whitehead's view; they could not do so and still be nonextensive. But they must occur *in* time; they must have dates even if they are without duration. But the events or occasions that are the products of such acts are also located in time. Indeed, they have both date and duration, according to Whitehead; the existence of each begins at one definite time, ceases at a later time, and extends through all the times between. But if both the act and the product of the act of becoming are in time, there must be some temporal relation between them. But what could this relation be? Certainly the act cannot be either altogether earlier or altogether later than the product; the act's date must coincide with one of the times through which the produced event exists. But we cannot say that the act is simultaneous with the event's time of cessation, for then we should have to grant that the event began before its act of becoming had occurred, which is absurd. Nor can we, for the same reason, say that the act occurs at any time later than that at which the event begins to be. Therefore we must conclude that an actual occasion's act of becoming coincides with the moment at which the occasion begins to exist.

But this conclusion will not stand. An event or occasion is said to exist from time t_0 to time t_1 because an act of becoming, the act whereby it comes into being, occurs at t_0. But what does it mean to say that an event or occasion comes into being? *Things* come to be, but events *occur* or *happen*.[7] Yet the products of acts of microscopic becoming *are* events or occasions according to Whitehead, and are not things or objects. What Whitehead must mean, therefore, when he says that actual occasions become, is just that they happen; or at any rate he must allow that what 'becoming' signifies, when used of actual occasions, is no different from what we should ordinarily call 'happening.' Substituting 'happening' for 'becoming,' then, the above conclusion reads: an actual occasion exists from t_0 to t_1 because it happens at t_0; the occasion, which is temporally extended, begins at the time of its happening, and its happening is itself instantaneous. Put in this way, however, Whitehead's doctrine is easily shown to be senseless. For it requires us to distinguish the happening of an event or occasion from the event itself, or from the event's existence. But how does an event differ from its happening, or how does its existence do so? The answer is that it differs not at all. An event is not one thing and its happening another; happening adds nothing to an event, as being or existing adds nothing to a thing or object. An event, in short, *is* its happening; to be an event and to happen are one and the same.

It follows that there is a crucial difference between happening and becoming in the proper sense and also between objects or things and events. For the being or existence of a thing is distinct from its becoming, but the "being" of an event just is its occurrence or happening, so that in the case of events "being" and "becoming" coincide. Things (objects) come into being and then are; their becoming precedes their being; and although nothing can come into being without thereby being, it is at least conceivable that a thing should be and not have come to be. But if an event "becomes" by happening it also "is" by happening. Then if we choose, with Whitehead, to use 'becoming' of events or actual occasions, we must acknowledge, as Whitehead himself does not, that our meaning is no different from what it would have been had we used 'being' instead.

Actual occasions, Whitehead says, are temporally extended, but their acts of becoming, which is to say their happenings, are not. But if an occasion is its happening, if it exists by happening, then Whitehead's doctrine ends in a contradiction: one self-same thing both is and is not extensive. And this is sufficient to show the unintelligibilty of Whitehead's view.

(2) But not only is Whitehead's epochal theory of becoming unintelligible; the argument on which it is founded is invalid as well. It is easy enough to show the invalidity of Zeno's Dichotomy argument in its original form, i.e., as it stands without the changes that Whitehead made in it. For in this form the argument assumes that because there is no *first* distance traversed by a moving body and hence no *first* motion, its motion can have no *beginning*. And this is clearly not the case. As Adolf Grünbaum has expressed it,

What is true in the "Dichotomy" argument as applied to the theory of events is that the dense ordering of the events [required by the "infinite divisibility of time"] entails the absence of a first subinterval among the continuum of events which elapse. . . . [But] the requirement that there be such a first sub-interval [is] entirely gratuitous. There is a first event in the motion process but no first motion, no first time interval and no first space interval. . . . Zeno was entirely successful in showing that there is no first motion but it does not follow that there is no motion, as he thought. . . . [T]here is no more reason why there should be [a first motion] than there is a reason for the existence of a first rational fraction greater than 0.[8]

So the question before us is this: Are the changes Whitehead makes in Zeno's argument sufficient or of the right sort to change it from an invalid argument to a valid one? And the answer is that they are not.

Whitehead changes Zeno's argument in two ways: (1) he makes it apply not just to motion but to becoming generally; (2) he adds the premise that "in every act of becoming there is the becoming of something with temporal extension" (PR 107). He then draws the conclusion that macroscopic becoming is discontinuous because composed of acts of microscopic becoming that are indivisible, on the grounds that if there were not such indivisible acts nothing having temporal extension would become in an act of becoming, which controverts the added premise. Whitehead must mean, therefore, that in every act of *microscopic* becoming, in every process of concrescence, there is the becoming of something with temporal extension. To use the terminology of a recent writer, Whitehead's view seems to be that 'becoming,' in the microscopic sense, is a "verb of accomplishment," i.e., that actions which count as becomings have a "set terminal point, . . . a 'climax,' which has to be reached if the action is to be what it is claimed to be"; such actions "proceed toward a terminus which is logically necessary to their being what they are." [9] Thus there is no becoming until the terminus has been reached and the accomplishment—viz., the creation of something with temporal extension—has been effected. Becoming cannot, then, be divided (into becomings), for the reason that the products of any division are logically precluded from being themselves becomings; to say that part of a becoming is itself a becoming would be to go against the meaning of the term 'becoming.'

But let us consider the nature of the accomplishment in the case of (microscopic) becoming. Becoming, Whitehead says, must issue in something with temporal extension. He does *not* say, something with a certain *minimum amount* of temporal extension. Nor does he mention any other condition that a thing must meet to count as an accomplishment or product of an act of becoming. Of course, actual occasions, the products of acts of microscopic becoming in Whitehead's view, do have other features, and features essential to their being what they are. But these features are not mentioned in Whitehead's statement of the premises of

Zeno's argument. The conclusion is to follow from the sole requirement that what becomes have temporal extension; the only condition necessary for something's being a product of an act of becoming that is relevant to the conclusion is this, that the thing in question be temporally extended. But if a thing need only be temporally extended in order to be an accomplishment of an act of becoming, there is no reason to deny that part of such a thing is itself such an accomplishment. Half a temporally extended thing is still a temporally extended thing, though it is not of course the original whole thing. Let us now suppose that an act of becoming, which by its nature must issue in some temporally extended thing, were itself temporally extended and so divisible into parts. There is then no reason to deny the existence, for each resulting part of the act, of a corresponding part of the accomplishment of the whole act, which, since it is a temporally extended thing, will also be divisible into parts. Nor is there any reason to deny that each such part of the accomplishment is *the* accomplishment of the corresponding part of the act. And finally, since each part of the accomplishment is itself something with temporal extension, there is no reason to deny that the part of the act of becoming whose accomplishment it is is itself an act of becoming. For an act of becoming need only, on the grounds actually stated by Whitehead, issue in something with temporal extension in order to count as an act of becoming.

I conclude, therefore, that the conclusion drawn by Whitehead from Zeno's Dichotomy argument, even as Whitehead amends it, does not follow; it does not follow from the premise that in an act of microscopic becoming something with temporal extension becomes that such an act is itself indivisible, not extensive, and "not in physical time." Zeno's argument is no more valid with the changes made in it by Whitehead than it is without them.

III

I want now to make some general points about Whitehead's philosophical procedure which are suggested and, I think, illustrated—though they are not, of course, established—by the results of my critical examination of the epochal theory. To begin with, I want to note how little of Whitehead's philosophical position as a whole is affected by my criticisms. If my claims are just, the epochal theory of time or becoming is both untenable and unnecessary; there is no sense to the doctrine that the process of concrescence or act of becoming that constitutes an actual occasion is temporally nonextensive, and no reason to hold such a doctrine. But this result, far from striking at the heart of Whitehead's philosophical position, only cuts off a minor appendage, an appendage which has no function other than that of protecting Whitehead's system from the—supposed—upshot of Zeno's argument, and which has no ground in or connection with any other element in the system. There are four major and essential tenets in Whitehead's position regarding actual occasions: (1) that there are real individuals with distinct identities and definite natures and that actual occasions are such individuals; (2) that the fundamental units of reality are temporally extended and, hence, that actual occasions are; (3) that actual occasions exist by becoming, that they are self-creative processes; and (4) that actual occasions are finally caused and hence have an atomic character, which is to say that the process that constitutes an actual occasion cannot be divided into processes that are themselves actual occasions. No one of these tenets is in the least affected by my criticisms of the epochal theory. Each of them is logically independent of the epochal theory and is held on grounds other than Zeno's argument—each, indeed, is held on grounds of a different sort from those provided by Zeno's argument, as I shall suggest in a moment. It might be thought that (4) above *is* the epochal theory, but this is not the case. For the epochal theory is not that the process of concrescence is indivisible in *any* way for *any* reason, but that it is indivisible in the *particular* way and for the *particular* reason that it is temporally nonextensive. And my criticism of the epochal theory was directed not against the notion that there are indivisible processes or that actual occasions are indivisible processes in general—because finally caused or for any other reason. My criticism was directed rather at the notion of a *temporally* indivisible process, the notion that actual occasions are indivisible because temporally nonextensive. I concluded that there is no reason to deny that actual occasions are temporally extensive and hence temporally divisible—divisible into parts that are themselves becomings of something with temporal extension. But this leaves altogether open the possibility that actual occasions may be indivisible in some other way and for some other reason. And Whitehead's basic reason for holding that actual occasions are indivisible unities, atomic drops of process, is, I think, his doctrine that they are finally caused, which doctrine is in no way required by or even related to the Dichotomy argument of Zeno.

The fact that the major elements in Whitehead's account of actual occasions are independent of Whitehead's own use of Zeno's argument and, hence, are untouched by my criticism of that argument and its alleged conclusion suggests that the role played by such arguments in Whitehead's philosophy is relatively slight. Since Zeno's argument is typical of many philosophical arguments and indeed is a paradigm of a certain important type of philosophical argument, we may say that the role played by philosophical arguments of this type in Whitehead's philosophy is small. To be sure, Whitehead often cites such arguments; he often mentions, develops, states, and even employs them in his writings. But their function is not, I believe, to *determine* the elements of his philosophical system, to settle *which* positions shall find a place in it—though

this is the function that they generally appear to have and that Whitehead himself perhaps thought they did have. Their function is rather to
provide a kind of negative *test* of positions already arrived at by quite
other means, and in particular by nonargumentative means. Whitehead's
philosophical position is not so much the *conclusion* of a philosophical
argument as an *imaginative construction*. This construction must, Whitehead says, meet certain tests, some internal or "rational," and some external or "empirical" (PR 4 ff.). Among the external tests Whitehead includes only (1) that the construction be "applicable," and (2) that it
be "adequate." But another external test that Whitehead actually employs, and employs frequently, is that the construction be secure against
traditional philosophical objections, the objections that arguments such
as that of Zeno bring to light. Hence philosophical arguments do have
a role in Whitehead's philosophy, but a subsidiary and secondary role.
They are used by Whitehead, at least for the most part, not to determine
what goes into the philosophical system, but to help make what has already been put there comfortable and safe. Hence they play their role
only after the main content of the system has been settled upon and
settled upon by altogether different means.

The fact that philosophical arguments, at least of the type represented
by Zeno's argument, play this subsidiary and relatively minor role in
Whitehead's philosophy is one thing, I think, that makes Whitehead's
later work uninteresting at best to many contemporary philosophers.
For the majority of present-day philosophers, or anyhow for those of an
"analytic" bent, a philosophical doctrine is essentially the conclusion of
a philosophical argument; philosophy is principally and distinctively
argumentative or dialectical in character, and imaginative construction,
whatever its own merits, is not a *philosophical* procedure—its use does
not result in *philosophical* theses. And it is pretty obvious, I think, that
the major tenets of Whitehead's philosophical position are not the
conclusions of philosophical arguments, for all that Whitehead does make
use of such arguments. The fact that his use of them is often careless
and unsuccessful, as I have argued it is in the case of Zeno's argument,
has seemed to many philosophers to confirm their low judgment of
Whitehead's philosophical prowess. But I think that in fact it does nothing of the kind. For not only do I think that Whitehead's use of philosophical arguments is different from the use these philosophers would
make of them and that such arguments are of less importance to him
than to them. I also think that their conception of philosophy, as argument and little else, is unwarrantedly narrow. Philosophy also, to my
mind, comprehends the sort of imaginative construction that was Whitehead's forte and that he practiced better, as I believe, than anyone else
has done in the present century. But this is itself a claim that requires
justification, and I have not tried to provide such justification here. I
have not even tried to justify my claim that philosophy for Whitehead

is essentially imaginative construction, although this too needs justifying. For there are some students of Whitehead's philosophy, I imagine, who might dispute it.

NOTES

[1] The process of concrescence can, however, be *analyzed* into its component *prehensions;* see, e.g., PR 35 and *passim.*

[2] Whitehead uses the word in both ways and explicitly contrasts the two uses in his article "Time" (*Proceedings of the Sixth International Congress of Philosophy*, 1926), pp. 63-64.

[3] *Physics* Θ, 8, 263a4-6; see *ibid.* Z, 2, 233a23 for the scholium. I have used the translation of Aristotle that is given by H. D. P. Lee in his book *Zeno of Elea* (Cambridge: University Press, 1936), except that I have used 'pass through' for 'διεξελθεῖν' and 'διεξιέναι' in place of Lee's 'complete,' which seems to me to make for awkward English. I have, however, preserved Lee's distinction between these two terms on the one hand and 'διελθεῖν' and 'διιέναι' on the other (a distinction not observed by the Oxford translators) by retaining Lee's "traverse" in rendering the latter two terms.

[4] See Simplicius's commentary on the *Physics*, 1013.4 ff. More recent commentators who take the same view are, e.g., V. Brochard, "Les arguments de Zénon d'Élée contre le mouvement," *Séances et travaux de l'académie des sciences morales et politiques*, n.s. 29 (1888), 555-568; G. Noel, "Le mouvement et les arguments de Zénon d'Élée," *Revue de métaphysique et de morale*, 1 (1893), 107-125; J. Burnet, *Early Greek Philosophy* (London: Black, 1892; 4th ed., 1930); Lee, *op. cit.;* and W. D. Ross, *Aristotle's Physics* (Oxford: University Press, 1936).

[5] Hence his statement that "the true difficulty" brought to light by Zeno's argument "is to understand how [anything] survives the lapse of time" (PR 106).

[6] The qualification is essential, Whitehead says, for Zeno's "difficulty is not evaded by assuming that something becomes at each non-extensive instant of time" (PR 106). But Whitehead does not always state the qualification in stating the premise. Indeed, in SMW he states Zeno's argument, and says that it is valid, without this added premise; see page 186. But this must be a slip, for Zeno's argument is obviously invalid without this added premise; see below, pp. 75-76 and footnote 8. It should be noted that the premise Whitehead adds to Zeno's argument can be added only after the argument has been generalized and made to apply to becoming. For there is no comparable premise, no analogous addition, that can be stated for the case of motion by itself.

[7] Cf. J. J. C. Smart, "The River of Time," *Mind*, 58 (1949).

[8] "Relativity and the Atomicity of Becoming," *Review of Metaphysics*, 4 (1950-1951), 177-178. Cf. Aristotle, *Physics* Z, 5, 236a14 and 26-27; also *ibid.*, Z, 6, 237b5-7; and R. M. Blake, "The Paradox of Temporal Process," *Journal of Philosophy*, 23 (1926), 653.

[9] Zeno Vendler, "Verbs and Times," *Philosophical Review*, 66 (1957), 145-146.

Whitehead's Theory of Prehensions

by Lucio Chiaraviglio

I. Position, Definiteness, Strains

According to Whitehead, actual entities function in the becoming of other entities (PR 38). An entity functions in the becoming of another if it contributes position or definiteness or both to the other entity. Each actual entity, feeling, nexus, and generally any entity that becomes has associated with it an extensive quantum. Also, each of these entities may be said to occupy the volume of its quantum. The volume of an extensive quantum is the set of all the interior points of the quantum. The position of entities is specified by the relative position of the points of their volumes. But a point is a special set of sets of entities, and the relative position of points is specified by the topology of the space of all points. In its turn, the topology of this space is specified uniquely by the volumes of the extensive quanta. The entities that become occupy their volumes, volumes are located relative to one another by their points, and the relative position of points is determined by the volumes of these entities. Thus we come full circle and may say that the entities that become position one another.

In a similar way, we may say that entities contribute to one another's definiteness. The definiteness of an entity is, for Whitehead, the exemplification by that entity of selected eternal objects. It would seem that, besides the entities and the sets of entities that become, our universe must also contain an entirely different kind of entity that is eternal. But it will be seen that we may construe eternal objects as special sets of becoming entities. These sets have the property of being independent of position. An entity that becomes will be said to exemplify an eternal object when it is a member of the object. If we conceive eternal objects to be special kinds of sets of entities, then we may say that the entities that become

"Whitehead's Theory of Prehensions." Part I is reprinted from the Whitehead Centennial Issue of the *Journal of Philosophy*, **58** (1961), 528-534.

mutually determine one another's definiteness as well as one another's position.

Even though entities determine one another's definiteness and position, these two features of entities are relatively independent of each other. Becoming entities acquire position through the agency of physical feelings, and they acquire definiteness through the agency of both physical and conceptual feelings. But neither does the position of an entity uniquely determine its definiteness, nor does the definiteness of an entity uniquely determine its position. Consider, for example, the case of a physical feeling. Among the eternal objects exemplified by feelings are the geometric elements. A given geometric element, say a specific flat locus of points contained in the volume of some feeling, is a special set of sets of sets of entities that is not eternal. On the other hand, flatness is an eternal object among whose members is the flat locus in question. Thus, many other feelings could exemplify flatness, but each such feeling would have a different position.

Yet position and definiteness are not absolutely independent features of every entity. For example, physical feelings must reproduce the definiteness of their objective data; hence every eternal property of the geometric elements of the data is reproduced in the feeling. If flatness is exemplified in the data, then the corresponding feelings may not occupy volumes that do not contain flat loci of points. Conversely, if the feelings occupy volumes that contain flat loci, then they must exemplify flatness.

There follows a brief sketch of the theory of feelings, together with an account of the connection between this theory and the theory of extensive abstraction. The purpose of this sketch is to obtain definitions of 'definiteness' and 'position.' In terms of these two concepts we shall elucidate the reproduction of eternal objects in physical feelings. The reproductive character of physical feelings will be illustrated by the particular case of strains. Since a strain is a physical feeling whose objective datum is dominated by flat loci of points, it will serve well to illustrate the reproduction of geometrical eternal objects (PR 472). Furthermore, the other eternal objects exemplified by the datum of a strain may be assigned to flat loci so that the corresponding flat loci of the strain will be qualified by the same eternal objects as the flat loci of the datum (PR 476).[1]

Let S be the set of all feelings, S_1 be the set of all physical feelings, and S_2 be the set of all conceptual feelings. $S = S_1 \cup S_2$ and S_1 'F' is to be read "is a physical feeling of." F is a many-one, asymmetric, and irreflexive relation whose domain is S_1 and whose range is S. 'R' is to be read "has the same subject as." R is an equivalence relation whose field is S. A is the set of all equivalence subsets of S with respect to R: $A = S/R$. The members of A may be called "actual entities." Some of the conditions satisfied by F, R, and A are as follows:

1. If $X \in A$, then $X \cap S_1 \neq \Lambda$ and $X \cap S_2 \neq \Lambda$.
2. If Rxy, then neither Fxy nor Fyx.
3. If Rxy and $x \neq y$, then there is no z such that Fxz and Fyz.
4. If $X,Y \in A$ and if there is an $x \in X$ and a $y \in Y$ such that Fxy, then there are no $x' \in X$ and $y' \in Y$, $x' \neq x$, $y' \neq y$, such that either $Fy'x'$ or $Fx'y'$.

The categories of subjective unity and subjective harmony seem to require that R be an equivalence relation. If different subjects had common feelings, then we could surely abstract these feelings from their subjects. The category of objective diversity seems to require that no feeling have two distinct objects. Thus, F must be a many-one relation. The category of objective identity seems to require that no two distinct feelings of one actual entity have the same object (PR 39-41). Hence the relation F is one-one from the physical feelings that are members of one actual entity to the members of some subsets of S.

The notion of "actuality" explicated so far is nonrelative. A relative notion of actuality may be explained in terms of 'Pre.' 'Pre,' to be read "prehends," is defined as follows: If $X \in A$ and $Y \in A$, then Pre XY if and only if there is an $x \in X$ and a $y \in Y$ such that Fxy. Since the set A and the relation Pre form a lattice without upper or lower bounds (PR 33, 95-126, 296, 486-489), we may introduce a relative concept of actuality as follows: Y is actual for X if and only if Pre XY. The set of all Y that are actual relative to X is the actual world of X (PR 34, 117-126, 294, 345-346, 351, 435-439). The actual world of X is a subset of A that has no terminal member relative to Pre. According to the fifth category of explanation, the actual worlds of distinct actual entities are distinct (PR 33-34). The actual world of Y is a subset of the actual world of X if and only if Pre XY. The actual worlds of any two actual entities have a nonnull intersection.

In order to explicate "position" we shall make use of some of the predicates of the theory of extensive abstraction. Among the predicates that we shall use are the following: "is a part of," "overlaps," "is a point," "is a flat locus," "is the volume of," and "is an ovoid" (PR 449-471). These predicates are defined by Whitehead in terms of the sole primitive predicate "is connected with." To these predicates we shall add two more: (a) "x is the aggregate of X" is to mean "any y overlaps x if and only if y overlaps some member of X"; and (b) "x is a connected entity" is to mean "there exist no y and z such that y is not connected with z, and x is the aggregate of the set whose only two members are y and z."

The field of the relation *is connected with* is constituted by the members of S and the aggregates of any subsets of S (PR 441-444). If $X \in A$ and x is the aggregate of X, then we shall say that x is the *satisfaction* of X. We assume that satisfactions are connected entities and that every connected part of a satisfaction is a member of S. Every satisfaction is a connected entity, and so is every feeling.

Let S_3 be the set of all satisfactions; then we have that the aggregate of S_3 is identical with the aggregate of S. Since R is an equivalence relation, no two distinct members of S_3 may overlap. In contradistinction, every member of S is overlapped by an infinite number of members of S. Indeed, every member of S must be a member of some abstractive set. In short, we suppose that the axioms of the theory of extensive abstraction are sufficient to show that every member of the field of the relation *is connected with* has a unique volume.

If every member of S and every aggregate of subsets of S has a unique volume, then all these volumes will be subsets of the volume of the aggregate of S. Let v be the volume of the aggregate of S, and let V be the set of all the volumes of the aggregates of subsets of S; then it may be ascertained that the ordered pair (v,V) is a normal topological space. This space is metrizable just in case there exists a denumerable subset S' of S such that every member of S is the aggregate of some subset of S'.

Once a metric for the space (v,V) is fixed, the distance between two points will receive a unique physical interpretation in terms of the relations that hold among the feelings whose volumes contain the given points. Any metric for the space (v,V) must have the property that the sets of points that are open in the sense of the metric are all and only those sets which are members of V. Since the members of V are the volumes of feelings and aggregates of feelings, the relative position of points is dependent only on the extensive relations that hold among feelings. The relative position of points is independent of the choice of a metric. Further development of the theory of position depends on the choice of the metric for the space (v,V).

Feelings may be said to occupy or to be positioned at their volumes (PR 458). Actual entities may be said to occupy or to be positioned at the volumes of their satisfactions. Similarly, we may say that sets of feelings or sets of actual entities occupy or are positioned at the volumes of the corresponding aggregates. Since the entities that are actual relative to some $X \in A$ are all of those which are members of the actual world of X, we may say that the position of some actual entities is determinate relative to X if these entities are members of the actual world of X. If $A_j \subseteq A$,[2] then the members of A_j are *positioned relative* to X if and only if A_j is a subset of the actual world of X. If x is a feeling and $S_j \subseteq S$, then the members of S_j are positioned relative to x if and only if there is an $X \in A$ such that $x \in X$ and every actual entity whose intersection with S_j is non-null is in the actual world of X. Similar definitions of "relative position" may be given for aggregates, sets of aggregates, and sets of sets of aggregates of subsets of S.

For the sake of simplicity we shall consider only those eternal objects which are subsets of the field of the relation *is connected with*. An eternal object is a subset of the field of *is connected with* such that its members are not positioned relative to any feeling. If S_j is a subset of the field of *is connected with*, then S_j is an eternal object if and only if there is no $x \in S$ such that the members of S_j are positioned relative to x (PR 38, 69-70, 283-287, 364-365, 443-447).

In our basic language there is a rule of subset formation which states that, given any sentential function 'F' in which 'S_j' and 'S' do not occur freely and given any set S, there exists a set S_j whose members are just those members of S which have the property F. F is independent of position if the set S_j is an eternal object. F is localized, or dependent on position, if S_j is not an eternal object.

The definiteness of an entity x may be conceived as the collection of all the properties of x that are independent of position. If $x \in S$, then D_x is the form of definiteness of x if and only if the members of D_x are all and only those eternal objects S_j such that $x \in S_j$. Since we are considering only feelings, the form of definiteness of x is a set of subsets of the field of the relation *is connected with*.

A physical feeling may be considered to be a transformation that reproduces the form of definiteness of the objective datum. This transformation is complex, since we require that every connected part of a feeling be again a feeling. If v_x is the volume of x and v_y is the volume of y, ten (v_x, V_x) and (v_y, V_y) are the topological spaces induced by the identity transformation of v_x and v_y into v. If the set v is the volume of the aggregate of S, and (v, V) is the space previously defined, then V_x is a set of subsets of v_x such that every member of V_x is the intersection of v_x with some member of V. Similar remarks hold for (v_y, V_y). If Fxy, then there must exist a continuous transformation of (v_y, V_y) onto (v_x, V_x) such that the nonlocalized properties of y and parts of y are transmitted onto x and corresponding parts of x. More precisely, we assume that:

5. If Fxy, then there exists a homeomorphism H of (v_y, V_y) onto (v_x, V_x) such that, for any z, v, and D, z is a part of y, v is the volume of z, and D is the form of definiteness of z, if and only if there is a w part of x, $H(v)$ is the volume of w, and D is the form of definiteness of w. (Note: the relation *is a part of* is here taken to be reflexive.)

The feeling x conforms to its objective datum y in the sense that the forms of definiteness of x and y are identical and the forms of definiteness of parts of x and parts of y that have corresponding volumes are likewise identical (PR 361-367, 441, 445-447). If p_x and p_y are points of v_x and v_y such that $H(p_y) = p_x$, then p_x and p_y will belong to the volumes of parts of x and y that have identical forms of definiteness. Similarly, if $v'_x \subseteq v_x$, $v'_y \subseteq v_y$ and $H(v'_y) = v'_x$ (i.e., v'_x is the image of v'_y under H), then v'_x and v'_y are subsets of the volumes of parts of x and y that have identical forms of definiteness. Thus, to every point $p_y \in v_y$ and to the corresponding points $p_x = H(p_y) \in v_x$ we may assign the set of all the forms of definiteness of parts of y such that p_y is a member of their volume. More generally, to every set of points $v'_x = H(v'_y) \subseteq v'_x$ we may assign the set of all the forms of definiteness of parts of y such that v'_y is a subset of their volume. If we let Dv'_y be the set of forms of definiteness that is assigned to v'_y, then we may say that Dv'_y is the set of qualities implicated in v'_y (PR 472-473). $Dv'_y = Dv'_x$, if $H(v'_y) = v'_x$.

Every sufficiently small part of y whose volume contains v'_y is an *ovoid* if and only if v'_y is a flat locus of points. If the set of all ovoids is an eternal object, then v'_y is a flat locus if and only if the set of all ovoids is a member of every member of a certain subset of Dv'_y. Thus, if $v'_x = H(v'_y)$ and v'_y is a flat locus, then so is v'_x.

If there is a collection G_y of flat loci of points that are subsets of v_y and such that any subset of v_y is the union or intersection of some members of this collection, then we may say that v_y is *dominated* by G_y (PR 472-473). If v_y is dominated by G_y and Fxy, then v_x is dominated by a corresponding collection G_x of flat loci, where $v'_y \in G_y$, if and only if $H(v'_y) = v'_x \in G_x$.

A feeling x whose objective datum y has a volume v_y dominated by a collection G_y of flat loci is called by Whitehead a "strain." The form of definiteness of the feeling x or of a part of x may be expressed in terms of the set of qualities implicated in the volume of x or in the volume of parts of x. Every volume of a part of x, where x is a strain, must be the union or intersection of a collection of flat loci that are members of G_x. The members of G_x and G_y are paired in one-to-one fashion. Consequently, the form of definiteness of the strain x may be expressed in terms of the set of qualities implicated in G_y.

Since corresponding parts of a physical feeling and its objective datum have identical forms of definiteness, the volumes of these corresponding parts must have identical nonpositional geometric properties. In general it is not easy to see how to separate positional from nonpositional geometric properties of arbitrary subsets of the volumes of the datum and the feeling. But in the particular case of strains the task is facilitated by the fact that these volumes are dominated by flat loci of points. Once the sets of corresponding flat loci are known, the nonpositional, or eternal, geometric properties of arbitrary subsets of the volume of the strain are likewise known. The eternal properties of any arbitrary locus of points of the volume of a strain are all of those geometric properties of the locus which are entailed by the flatness of the component loci.

II. Nexūs, Eternal Nexūs, Eternal Objects

Whitehead's failure to provide the one-substance cosmology required by his ontological principle has been abundantly noted. Critics have contended that the philosophy of organism perpetuates the mind-body split, that it weights the account heavily toward mental substances, and that it commits the fallacy of misplaced concreteness. Such criticisms usually hinge on the fact that Whitehead postulates the existence of eternal objects but does not show how this postulate may be justified by the facts of immediate experience.

Indeed, the ontological principle, the cornerstone of the philosophy of organism, does not mention eternal objects. In the introductory chapters of *Process and Reality* we are told that "[t]he ultimate facts of immediate actual experience are actual entities, prehensions, and nexūs. All else is, for our experience, derivative abstraction" (PR 30). But farther along in the book we find that his nineteenth category of explanation states: "That the fundamental types of entities are actual entities and eternal objects; and that the other types of entities only express how all entities of the two fundamental types are in community with each other, in the actual world" (PR 37). This category seems to be inconsistent with the former uncompromising appeal to immediate experience and the ontological principle. Harmony is re-established between these disparate features of the philosophy of organism by the assumption that the locus of eternal objects, the Platonic world of ideas, is an actual entity. It is apparent that this actual entity is not very similar to her less exalted sisters.

It would be interesting to know how the principal features of Whitehead's cosmology are altered when the categoreal notion "eternal objects" is abandoned. One procedure which will demonstrate this alternative to his philosophy is as follows: (1) 'nexus' is defined in terms of "prehends" and "actual entity"; (2) a subset of nexus called "eternal nexus" is singled out; (3) 'forms of definiteness' is defined in terms of "eternal nexus"; and (4) 'eternal object,' 'conceptual prehension,' and 'illustrates' are defined in terms of "forms of definiteness" and "eternal nexus." Since eternal objects are to be conceived as special kinds of nexūs, there will be no need of postulating the existence of a realm in which these objects are located.

The set A of all actual entities is the field of the relation *prehends*. 'Prehends' is to be understood in the same sense as Whitehead's 'positive pure or hybrid physical prehension.' The basic features of *prehends* are as follows: (1) *prehends* is transitive and irreflexive; (2) any two members of A are prehended by a third; (3) any two members of A prehend a third; and (4) every member of A has at least one immediate successor and predecessor relative to *prehends* (PR 101-108, 467-471). Of course, a complete discussion of Whitehead's cosmology requires consideration of further axioms which jointly characterize 'prehends' and 'extensive connection.' There is no need to be concerned with all of them here, but it may be noted that these axioms should entail a theorem to the effect that the union of all the volumes of the extensive quanta of the members of A is an extensive continuum.

Conditions (2) and (3) above state that the universe A does not split up into noncommunicating parts. Whitehead achieves the same end by the postulate of the existence of God. The assumption that God's consequent nature exists entails condition (2). The assumption of the existence of God's primordial nature entails an analogue of condition (3). But this assumption also requires that *prehends* have a terminal member in A. In contradistinction, conditions (2) and (3) entail that *prehends* has no terminal and no initial members. The ontological principle and the principle of process jointly imply that every actual entity is both a first-place and a second-place member of *prehends*. Therefore, the postulate of the existence of God's primordial nature is inconsistent with these principles.

Any subset B of A is a nexus if and only if *prehends* restricted to B is transitive and irreflexive, and the members of B satisfy at least one of the following conditions: (1) for any two a and b in B there is a c in B which prehends both a and b; or (2) for any two a and b in B there is a c in B that is prehended by both a and b. Since the elements of A satisfy both conditions, A is a nexus. Furthermore, this definition covers the particular cases of societies, personal orders, enduring objects, indicative nexūs, routes of physical transmission, and actual worlds.

According to Whitehead: (1) a subset B of A is a society if *prehends* has one terminal member in B (PR 50-51); (2) if B is a society and *prehends* is a series on B, then B is a personally ordered nexus or an enduring object (PR 51-52); (3) an indicative nexus is a subset of A on which *prehends* is a series with one initial member (PR 296-297); (4) a route of physical transmission is a subset of A on which *prehends* is a series without initial or terminal members (PR 268, 438); and (5) the actual world B of an entity b is the largest subset of A which has b as its only initial member (PR 345, 351). All of these subsets of A satisfy the specifications of nexūs stated above.

As we have seen in Part I, Whitehead wishes to define 'position' in terms of "prehends," "nexus," "extensive quanta," and "extensive connection." A nexus B is temporally located relative to an actual entity b if B is a subset of the actual world of b, or if B is a subset of the future of b, or if B is disjoint from both the future and past of b. In other words, a nexus B has a temporal location relative to b if either b prehends every member of B, or every member of B prehends b, or no member of B prehends b and *vice versa* (PR 486-487).

The predicates 'eternal' and 'everlasting' may now be defined in terms of "relative temporal location." The nexus B is not temporally located relative to b if and only if B overlaps the past, the future, and the set of contemporaries of b. The nexus B is eternal if and only if B is not temporally located relative to any b in A. The nexus B is everlasting if and only if there is a b such that B is temporally located relative to b, and either B is not temporally located relative to every entity in the past of b or B is not temporally located relative to every entity in the future of b.

Neither societies, personal orders, enduring objects, indicative nexūs, nor actual worlds are eternal. Actual worlds are everlasting, because *prehends* has an initial and no terminal members in an actual world. Similarly, some societies, personal orders, enduring objects, and indicative nexūs may be everlasting if they have initial and no terminal members, or terminal and no initial members. Routes of physical transmission are eternal. Furthermore, every nexus that is eternal is the union of a set of routes of physical transmission. For example, the nexus A is eternal and is the union of all the routes of physical transmission.

In order to define 'eternal objects,' consider what Whitehead writes about the definiteness of actual entities and nexūs. The category of conceptual valuation stipulates that from each prehension there arises a purely conceptual prehension of an eternal object that determines the definiteness of the actual entity or nexus prehended (PR 39, 40). According to the eighth category of explanation, there are two kinds of description of an actual entity: the first describes how the actual entity may be prehended by others, the second describes how the actual entity prehends others (PR 34). Furthermore, the definiteness of actual entities or nexūs is what is described when they are abstracted from position (PR 38).

The above train of reasoning suggests that the definiteness of actual entities or nexūs is to be described by statements which refer to the past that generates them and the future which emerges from them. For example, if B is a physical route of transmission, then the statement *"b is a member of B"* partly describes the definiteness of b. Also such a statement abstracts from b's position, since it does not state where in B b is located. Similarly, if B is a physical route of transmission and B' is any nexus, then the statement *"B overlaps B'"* partly describes the definiteness of B'.

The form of definiteness D of an actual entity b is the union of all the physical routes of transmission to which b belongs. The statement *"b belongs to D"* does not specify how b is related by prehensions to the other members of D. Since the nexus D includes all of b's past and future, such a statement fully describes b's definiteness in complete abstraction from b's position in D. Also, note that the nexus D is eternal.

Entirely similar considerations to the ones presented suggest that the form of definiteness of a nexus is the union of the forms of definiteness of its members. Every form of definiteness, either of nexūs or of actual entities, is the union of some set of routes of physical transmission. Consequently, every route of physical transmission and every other eternal nexus that is also a form of definiteness is here called an "eternal object."

Definitions of 'conceptually prehends' and 'illustrates' now may be given in terms of "eternal object." The range of the relations *conceptu-*

ally prehends and *illustrates* is the set of all eternal objects. Thus, first, the structure of this set must be specified.

If E and E' are eternal objects and E' is a subset of E, then E is a complex eternal object and E' is one of its components. It may be easily seen that all eternal objects have components and that every eternal object is a component of A. Furthermore, every eternal object is the least upper bound of the set of its components. Thus, the relation *is a component of*, which holds among eternal objects, is a semi-lattice with least upper bound A. That is to say that for every two eternal objects E and E' there exists an eternal object E'' such that both E and E' are components of E'' and any other eternal object which has E and E' as components must also have E'' as a component. Also every eternal object must be a component of A.

Consider a set C of eternal objects on which the relation *is a component of* is a semi-lattice with the following specifications: (1) E is the least upper bound of C and of course a member of C; (2) there is a subset G of C composed entirely of eternal objects which are components of the forms of definiteness of some actual entities; (3) the least upper bound of G is E; and (4) G is the largest set composed of components of the forms of definiteness of actual entities that has least upper bound E. According to Whitehead: C is an abstractive hierarchy; G is the base of C; and E is the vertex of the hierarchy C (SMW 150-152).

An actual entity *illustrates* an eternal object if and only if the entity is a member of the eternal object. An actual entity does not illustrate every component of its form of definiteness. For example, if b is an actual entity that belongs to the route of physical transmission B, then there are many routes of physical transmission B' subsets of B such that b is not a member of B'.

The actual entity b *conceptually prehends* E if and only if b prehends every member of a nexus B and B is a subset of the eternal object E. If b conceptually prehends E, then b conceptually prehends every eternal object in which E is a component. On the other hand, it is not the case that if b prehends every member of B, then b thereby conceptually prehends every component of E. There may be components of E which are disjoint from B.

The above definitions of 'eternal object' and 'conceptual prehension' satisfy Whitehead's categories. It would appear that categoreal obligations IV, V, and VI are entailed by the definition of 'conceptual prehension' given here (PR 39-40). If B is the actual world of b, then b conceptually prehends every eternal object illustrated by the members of B. Also b conceptually prehends all the eternal objects that have as components the forms of definiteness of the members of B. Thus b has conceptual prehensions of the forms of definiteness of the actualities it prehends, and conceptual prehensions of eternal objects partly diverse from these forms of definiteness. Similarly, if b prehends all the members of a nexus, then *b* conceptually prehends the form of definiteness of the nexus.

If an actual entity *b* illustrates *E*, then *b* conceptually prehends *E*. The converse statement is not generally true. But if *b* conceptually prehends *E*, then *b* will *illustrate* some eternal object that has *E* as a *component*. For example, let *b* and *c* be contemporaries; then there is a *d prehended* by *b* and *c*; *b* and *d* will belong to a route *E*, and *c* and *d* will belong to a route *E'*. But *c* does not belong to *E*, and *b* does not belong to *E'*. Nevertheless, *b* prehends every member of a nexus contained in *E'* and *c* prehends every member of a nexus contained in *E*. Hence *b* conceptually prehends *E'* but does not illustrate *E'* and *c* conceptually prehends *E* but does not illustrate *E*. Both entities *b* and *c* conceptually prehend and illustrate the eternal object *E'* which is the union of *E* and *E'*.

It would seem reasonable to say that *b* has a negative conceptual prehension of *E* if *b* conceptually prehends *E* but does not illustrate *E*. Since the actual world of each actual entity is overlapped by every eternal object, we can say that every actual entity prehends positively or negatively every eternal object. This would seem to be a possible interpretation of the fifth category of explanation, which states that the eternal objects are the same for all actual entities. According to the same category no two actual entities may have identical actual worlds, and consequently no two actual entities will illustrate the same set of eternal objects. *Positive conceptual prehensions* and *negative conceptual prehensions* are disjoint subrelations of the relation *conceptually prehends*.

It is not clear what a negative physical prehension might be. It seems trivial to suggest that *b* negatively prehends *b'* whenever it is not the case that *b* prehends *b'*. A negative prehension according to Whitehead is one which holds its datum inoperative. In the case of conceptual prehensions it is relatively easy, as has been shown, to give a reconstruction of 'inoperative' in terms of "conceptually prehends" and "illustrates." In the case of physical prehensions the data would be inoperative only if they were not members of the actual world of the prehending subject. Whitehead seems to have entertained such a view (PR 435). If this interpretation is correct, the predicate 'prehends physically negatively' is not useful.

The procedure outlined above may be summarized as follows: (1) 'nexus,' 'eternal objects,' 'conceptually prehends' and other constants of Whitehead's philosophy are defined in terms of "prehends" and "actual entity"; (2) the structure of the set of all actual entities *A* is partly characterized and it is assumed that *prehends* has neither terminal nor initial members; (3) nexūs are subsets of *A* on which the product of *prehends* with its inverse, or the product of the inverse of *prehends* with *prehends,* is connected; (4) eternal objects are nexūs that are the union of subsets of *A* on which *prehends* is a series without initial or terminal members; (5) the relation *is a component of* is a semi-lattice on the set of all eternal objects with least upper bound A; and (6) *conceptually prehends* is a relation whose domain is the set A, whose range is the set of all eternal objects, and such that the set of all eternal objects conceptually prehended by any one actual entity forms a semi-lattice with least upper bound A.

The main differences between Whitehead's theory and the one presented here are as follows: (1) the relation *positive pure* or *hybrid physical prehension* has, for Whitehead, a terminal member while the analogous relation *prehends* explicated here has no terminal members; (2) according to Whitehead every eternal object is included in God's primordial nature, which is an actual entity, while in the reformulated theory every eternal object is a subset of A.

The point of introducing the category 'eternal objects' into either theory is to facilitate the description of the structure of A. Whitehead elects to do this by postulating a realm of eternal objects and then selecting all the subsets of A that are obtained by considering all the actual entities which prehend given eternal objects positively. The alternative procedure followed here is to specify this set of subsets of A directly. That this can be done suggests that the categoreal notion 'eternal object' may be superfluous.

NOTES

[1] Such an assignment of eternal objects to flat loci is what Whitehead calls a "projection."

[2] To be read: "Aj is either a proper subset of or equal to A."

Whitehead's Explanation of
the Past

by William A. Christian

Under this general heading I shall discuss two topics: (I) how Whitehead introduces the concept of pastness into his system, and (II) what
explanation of the past his principles require him to give. The chief
value of the discussion may be to raise certain questions, first about the
way his system is constructed and second about the way it can be used.

I

By "pastness" I mean the relation *being in the past of*, the converse
of which is *being a successor of*. X is in the past of A (and A succeeds
X) if X conditions A, if A does not condition X, and if their durations
do not overlap. If X is in the past of A, then, when A exists, X has come
to an end.

To see how Whitehead introduces this concept into his system, let us
begin with the scheme of categories stated in *Process and Reality* (I, ch.
II, secs. II and III). As Whitehead says, Part I is practically unintelligible
by itself. But suppose we have studied the rest of the book, and his other
writings, with care, and then return to the categoreal scheme. We shall
understand better what it says, but there is also a danger that we may
read into it some things it does not say.

For example, having read many later passages where Whitehead points
to experiences of causal efficacy and others where he explains transition
from past to present in systematic terms, we are strongly tempted to
suppose that the concept of pastness is a part of the categoreal scheme.
Is this true? Clearly, the scheme does not rule out this concept. My question is: Does the scheme itself require this concept?

Whitehead does not claim to introduce all his systematic concepts in
the categoreal scheme. On the contrary, he explicitly introduces concepts

"Whitehead's Explanation of the Past." Reprinted from the Whitehead Centennial
Issue of the *Journal of Philosophy*, 58 (1961), 534-543.

that the scheme permits but does not require, for example, the concept of God, the concept of the extensive continuum, and the concept of enduring objects. These he introduces in Chapter III under the title, "Some Derivative Notions." So these are systematic concepts but not categoreal concepts. They are required to interpret certain generic but contingent features of the world we experience.

This distinction is important for seeing what sorts of truth claims are made in Whitehead's philosophy. We can distinguish categoreal statements (like "Every actual entity attains a satisfaction") which, in order to be true, must be required by the categoreal scheme, from other systematic statements (like "There is a nontemporal actual entity") which, in order to be true, must be permitted by the scheme.[1] Then we can ask: Is "Some actual entities are in the past of others" categoreally true?

Let us put our question into a larger setting by looking at some of the key concepts in Whitehead's theory of time, as follows:

1. Concrescence (and satisfaction)
2. Transition (inheritance, causal efficacy, influence)
3. Duration (contemporaneousness, unison of becoming)
4. Coordinate divisibility of regions (*qua* temporal quanta)

Let us ask whether all these are required by the categoreal scheme or whether, on the contrary, some are derivative notions. We can dispose of the clear cases first and then deal with the doubtful ones.

1. Concrescence is clearly one of the basic concepts in the categoreal scheme. A whole set of categories (the categoreal obligations) is devoted to explaining the categoreal conditions a concrescence must satisfy. But we must remember Whitehead's often-repeated remark that the process of concrescence is not in "physical time."

2. It is equally clear that coordinate divisibility is not a categoreal concept but a derivative notion, belonging to the larger concept of the extensive continuum. Whitehead says plainly (PR 53) that extensive continuity is not a necessary feature of all possible cosmic epochs. This implies that it is not a categoreal concept.

3. The concept of contemporaneousness, on which the concept of a duration depends, is not expressed or explained in the categoreal scheme, not even in the category of transmutation (categoreal obligation vi) where it would be most likely to appear. Whether it is required by the scheme depends in part on what we discover about transition. For Whitehead's explanation of contemporaneousness depends on the concept of pastness, which belongs to the concept of transition.

4. Let us see, first, what passages in the statement of the scheme seem to require the more general notion of transition or some of its elements and, second, whether any of these require the more specific concept of

pastness. I find five points that require attention, and beg the reader's patience through some exegesis: (a) a concrescence "originates from" an actual world (category of explanation v); (b) one actual entity is "objectified" in another (cats. exp. viii, xxiv); (c) the ontological principle can be termed "the principle of efficient, and final, causation" (cat. exp. xviii); (d) the subjective aim of an actual entity is at intensity of feeling in "the *relevant* future" as well as in the immediate subject (cat. ob. viii); and (e) "in each particular instance" the process of becoming (concrescence) "ceases" with the attainment of coherence (cat. exp. xxii).

Now, though (a), (b), and (c) introduce certain elements of the full concept of transition (e.g., "objectification"), they do not introduce the concept of pastness. The reason is that they do not require a distinction between past and contemporary actual entities. We are not told in (a) that the actual world of an actual occasion consists of only those actual entities in its past, though we know this from later developments. Nor is causal objectification distinguished from presentational objectification (i.e., of the contemporary world) in (b). Similarly, (c) does not say or imply that there is no efficient causation between contemporaries, though we know this is a cardinal principle in Whitehead's cosmology.

So there is room to argue that the categoreal scheme does not of itself require that influence run from past to present. We could put this by saying that the scheme leaves open the question whether contemporary actual entities influence one another. But it would be much better to say that this question is not even raised, much less decided, because the concepts of pastness and contemporaneousness are not introduced.

Now consider passages (d) and (e). Since (d) involves a distinction between present and future, we might think it required the concept of pastness. But the reference to a relevant future does not need to involve pastness. Its meaning could be satisfied by saying that some actual entities come into existence (or that they continue to exist) while others are in existence. It does not strictly imply that the coming into being of a relevant future involves the ending of the present subject. Nor does it deny this. My point is that the question is not raised.

The point of category of explanation xxii (e) is to explain the self-formation of an actual entity. This is done formally in the first sentence of the statement and more vividly in the second ("self-creative" for "self-formation"). The third sentence, beginning with 'Thus', uses the explanation to elucidate "becoming" and, in its second clause, *adds* the remark about cessation. What is it that ceases? Clearly, the process of becoming (concrescence). But this is not the same as saying that the actual entity ceases. The specific point of the clause is not to say that an actual entity "perishes" but to say that every actual entity achieves a satisfaction. This is the "attainment" at which the process of self-formation is directed. Here as elsewhere the problem is to read the categoreal scheme for what it says and strictly implies, and not to read into it the systematic development that follows after derivative notions have been introduced.

Thus there are reasons for saying that the categoreal scheme does not introduce the concept of pastness either explicitly, by using and explaining it, or implicitly, by requiring it. This conclusion can be put by using the following statements:

P: Every actual entity succeeds some other actual entity.
Q: Some actual entities succeed other actual entities.
R: No actual entity succeeds another actual entity.

Then *P, Q,* and *R* are all categoreally permitted; *Q* is systematically true; and *P* and *R* are systematically untrue. *P* is systematically untrue because Whitehead introduces, as a derivative notion, the concept of an actual entity (God) that does not succeed [2] any other actual entity. God is "primordial." *Q* is systematically true because Whitehead introduces the concept of temporal actual entities (i.e., actual occasions) which, if the concept of a nontemporal actual entity is derivative, must be a derivative notion also. And if *Q* is systematically true, *R* is systematically untrue.

If this conclusion is justified—and I do not suppose I have proved it, but I hope I have shown how it is arguable—it has two important consequences.

1. The categoreal scheme would permit the possibility of a universe (or a "cosmic epoch") in which the relation *being in the past of* was not instantiated. All actual entities would be conditioned by others, as some *A* by some *X*. But since *X* would not come to an end, *X* would not be unambiguously in the past of *A*. For all we are told in the categoreal scheme, a universe like this is abstractly conceivable. It happens that our world is not like this, for in our world the relation *being in the past of* is abundantly instantiated. It is clearly, but contingently, true that in our world some things are unambiguously in the past of others. Hence if the categoreal scheme is to apply to this world, there must be some actual entities that come to an end. Whitehead says:

> In the temporal world, *it is the empirical fact* that process entails loss: the past is present under an abstraction. But there is no reason, of any ultimate metaphysical generality, why this should be the whole story (PR 517, my italics).

2. The categoreal scheme would permit (though it does not require) the conception of an actual entity that is not unambiguously in the past of any other actual entity (since it never comes to an end) and does not succeed any other actual entity (since it has no beginning).

II

The second question I wish to raise is this: What sort of explanation of the past do Whitehead's principles of explanation require? With all due respect, this is not the same as asking what Whitehead thought they required.

Whitehead's conception of speculative philosophy requires three sorts of statements involving references to the past. I shall call these (1) *descriptions,* (2) *interpretations,* and (3) *explanations.*

1. First he must assemble the main facts about our experience of the past, drawing on our ordinary experience, on science, and on the reflections of earlier philosophers, putting these facts into descriptive statements. So he describes our sense of the efficacy of the immediate past, acts of remembering, and our practical reliance on causal influence, in what might be called *phenomenological* or *presystematic* statements. He remarks, among other facts, on the "roughness" of our experience of time. Instead of a steady stream of time, smoothly flowing, there are discrete happenings. Events occur after other events. This is why a systematic concept of pastness will be needed.

2. Then, in *postsystematic* statements, he must interpret the facts he has described. For example, the following would be an interpretation of some particular experience of efficacy: "In this experience the subject is directly prehending some immediately past actual occasions." In statements like this both nonsystematic terms (e.g., 'experience') and systematic terms ('prehend,' 'actual occasion') occur. The nonsystematic terms are taken over from ordinary language, from science, from traditional philosophical usage, or from other sources.

3. The systematic terms require explanation in *systematic* statements, telling, for example, just how an actual occasion prehends an immediately past occasion. Whitehead must explain how, in objectification, an objective datum is derived from an initial datum by abstraction, involving negative prehensions, and how subjective forms of feeling are repeated.

Two points about interpretations (postsystematic statements) should be noticed in passing. First, they are not immediately deducible from descriptions, because their systematic terms express constructed concepts, not (we might say) natural concepts (including here those scientific and traditional philosophical concepts which have become, so to speak, naturalized). The meaning of these terms is given in the categoreal scheme and in later systematic developments. So the truth of interpretations depends not only on the truth of the descriptions but also on the truth claim of the system as a whole. The second point is that, if the conclusion of section I (above) is justified, interpretations of the past cannot be explained by reference to the categoreal scheme alone. This is

because the categoreal scheme does not tell us that for some actual entity
A, some of the actual entities objectified in *A* are in *A*'s past. So derivative
notions as well as categoreal concepts are involved in the explanation.

One of Whitehead's principles of explanation is the "ontological principle" (cat. exp. xviii). How does this principle apply to the explanation
of the past? It is a rule governing systematic explanations and might be
put in the following way: When you mention some condition to which a
particular process of becoming conforms, you must refer to some actual
entity (or entities) as the reason for the condition. So the principle
governs systematic explanation of all the conditions of a concrescence,
including conditions from the past, if any. (Incidentally, the principle
clearly rules out creativity as an ontological ground. It calls for actual
entities, and creativity is not an actual entity, nor indeed an entity of
any other systematic kind.)

Now, when the concept of pastness is introduced into Whitehead's
system, does this put an additional strain on the ontological principle?
Are we required to explain, under the ontological principle, not only
why a condition of a concrescence has the character it has but also how
it comes to be an effective condition *now?*

The reason that this is at least a specious problem, if not a real one, is
as follows. Whitehead undertakes to describe and interpret the discon-
tinuity of experience in time. Some things happen after other things
have stopped happening. In this way the world is "rough" in its temporal
dimension as well as spatially. It is not the smooth world of classical
mechanics.[3] To interpret this feature of experience Whitehead introduces
the concept of temporal actual entities (actual occasions), which can be
serially ordered in such a way that some are in the past of others. Conversely, some succeed others. This makes possible a systematic explanation
of the epochal character of time.

Now, if some actual occasion *X* is succeeded by some actual occasion *A,*
it is clear that *X* can be the reason (under the ontological principle) for
what is given for *A;* but it is not so clear that *X* can be the reason *why*
this is in fact given for *A.* So the question arises whether the ontological
principle properly applies to the givenness of the past as well as to the
character of the data from the past. And if it applies, what systematic
explanations of givenness are possible?

All I propose to do about this puzzle is to set out briefly three arguable
views on the matter, though I should add that the arguments for the
first two views are stronger than I used to think.

1. One view is that the ontological principle does not properly apply
to the givenness of the past. What is to be explained under the principle
is not the fact that a concrescence conforms to conditions, but only the
conditions to which it conforms. The concept of conformity to some
conditions or other is built into the categoreal scheme to interpret a

pervasive feature of experience. So the fact of conformity as such, in any particular case whatever, does not call for any special systematic explanation under the ontological principle. Now if conformity as such does not require special explanation, then givenness as such does not require special explanation, for the concepts of conformity and givenness are tightly linked together. What is to be explained under the ontological principle, in a particular case, is not that something is given but only what is given. On this view, the problem about a ground of the givenness of the past is only a specious problem, not a real one.

The main strength of this view is its simplicity. Also, the fact that Whitehead does not clearly mention the problem in his writings is a reason for attributing this view to him. But our question is: what do his principles require?

2. A second view is only a little less simple. This is that the ontological principle properly applies to the givenness of data from the past as well as to the character of the data and that the objectified actual occasions are the reasons for their own givenness for the present.

The natural (but not conclusive) objection to both these views is that they are too simple. They leave us with a mystery on our hands—namely, the mystery of how something past can be effective in the present. We may say that this is simply part of the general mystery of time. But when we are interpreting Whitehead, our problem is not whether we are able to admit such mysteries but whether Whitehead can admit them. Do his principles permit him to leave this mystery on our hands? Perhaps they do. Perhaps, indeed, they require him to do so, but I am not sure that this is the case.

One way this mystery could be avoided is by saying that there really are no endings. Things live on and on, as real as ever they were. So we would have no good use for the concept of pastness. But Whitehead needs and uses this concept. Another way to avoid the mystery is to say that there really are no beginnings. What seems like a birth is really a sleep and a forgetting. But I suppose it is clear that Whitehead thinks there are real and novel beginnings. The mystery appears because Whitehead wants his speculative philosophy to do justice both to real endings and to real beginnings.

3. A third arguable view is that the ontological principle applies to the givenness of the past and that God is the ground of the givenness of the past. There are at least three objections to this view, as follows:

(a) Whitehead does not clearly assign this function to God.

(b) The explanatory mechanism we would have to construct[4] is bound to seem somewhat artificial. (However, if pastness is a derivative concept, some categoreal difficulties would be mitigated.)

(c) This would leave us liable for an explanation of the ground of givenness of the data of God's physical prehensions. (But since no actual occasion is in the past of God—nothing happens before God—this is not the same problem as in the case of actual occasions. Here, applying the ontological principle would not mean asking for a ground of the givenness of the *past*.)

As I have meant to suggest, these objections are not conclusive, though they have some weight. But suppose we should reject view 3 for these or other reasons. Then we should still have to recognize two functions of God in relating a present actual occasion (as A) to a past occasion (as X). First, God makes it *possible* for A to absorb some abstraction from X into its own satisfaction, in the following way. A can be positively influenced by X because A's subjective aim permits this. Now A's initial conceptual aim is derived from a hybrid physical prehension of God. And the ordering of pure possibilities (eternal objects) that conditions this hybrid prehension is determined in part by A's past, including X. But this implies a constant aim in God's experience, something determinable but constant in God for X to determine. In this way God's constant subjective aim at maximum intensity is a reason (under the ontological principle) for the possibility of A's having positive prehensions of X. Also, X is a reason for the particular pattern of divine experience which orders the relevance of possibilities for A's subjective aim.

Second, God makes it *necessary* for A to conform to the past, in the following way. A's subjective aim, inherited from God (but with modifications), is such that it can be achieved only if A conforms to X in some way. A macroscopic example: If I am ill and want to be well, I must treat the causes of the illness. Only by taking account of the past can the aim of a finite concrescence be achieved. In this way conformity to God requires conformity to the past also.

Neither of these functions, nor both together, amount to quite the same thing as being the ground of the givenness of the past. But they make God an essential condition—though not the only condition, of course—of the effectiveness of the past in the present, and are in this way part of Whitehead's systematic explanation of the past. They help to give an interpretation, in systematic terms, of the following: "We owe to the sense of Deity the obviousness of the many actualities of the world . . ." (MT 140).

NOTES

[1] But not all statements permitted by the scheme are systematically true (e.g., "There is no extensive continuum"). His philosophy also includes many presystematic statements (like "We remember past events") and postsystematic statements (like "A stone is a nexus of actual occasions"), and these have to be judged in other ways. We shall come to these later.

[2] In the sense defined at the beginning of this section. Of course, all other actual entities affect God.

³ Of course, Whitehead also undertakes to explain the smoothness of the world of classical mechanics. That world is an abstraction from the world of concrete experience, and he tries to show how that abstraction is made.

⁴ See *An Interpretation of Whitehead's Metaphysics* (New Haven: Yale University Press, 1959), pp. 327-330.

Of What Use Are
Whitehead's Eternal Objects?

by Everett W. Hall

I

Professor A. N. Whitehead's analysis of what he variously calls 'events,' 'occasions,' and 'actual entities' is always highly acute, and in some respects it makes contributions of lasting philosophical importance. Besides actual occasions, however, he gives us a realm of shadowy "eternal objects," whose function and status are not always clear. In fact, if he admits that his division between actual occasions and eternal objects is metaphysically ultimate, he seems to have fallen into a fallacy which, in other connections, he has himself forcefully and correctly condemned: viz., the fallacy of "bifurcation." Hence it is natural to wonder whether "eternal objects" play any role which could not be legitimately taken over by actual occasions, if these latter were reinterpreted in certain ways. We are strengthened in this hypothesis by Whitehead's recent Gifford Lectures, *Process and Reality*. For in them it almost seems that all the distinctive functions of eternal objects are taken over, in one way or another, by actual occasions. This tendency is present in Whitehead's earlier works, but in *Process and Reality* it seems to be expressed more explicitly.

It might be well, at the outset, to inquire briefly as to what functions eternal objects are supposed to perform according to Whitehead's earlier works. Among other things, eternal objects are made to account for identity, permanence, universality, abstractness, and potentiality—all of which are essential to knowledge, but none of which, supposedly, is to be ascribed to concrete occasions as they directly come. Let us note briefly what Whitehead has to say on each of these heads.

It is clear that there can be no knowledge unless there are some identities which are exemplified in more than one specific case and hence are not shattered by the diversities between occasions, and unless there are some permanences which persist through changing experiences of them. Now if an actual occasion is such that when it is gone it is wholly and

"Of What Use are Whitehead's Eternal Objects?" Reprinted from the *Journal of Philosophy*, **27** (1930), 29-44.

irretrievably annihilated, if each occasion is identical only with itself as it immediately occurs, then it is plain that we must look elsewhere for the identity and permanence required by knowledge. This elsewhere is the realm of eternal objects. Knowledge involves recognition, and what is recognized is always an eternal object.

> Objects convey the permanences recognised in events, and are recognised as self-identical amid different circumstances; that is to say, the same object is recognised as related to diverse events. . . . The object is permanent, because (strictly speaking) it is without time and space; and its change is merely the variety of its relations to the various events which are passing in time and in space (PNK 15.1, 15.2).
>
> Objects are elements in nature which do not pass. The awareness of an object as some factor not sharing in the passage of nature is what I call "recognition." It is impossible to recognise an event, because an event is essentially distinct from every other event. Recognition is an awareness of sameness. . . . Events are only comparable because they body forth permanences. We are comparing objects in events whenever we can say, "There it is again." Objects are the elements in nature which can "be again" (CN 143-144; cf. 169).

This function of bringing identity into the diversities of actual occasions Whitehead calls the "ingression" of eternal objects into occasions. The modes of ingression of an eternal object vary with different occasions, but the eternal object remains the same. (Cf. SMW 222.) By the principle of the "Translucency of Realisation," Whitehead means "that any eternal object is just itself in whatever mode of realisation it is involved. There can be no distortion of the individual essence without thereby producing a different eternal object" (SMW 247-248). That is, the changing, diverse exemplifications of an eternal object in particular occasions do not affect the persistent identity of the eternal object.

Just as eternal objects furnish the permanence and identity lacking in the fluency and diversity of actual occasions, so they likewise take care of universality, which is not a character of particular actualities, as such. Each occasion is restricted—itself and no other. But an eternal object, by ingressing into any one occasion, ingresses into all. That is, it is not a particular. Whitehead makes eternal objects absolutely universal; each is to be found throughout the whole actual world and is present in every occasion. Hence he has to bring in the doctrine of grades of entry into, or relevance of, different eternal objects to a given occasion. These grades vary from the inclusion to the exclusion of the essence of any eternal object. When the essence of an eternal object is excluded from an occasion, it is "ingredient in the occasion" simply in the way that occasion leaves it as a merely unfulfilled alternative or possibility. (Cf. SMW 226-227.) As Whitehead says, ". . . each object is in some sense ingredient throughout nature; though its ingression may be quan-

titatively irrelevant in the expression of our individual experiences"
(CN 145). The basis of the universality of eternal objects is the fact that
they are expressions of content or character, not of numerical existence.
They are natures, not actual facts.

> An object is an ingredient in the character of some event. In fact the char-
> acter of an event is nothing but the objects which are ingredient in it and
> the ways in which those objects make their ingression into the event
> (CN 143-144).

Eternal objects thus take the place, in Whitehead's terminology, of
what are generally called universals, qualities, characteristics, etc. Whitehead likewise insists that eternal objects are abstractions. They are not
total concrete experiences, in all the complexity and completeness of
the latter. Hence we can grasp an eternal object independently of its
concrete settings in this or that occasion. "By 'abstract' I mean that what
an eternal object is in itself—that is to say, its essence—is comprehensible
without reference to some one particular occasion of experience" (SMW
228). However, though eternal objects are abstractions from actual occasions, it does not follow that they are unreal or merely subjective:
". . . I have already explained to you that to be an abstraction does not
mean that an entity is nothing. It merely means that its existence is only
one factor of a more concrete element of nature" (CN 171).

Finally, eternal objects are made to account for possibility and potentiality. Occasions are thoroughly actual, are just what they are, are
devoid of all potentiality: ". . . an event is just what it is, and is just
how it is related; and it is nothing else" (PNK 15.4). "Time and space,
which are entirely actual and devoid of any tincture of possibility, are to
be sought for among the relations of events" (PNK 14.2). Hence we
must localize possibility elsewhere than in actual occasions and their
relations. Eternal objects *are* the sum total of possibilities. Occasions are
realizations, actualizations, of these possibilities. "Every actual occasion
is defined as to its character by how these possibilities are actualised for
that occasion. Thus actualisation is a selection among possibilities"
(SMW 229). And this "selection," we may suppose, implies the previous
reality of that which is selected; i.e., it implies the reality of possibilities
before they are exemplified in actualities.

From this rapid survey, we can conclude that Whitehead's eternal
objects have quite definite work to do. They are made to account for
identity, permanence, universality, abstractness, and possibility. All of
these tasks are essential to knowledge, but none of them, supposedly, is
performed by actual occasions as such. Even in these earlier works of
Whitehead, however, we often wonder whether actual occasions do not
themselves encroach upon the special sphere assigned to eternal objects.
Especially is this the case when Whitehead is treating of the spatio-

temporal aspects of occasions. And when we come to *Process and Reality* our suspicions, if not completely vindicated, are at least justifiably augmented. It is true that in these Gifford Lectures all of the above-considered differentiae are still ascribed to eternal objects. But at the same time, every one of them is ascribed, in some fashion, to actual occasions as such. And since we now learn that identity, permanence, universality, abstractness, and possibility are all definable in terms of occasions, we cannot avoid wondering whether eternal objects have not virtually become so much useless baggage. Let us turn to *Process and Reality*.

II

In the first place, we have seen that knowledge requires that there be identities not shattered by the diversities between immediate experiences. But we now learn that this requirement can be met by actual occasions themselves—through their "objectification" or "objective immortality" in other occasions. Several different occasions can "prehend" the same occasion—in fact, all occasions prehend each.

> All actual entities in the actual world, relatively to a given actual entity as "subject," are necessarily "felt" by that subject, though in general vaguely. An actual entity as felt is said to be "objectified" for that subject (PR 66; cf. also, e.g., 79).

Since an immediate occasion can thus retain its identity beyond itself and be a constituent of other occasions, Whitehead would seem to be endangering its intolerant immediacy. But he avoids this by drawing a distinction between an occasion considered as "subject" (i.e., as immediate and specific) and as "superject" (i.e., as an identity not destroyed by the diversities of exemplification of itself). "An actual entity is to be conceived both as a subject presiding over its own immediacy of becoming, and a superject which is the atomic creature exercising its function of objective immortality" (PR 71). Thus a given occasion, after its completion or "satisfaction," passes over into the actual worlds, the "data," of other occasions, and thus contributes its part to the "creative advance." Certainly there is a problem as to how an occasion, as it immediately exists for itself and as it functions in the data of other occasions, can be identical. But for the present it is sufficient to point out that through the diversities of these immediate experiences, the occasion does remain identical. So we are led to ask: Since objectification of actual occasions gives us the identity between immediate occurrences which is required for knowledge, why retain the doctrine of the ingression of eternal objects? Why do we need eternal objects any longer?

Again, eternal objects, as we have seen, account for permanence; they stand aloof from flux. But in *Process and Reality* we seem to be given permanence in the world of actualities and without recourse to eternal objects. It may be that the type of permanence we get in this way is both relative and restricted. Still Whitehead presents it as real permanence, and so he takes away the necessity of seeking permanence in some other type of entity than actual occasions themselves. I refer to Whitehead's doctrine that permanence signifies a repetition or grouping of occasions which stand in the relation of "inheritance." "In the [actual] world there is nothing static. But there is reproduction; and hence the permanence which is the result of order, and the cause of it" (PR 365). More particularly, we hear of "enduring objects," "lines of inheritance," "historic routes," "events" (as distinguished from single occasions), "stabilized societies," etc. An enduring object sustains a given character through change. It is a society of occasions where a common characteristic is inherited through a single line of inheritance. (Cf. PR pt. I, ch. III 2.) Whitehead tells us that "each historic route of like occasions tends to prolong itself, by reason of the weight of uniform inheritance derivable from its members" (PR 88). A "stabilized" society is another example of this type of permanence. "A society is 'stabilized' in reference to a species of change when it can persist through an environment whose relevant parts exhibit that sort of change" (PR 153). Societies gain stability in the midst of environmental novelties by the elimination of diversities of detail (in the case of inorganic societies) and by the origination of novelties of conceptual reaction (in the case of living societies).[1] Thus we can account at least for a relative degree of permanence in terms of occasions and their groupings and repetitions. And if there be any society embracing all occasions or all durations (and there seems to be one, namely, that whose defining characteristic is extensive connection), then we can speak of absolute permanence. Whitehead might object that repetition itself implies that the same eternal object is ingredient in several occasions. But it seems to me that the objectification or objective immortality of actual occasions could very well be taken as performing this function; that is, an objectified occasion of a certain degree of relevance can define that common characteristic or similarity of many occasions in virtue of which they are spoken of as being "repetitions" or forming one "line of inheritance."

Societies of actual occasions also seem to account for the general and universal aspect of experience. Every society presupposes an environmental background which is permissive of the self-sustenance of the society and contributes the more general characteristics presupposed by the special characteristics of the society. "In reference to any given society the world of actual entities is to be conceived as forming a background in layers of social order, the defining characteristics becoming wider and more general as we widen the background" (PR 138). A "cosmic epoch" is the widest society immediately relevant to a given one. The whole environment in which our cosmic epoch is set is a society whose defining characteristics are the general properties of extensive connection. Within this widest society is a more specialized one, which yet is more inclusive than our cosmic epoch—the geometrical society. Our present epoch is an electromagnetic society. Within it there is a bewildering complexity of even more restricted and special societies, such as "regular trains of waves, individual electrons, protons, individual molecules, societies of molecules such as inorganic bodies, living cells, and societies of cells such as vegetable and animal bodies" (PR 150). Hence occasions form a vast and complex hierarchy of societies, the higher of which are more inclusive than the lower. Thus the order within the actual world itself (for I do not understand that a society is an eternal object) furnishes a basis for all degrees of generality up to absolute universality (extensive connection).

It may, of course, be objected that these societies of occasions are simply classes of particulars, and hence are not universals in the sense in which eternal objects are universals—i.e., as elements of quality or character. But we have already seen that in objectification one occasion enters into the very nature or content of another. Whitehead seems to be perfectly clear on this: ". . . every so-called 'particular' is universal in the sense of entering into the constitutions of other actual entities" (PR 76). And again, he says: ". . . every item of the universe, including all the other actual entities, are constituents in the constitution of any one actual entity" (PR 224). Certainly Whitehead does not mean that an occasion can be objectively immortal—i.e., pass into the "constitution" of another occasion—precisely in its role of mere immediate existence. Its immediate existential status is peculiar to it, and is annihilated as soon as it ceases. Hence its immortality must be qualitative; it contributes its nature to the nature of the prehending occasion. Thus if we consider both societies of occasions and objectifications of occasions, we appear to have in occasions themselves both kinds of universals (if there are two kinds), and hence we hardly need eternal objects any longer in order to account for universality.

Another function we had thought peculiar to eternal objects is that of being abstract. Actual occasions, we supposed, are total concrete occurrences invested with all their detail and complexity. But now we learn that, as objectifications, occasions are themselves abstract; as data in other occasions, they omit from their total detailed nature as immediate occurrences. Thus, for example, we are told that

> objectification relegates into irrelevance, or into subordinate relevance, the full constitution of the objectified entity. Some real component in the objectified entity assumes the role of being how that particular entity is a datum in the experience of the subject (PR 97).

Or again, we read:

The objectified particular occasions together have the unity of a datum for the creative concrescence. But in acquiring this measure of connection, their inherent presuppositions of each other eliminate certain elements in their constitutions, and elicit into relevance other elements. Thus objectification is an operation of mutually adjusted abstraction, or elimination, whereby the many occasions of the actual world become one complex datum (PR 321).

Thus it is clear that occasions, in their role of data for other occasions, exemplify abstractness.

Finally, let us consider potentiality. One of the most characteristic and differentiating functions of eternal objects, we supposed, is to account for the reality of possibility, for that which is real and yet is not actually determinate. Occasions, we thought, are thoroughly actual and matter of fact. But now we are led to believe otherwise. For we now learn that actual occasions, as well as eternal objects, can exemplify potentiality. (Cf. PR 33.) Besides the "general" potentiality furnished by the multiplicity of eternal objects, we are now introduced to a "real" potentiality located in the actual world. This real potentiality refers to the possibilities of future objectifications of a given occasion in other occasions. (Cf. PR 102.) It is in terms of this real potentiality that we can define all possible standpoints of occasions and hence gain an "extensive continuum" which is infinitely divisible, though every actual occasion is incurably atomic. The extensive continuum

> is one relational complex in which all potential objectifications find their niche. . . . The notion of a "continuum" involves both the property of indefinite divisibility and the property of unbounded extension. There are always entities beyond entities, because nonentity is no boundary. This extensive continuum expresses the solidarity of all possible standpoints throughout the whole process of the world (PR 103).

Every actual occasion is somewhere in the continuum, but by including objectifications of the whole actual world, it also includes the continuum.

> Thus the continuum is present in each actual entity, and each actual entity pervades the continuum. . . . The potential scheme does not determine its own atomization by actual entities. It is divisible; but its real division by actual entities depends upon more particular characteristics of the actual entities constituting the antecedent environment (PR 105).

Hence, so it would seem, besides being just what they actually are, occasions are also potentially all that they may become in future concrescences. Each is potentially the whole future, at least so far as the future is expressible in terms of extensive connection. Thus we are once more led to wonder whether occasions have not taken upon themselves the special task assigned to eternal objects.

We now see that all the characteristics supposedly peculiar to eternal objects are shared by actual occasions. Actual occasions are identical, universal, permanent, abstract, and potential (as well as diverse, particular, changing, concrete, and determinately actual). It is true that eternal objects are still characterized by these features now possessed by actual occasions. But as long as these features are taken care of by the actual world, why retain a further realm any longer? Why not dispense with eternal objects altogether? Why not say that the only real entities are actual entities?

But at this point, one can very well ask: You assume that eternal objects are quite other than actual occasions, but does not Whitehead hold that they are simply aspects of occasions, that they have no standing of their own, and that their nature and reality are wholly dependent upon the actual occasions exemplifying them? This, of course, is a basic question, and we must now turn to a direct consideration of it.

III

It seems to me that Whitehead, in *Process and Reality*, gives at least three answers to the question, Are not eternal objects simply aspects of actual occasions, with no status of their own or by themselves? One is "yes," another is "no," and a third is "yes and no." Let us turn to the affirmative answer first.

The "ontological principle," at least in one of its meanings, is an unequivocal expression of the view that eternal objects, taken by themselves, are nothing. For the ontological principle states that only actual occasions are real. It affirms that "everything is positively somewhere in actuality . . ." (PR 64). Actual occasions are "the final real things of which the world is made up" (PR 27). Whitehead tells us that "all things are to be conceived as qualifications of actual occasions; . . . the whole universe consists of elements disclosed in the analysis of the experiences of subjects" (PR 252). And again: ". . . apart from the experiences of subjects there is nothing, nothing, nothing, bare nothingness" (PR 254). And once more: ". . . in separation from actual entities there is nothing, merely nonentity—'The rest is silence' " (PR 68). Hence it would seem perfectly clear that eternal objects are simply aspects of the actual occasions exemplifying them, and have no reality by themselves. Of course, it might still be held that there is a division of labor between the total actual occasion and partial aspects thereof, and that only the latter express permanence, universality, etc. But if the only real entities are occasions, if eternal objects are simply aspects of occasions, then it becomes just as legitimate to say that the total occasion is permanent, universal, etc., as that it is changing and particular. That is, we have no right tacitly to equate total occasions with only one side of their dual nature and then leave the other side over to be accounted for in terms of another set of entities called 'eternal objects.' Rather, we would have to say that the total occasion includes both aspects, neither of which is independent of the other nor a real entity by itself.

In the second place, Whitehead seems to answer "no" to the question, Are not eternal objects simply aspects of actualities, with no status of their own? This answer seems to be explicitly upon his lips when he tells us about the original disjunctive multiplicity of eternal objects, which, by means of creativity, passes into the conjunctive unity of particular occasions. Creativity "is that ultimate principle by which the many, which are the universe disjunctively, become the one actual occasion, which is the universe conjunctively" (PR 31). Eternal objects are themselves without novelty. Creativity introduces novelty into the disjunctive multiplicity of eternal objects through the unique togetherness of the actual occasion. "The ultimate metaphysical principle is the advance from disjunction to conjunction, creating a novel entity other than the entities given in disjunction" (PR 32).

Now it seems to me that if eternal objects ever exist (or subsist) or ever have existed (or subsisted) in a state of disjunctive multiplicity, then they must have a status and reality of their own, for as aspects of actual occasions they are always in conjunctive unity. This conviction is strengthened by Whitehead's retention of the doctrine of "ingression," whereby what was previously an eternal object or potentiality becomes ingredient in an occasion. Furthermore, the doctrine that eternal objects enter into occasions by being "together" in them certainly leaves the impression that the eternal objects are something by themselves and when not together, for 'together' as ordinarily used implies the previous or at least the possible existence of the elements apart from each other. And so I cannot avoid the view that Whitehead means explicitly to deny that objects are merely aspects of occasions, with no status by themselves.

I think Whitehead makes this same denial implicitly or by implication, also. In so far as he still clings to the doctrine that occasions are *merely* specific and *merely* perish, i.e., simply cease to be, in the sense of being completely annihilated, he must seek for all permanence and identity in something entirely other than they. Consider, for example, the following: "Actual entities perish, but do not change; they are what they are" (PR 52). "Its [the occasion's] birth is its end" (PR 124). Each occasion is what it directly and immediately is for itself. Hence when it loses its own immediacy, it is simply gone, wiped out. Now, of course, if this be the case there can be no objectification of occasions as *occasions* (i.e., as wholly immediate occurrences), and we must look to something entirely other than occasions to give us universality, possibility, etc. And eternal objects, as possessing these latter characteristics, must have a nature and reality of their own, not reducible to the nature and reality of occasions.

So to the question, Are eternal objects simply aspects of occasions, having no real status by themselves?, Whitehead seems to give affirmative and negative answers. But he also, so it seems to me, gives an ambiguous answer, an answer which is *both* affirmative and negative at once. I refer to God and particularly to God's "primordial nature." For God's primordial nature is the actual home of the multiplicity of eternal objects, and yet its actuality is different from that of any other occasion. The fact is that God saves Whitehead from taking his own "ontological principle" seriously. For Whitehead wishes to retain the multiplicity of disjoined eternal objects as real in their bare potentiality, apart from their exemplifications in particular occasions. And so he makes this multiplicity itself "actual" and calls it God's "primordial nature," as though it were something existent before any creative process of concrescence ever occurred. The general potentiality of the universe, since it is real, must be "somewhere" (i.e., an actual occasion). This "somewhere" is God's primordial nature. (Cf. PR 73.) It is natural that such an actuality should prove startlingly different from all other actual occasions. Whitehead states the paradox of God's status as an actuality very aptly: "The concept of 'God' is the way in which we understand this incredible fact—that what cannot be, yet is" (PR 531). God's primordial nature is timeless, whereas all other occasions are in ceaseless flux.[2] Furthermore, it possesses no more than a "deficient actuality," for its realization of eternal objects is "conceptual" only, not "physical." (Cf. PR 521.) Finally, this peculiar actuality is not only outside the creative process comprising all other actualities; it is also entirely independent of the latter. God's primordial nature, "which is his complete envisagement of eternal objects, . . . is not . . . directly related to the given course of history. The given course of history presupposes his primordial nature, but his primordial nature does not presuppose it" (PR 70). It explains the world of actualities, for it gives all eternal objects their gradation of relevance to every possible occasion.

God's complete, yet merely conceptual, realization of all eternal objects in his actual, yet peculiarly nonactual, "primordial nature" seems to express Whitehead's final hesitancy before the question, Are eternal objects merely aspects of occasions, or do they have a real status of their own when taken by themselves?

IV

What I have wished to show in this paper is that in *Process and Reality* Whitehead has approached very closely to making his eternal objects quite otiose, and to confining the metaphysical entities required by his epistemology wholly to actual occasions. But though he approaches this result, he does not attain it. In this last section of my paper, I wish first to point out the reason why he does not attain this result, and then to suggest a modification of his "occasions" which will eliminate the cause of his failure to attain it.

It seems to me that Whitehead, more clearly than any other contemporary philosopher, has come to grips with the central philosophic problem of our times: namely, the problem as to the union of the principles of "internalism" and "externalism." [3] But it seems to me that he has not completely succeeded in bringing about a thorough reconciliation. For he still seems to cling to the unmodified externalistic belief in merely atomic, self-enclosed, wholly perishing particulars (occasions). And so long as occasions are treated as intolerantly specific, it is necessary to find identity and connection and universality in some other type of entity.

Now the doctrine of "objectification" does try to overcome this retention of an unmodified externalism and to find a place for internalism within the actual occasion itself. But it seems to me not to be finally successful. For it tries to substitute repetition of particulars for permanent identity, and it does this because of the supposal that the special characteristic of an occasion is its immediacy. That is, it supposes that no one occasion can be immediate more than once; differences in immediacy are absolute and destroy all identity as far as occasions are concerned. Thus, though occasions gain objective immortality, they " 'perpetually perish' subjectively. . . . Actuality in perishing acquires objectivity, while it loses subjective immediacy" (PR 44). The result of this final unresolved externalism is that Whitehead bids us look for a way in which the creative process of actuality does not involve the ceaseless loss of immediacy. And by a *tour de force* he finds the solution in God—where all occasions are conserved, not only as objectified, but in their very immediacy of occurrence. God's "consequent nature," Whitehead tells us, is "everlasting"—it combines "creative advance with the retention of mutual immediacy . . ." (PR 524-525). This result is due to the perfect completeness of God's primordial nature, which issues in a perfect whole of actual immediacy in his consequent nature. "He saves the world as it passes into the immediacy of his own life" (PR 525).

> Each actuality in the temporal world has its reception into God's nature. The corresponding element in God's nature is not temporal actuality, but is the transmutation of that temporal actuality into a living, ever-present fact (PR 531).[4]

Thus, in the last analysis, Whitehead tries to unite the externality and the internality of occasions by calling in God, in whom occasions lose their exclusiveness and yet retain their immediacy. The only trouble is that we mean by immediacy precisely that which is not retained. Of course God can do anything. But it may be presuming to suppose that he does just those things which our metaphysical difficulties require. Whitehead himself tells us: ". . . God is not to be treated as an exception to all metaphysical principles, invoked to save their collapse" (PR 521). Yet it almost seems as though Whitehead's own invocation is for this very purpose.

It seems to me that the resolution of the conflict between externalism and internalism remains impossible so long as one localizes either in an entity of its own, so long as one separates their spheres of functioning, so long as one makes any such ultimate distinction as that between eternal objects and actual occasions. My constructive suggestion is hardly anything more than a reformulation of Whitehead's doctrine of occasions, with their intolerant specifism so modified that they can truly and thoroughly take over the functions previously ascribed to eternal objects. Briefly, my suggestion amounts to this:

Occasions are immediate, matter of fact, specific. But this does not destroy their mediate identity, their permanence and universality. This being so, it might be well to change our designation of these entities from 'occasions' to 'things' or perhaps simply to 'entities.' Now the total thing is not restricted to what directly occurs at this or that moment in its history. The total thing includes all cases of its immediate occurrence, all changes, all details, all predicates, however trivial or however far apart in time, that can truly be ascribed to it. Within this mass of features truly predicable of the total thing, we must distinguish between those which are basic or central and those which are mere details. The basis for this distinction is degree of necessity to the identity of the thing. There are some features which are, in their specific nature, rationally necessary for the continued identity of the thing. There are other features which are as a matter of fact possessed by the thing but are not, in their specific character, rationally necessary to its identity. This distinction is analogous to Whitehead's doctrine of degrees of relevance within an occasion, and like it, the distinction is not absolute; i.e., there is no clear-cut dividing line between the focal features and the mere details within the total thing.

No amount of change in the detail of a thing will destroy that thing's identity. The change must permeate the structure of its focal features, before the thing ceases to be itself. But we are not to conclude that there are two sorts of entity—the total thing and its focus of central features. There is only one entity—the total thing focalized more especially in some of its features than in others. The thing *is* both its details and its focal nature, but it is *more truly* the latter than the former, for the former might (theoretically) have been different and we would nevertheless have had the "same" thing, but the latter could not have been different without destroying the total thing in question. Thus it is possible to distinguish between the total thing and its focal identity, without implying that we have here two entities separately real. The real thing is the total thing focalized in its own peculiar way.

With this change of what Whitehead calls actual occasions into what we have called real things, it becomes possible to account for all the functions which he ascribes to eternal objects without positing the real existence, as entities in themselves, of such eternal objects.

First, then, how are we to account for the identity between immediate experiences required by knowledge? It is obvious that knowledge never exhausts the total thing which is its object. But it can grasp the most essential features of some things. Hence, despite the diversities between the immediate occurrences of the thing, there can be one identical thing known, providing we do actually get hold of essential features of the thing. Differences, for example, due to spatial perspective, differences of visceral, auditory, and thermal sense data, etc., do characterize our various immediate experiences of a table. But still we may, through all of them, have as the object of our knowledge one thing, the table—not because these details are not truly included in the life history of the table, but because they are mere details in the total thing called the table and so do not destroy its identity.

This leads us directly to the problem of permanence and change. Change is always change of that which remains identical. This is why Whitehead cannot ascribe change to his occasions; they merely perish, for their identity refers to their whole nature as it immediately occurs at some specific time. The result is a series of specific, perishing identities rather than a single identity which changes. On our view, however, a thing is *both* changing and permanent. Its permanence lies in its focal structure. But this focal structure is not something apart from the change, for it is the essential nature of the total thing, and the details of the thing do really change. Hence both permanence and change are abstractions; really you always have a permanent thing changing.[5] But may not the *total* thing change? Surely. It does so whenever the change works into its focal features. In such a case, that specific thing ceases to be; *it* perishes. But it is hard to put our finger upon the precise change forming such a cessation, because there is no sharp dividing line between focal features and irrelevant details. This accounts for the fact that in many instances people differ on the question, Has the identity of the thing ceased to be? In remodeling a house, there comes a time when it is hard to say whether it is the same house changed or a new house. This does not mean, however, that degree of focality is wholly dependent upon subjective point of view.

I must add one more word on permanence and change. Cessation is always itself a case of change. Thus, whenever a thing ceases, there is involved another thing which does not cease, but changes. Even in cessation there must be an identity which remains permanent. This can

be expressed by saying that every change entering the focal features of
a given thing can be viewed as a change in detail, but not in focal nature,
of some other thing which possesses some features in common with the
first thing. Thus "things" are not separate and mutually exclusive. They
overlap in various, complex ways. There is never any cessation which
is not also a change. And there is no change which is not a change of
some identity which remains permanent through the change, though it is
truly characterized by the change.

Universality is an abstraction. It is legitimate, but it is never itself
a real entity or group of such. A universal is any feature (or group of
such) which is taken as focal to some real thing, and thus as actually
embedded in a host of details, but is considered without respect to the
specific nature of these details. To seek the universal is to seek the relatively abstract and simple. This is legitimate just so far as one does, in
this process, hit upon essential features of the total thing in question.
Various instances of one sort of thing do not destroy the essential identity
of that thing. It is this essential identity, amidst the complex differences
of detail between specific instances, which furnishes the basis for universals and makes abstraction legitimate. Universals are never real, if
taken by themselves. Only the total thing is real. But the total real thing
is focalized, and so it is legitimate and highly valuable, in many cases,
to neglect those differences of detail within the real thing which mark
off different "occurrences" or "instances" of it.

Finally, potentiality, as against actuality, refers to the recognition that
some of the features truly predicable of the total thing have been
neglected. It refers to the fact that we have got a group of features which
comprise the focal nature of some real thing, but do not exhaust its
complete nature, and so are compatible with various concrete settings of
detail. Thus the potential is never, as such, real; only the actual, total,
concrete thing is real. Potentialities are always abstractions within
knowledge, and do not wander through the world on their own feet.
But they are not arbitrary creations on our part. For they do express the
fact that an indefinite number of settings of concrete detail is compatible
with the focal nature rationally necessary to a certain identity. Hence
what particular exemplifications a certain potentiality may have is a
matter of fact not yet determined by its own nature.

Thus we have, in outline, accounted for identity, permanence, universality, abstraction, and potentiality, without creating a special type
of entity to perform these functions. And yet we have not for a moment
questioned the reality of diversity, change, particularity, concreteness,
and actuality. In short, it seems to me we have unified externalism and
internalism, not by flatly identifying them, not by calling in God's aid,
but by giving each a distinctive, though not independent, place in every
real entity. For an entity is its own total complexity, yet it is peculiarly

brought to a head or focalized in some part or parts of itself. And this, it seems to me, is not such a great modification of Whitehead's doctrine of occasions.[6]

<h1 style="text-align:center">NOTES</h1>

[1] Another type of permanence found in actual occasions is that required for the permanence of instruments in measuring. This Whitehead calls 'congruence,' and he accounts for it in terms of analogy of function of straight lines in a "strain-locus." Cf. PR pt. IV. ch. V. § § 4, 5.

[2] Cf. PR 73 where he calls it 'non-temporal.' However, in his last chapter, Whitehead urges that permanence and flux cannot be localized in diverse actualities, such as in God and the actual world, respectively. In this last chapter Whitehead seems to want to identify permanence and flux completely—somewhat after the fashion in which Hegel, at times, flatly identifies the opposites he has shown to be correlative. It is needless to say that on this basis the distinction between eternal objects and actual occasions collapses.

[3] By 'internalism' I mean the principle of immanent wholeness, of the internality of relations, of systematic connection, etc. By 'externalism' I mean the principle of atomic specifism, of the externality of relations, of mere factual togetherness, etc.

[4] This reminds one of Royce's *"totum simul."*

[5] I do not mean flatly to identify change and permanence. I simply mean that they are correlative aspects of every real entity.

[6] I might say, however, that I did not derive this doctrine, in the first instance, from Whitehead, though his works have proved very stimulating to me.

Whitehead and the Problem
of Extension

by Ivor Leclerc

In all periods of his thought the fundamental problems of cosmology were Whitehead's primary concern, and his preoccupation with them resulted in his most original contributions to philosophy. The advance of his thought from the paper "On Mathematical Concepts of the Material World" in 1905 to *The Principles of Natural Knowledge* and *The Concept of Nature* in 1919 and 1920 and on to *Process and Reality* in 1929 has been an advance from a restricted to an ever more comprehensive handling of the issues. The advance was constituted by an increasing penetration into these problems and an increasing realization of which issues are truly basic.

Even in the early paper it was clear to Whitehead that in an important respect the cosmological issues centered on the problem of extension; it was with some aspects of this problem that this paper was concerned. At that stage of his thought Whitehead assumed, along with the whole philosophical tradition, that extension was essentially spatial extension. Even then, however, he realized that the recent advances in scientific theory, culminating in the theory of relativity, had made time crucial. But it was only in his middle period, with his doctrine of "events," that he was able coherently to bring time into the notion of extension: events are essentially spatiotemporal—they have a temporal extensiveness as well as a spatial extensiveness.

The fundamental position of this doctrine is that extensiveness is the extensiveness of events: "Every event extends over other events, and every event is extended over by other events" (CN 59). Extension is an ultimate and intrinsic feature of actuality.

One of the most important aspects of this feature of extension is that it is continuous. As Whitehead wrote, "The continuity of nature arises

"Whitehead and the Problem of Extension." Reprinted from the Whitehead Centennial Issue of the *Journal of Philosophy*, 58 (1961), 559-565.

from extension" (CN 59); that is to say, "The continuity of nature is the continuity of events" (CN 76).

This doctrine of events is a formulation, in a philosophical theory, of the unification of space, time, and matter (or "the physical"), achieved by the scientific theory of relativity. The three kinds of real existence of the Newtonian cosmology are, in the doctrine of events, replaced by one real existent, namely, a continuous nature constituted by a continuity of events.

The analogy of Whitehead's position with that of Descartes is noteworthy. Descartes had unified spatial extension and the physical or material as *res extensa;* for Descartes the physical *res* is a continuous spatial extension. That is, for Descartes, matter and spatial extension are not two reals; the two concepts are integrated as one real existent. Whitehead has gone one step further and analogously integrated the physical with a continuous spatiotemporal extensiveness as one real existent. Einstein has pointed to the analogy of the position of the scientific theory of relativity—especially of the general theory—with that of Descartes.[1] Whitehead's doctrine at this stage was, in respect to this basic ontological issue, close to that of Einstein—despite the important differences between the theories of Whitehead and Einstein. The two are fundamentally in agreement in integrating the physical with space and time into a single real existent and in maintaining continuous extensiveness as an ultimate feature of the real.

After writing *The Principle of Relativity* (1922), however, Whitehead began to see that his doctrine involved some very grave difficulties. A crucial difficulty concerned the relativity of space and time. Whitehead had maintained a relativistic theory; but is it possible consistently and coherently to do so on the basis of a conception of spatiotemporal extension as the ultimate feature of the actual? For does not this imply that spatiotemporal extensiveness is absolute and not relative?

Whitehead came to recognize that the central problem that has to be explicitly faced is the ontological status of extension. Can continuous extension consistently be accepted as a real? That is, can actuality consistently be regarded as continuously extensive? In the few years before the appearance of *Science and the Modern World* (1925) Whitehead subjected this problem to a scrutiny and analysis strikingly analogous to that to which Leibniz had subjected the Cartesian conception of extension. Whitehead's analysis was made in independence of that of Leibniz, and it is thus all the more interesting and significant that the outcome in both cases should be so similar.

The outcome of Whitehead's reflection on this problem is expressed in the following extremely important passage in *Process and Reality:*

It cannot be too clearly understood that some chief notions of European thought were framed under the influence of a misapprehension, only partially corrected by the scientific progress of the last century. *This mistake consists in the confusion of mere potentiality with actuality. Continuity concerns what is potential; whereas actuality is incurably atomic* (PR 95, my italics).

The recognition that continuity pertains to potentiality and not to actuality is central to the enormous advance in thought of Whitehead's later period. Herein lies a basic factor making the doctrine of *Process and Reality* importantly different from the doctrine of *The Concept of Nature*. For the doctrine of his middle period still involved that confusion.

In his later period Whitehead argued that "Newton, in his treatment of space, transforms potentiality into actual fact, that is to say, into a creature, instead of a datum for creatures" (PR 123). In other words, "Newton in his description of space and time has confused what is 'real' potentiality with what is actual fact" (PR 113). This is also true of Whitehead's own doctrine in his middle period: that events are the actual existents and that events are essentially continuous. Thus this doctrine ascribes continuity to actuality.

I have said that the outcome of Leibniz's reflections on this problem is strikingly close to that of Whitehead. Leibniz saw very clearly that the basic problem was the ontological status of extension, which is why he subjected the Cartesian and Newtonian doctrines to such careful analysis. His conclusion was that extensive continuity could not be a fundamental feature of the actual, either as itself a kind of actuality (Newton) or as the essential character of the physical (Descartes). On the contrary, like Whitehead later, Leibniz saw that extension involved continuity and that continuity pertained to possibility (or potentiality), not to actuality. He states the point as follows in a letter to De Volder:

> But a continuous quantity is something ideal which pertains to possibles and to actualities only insofar as they are possible. A continuum, that is, involves indeterminate parts, while, on the other hand, there is nothing indefinite in actual things, in which every division is made that can be made. Actual things are compounded as is a number out of unities, ideal things as is a number out of fractions; the parts are actually in the real whole but not in the ideal whole. But we confuse ideal with real substances when we seek for actual parts in the order of possibilities, and indeterminate parts in the aggregate of actual things, and so entangle ourselves in the labyrinth of the continuum and in contradictions that cannot be explained.[2]

Because continuity pertains to possibility and not to actuality, Leibniz comes to the following conclusion as to the status of spatial and temporal extensiveness, expressed in his third letter to Clarke:

As for my own opinion, I have said more than once that I hold space to be
something merely relative, as time is; that I hold it to be an order of co-
existences as time is an order of successions. For space denotes, *in terms of
possibility,* an order of things which exist at the same time. . . .[3]

Space is an order of things coexisting, but not simply that; it is an order
"in terms of possibility." As he stated the point in a letter to De Volder:

For *space* is nothing but the order of existence of things possible at the
same time; while *time* is the order of existence of things possible successively.[4]

Since extensiveness is not a character of actuality, but pertains to
possibility, this means, Leibniz held, that the ontological status of extension as possibility must be that of "ideality." Leibniz went one step
further, maintaining that "ideality" must be interpreted as "phenomenality." The Kantian doctrine follows Leibniz in this, as Gottfried Martin
has shown.[5] And many interpreters of the scientific theory of relativity
have, implicitly or explicitly, adopted an essentially Kantian position in
regard to the ontological status of extension.

Whitehead explicitly rejects this position. He would agree with
Leibniz in maintaining that the ontological status of extension as possibility must be that of "ideality." He differs from Leibniz and the
Kantian tradition following Leibniz, however, in regard to the interpretation of "ideality." Whitehead rejects the view that there is no
alternative but to interpret "ideality" as "phenomenality." This rejection
is a rejection of the whole post-Cartesian tradition of subjectivism based
on an ontological dualism, in accordance with which "ideas" are essentially mental existents. Instead Whitehead returns to an Aristotelian
conception of "Idea" or "Form." Like Aristotle, he regards "Ideas" or
"eternal objects" as the "forms of definiteness" of actuality. In their essential nature forms transcend actuality—which does not mean that they exist apart from actuality. Whitehead's chief difference from Aristotle is in
regard to this "transcendence" of form. Form *qua* form is a metaphysical
ultimate which constitutes the "possibility" for actuality; eternal objects
are "pure potentials for the specific determination of fact" (**PR** 32).
"Possibility" (or "potentiality") is the correlative of "actuality"; it is
thus not reducible to "actuality." The factor of possibility in the universe
belongs to form. So Whitehead is at one with Leibniz in maintaining
that the ontological status of extension as possibility must be that of
"ideality," but Whitehead's interpretation of "ideality" enables him to
develop an important new doctrine.

Leibniz, on his interpretation of "ideality," regards all order as phenomenal. Thus, "in themselves [the] monads have no situation [*situs*] with
respect to each other, that is, no real order which reaches beyond the

order of phenomena." [6] This means that Leibniz held a doctrine of *relatio rationalis*. Whitehead, on the other hand, with his different conception of form or ideality, is able to admit real relations. Relations are real because every relation is a relating, an actualization of form.[7] That is, actualities are really (as opposed to merely phenomenally) related by their actualizing a form in common. Any specific structure, pattern, or character displayed by a number of actualities results from their common actualization of a particular form—for structure, pattern, character, are nothing other than form. The actual existence of a structure is the actualization of that structure which, in abstraction from the actualization, is a pure form, and as such a pure possibility. Order is constituted by the exemplification of some structure, some pattern, some character actualized by the actualities in question. Order is an exemplification of some real relatedness between actualities.

Leibniz had seen that extension must be regarded as an order of relatedness between actualities, for extension cannot itself be an actuality. But he conceived the order of relatedness as phenomenal, not real. Descartes, on the other hand, maintained that extension was real by regarding it as itself actual. Whitehead holds, with Leibniz, that extension must be an order of relatedness between actualities and not itself an actuality; but he is able to maintain that the order is a real relatedness. Thus he says:

> We diverge from Descartes by holding that what he has described as primary *attributes* of physical bodies, are really the forms of internal relationships *between* actual occasions, and *within* actual occasions" (PR 471).

The most general "form of relationship" between actualities is the generic form of "extension" or "extensive connection":

> For Descartes the primary *attribute* of physical bodies is *extension;* for the philosophy of organism the primary *relationship* of physical occasions is *extensive connection* (PR 441).

In the cosmology of *Process and Reality,* therefore, unlike that of *Concept of Nature,* continuous extension is not a basic feature of actuality; actuality as such is not seen as continuously extensive. In the earlier doctrine events are continuously extensive; extensive continuity belongs to their essential nature as events. The new doctrine is that "the ultimate metaphysical truth is atomism. The creatures are atomic" (PR 53). That is, actuality is fundamentally and by metaphysical necessity atomic. This does not mean that continuity—and extensiveness—are phenomenal. On the contrary, Whitehead maintains that extensive continuity is real. But its reality is the reality of a relation and not of actuality as such. Also, the character of extensiveness and the character of continuity derive from form and not from actuality. That is to say, for these characters we are to look not to actuality or actualization as such, but to the particular form that is actualized. It is by virtue of the actualization of a particular form that there is extensive continuity. Whitehead acknowledges that "[i]n the present cosmic epoch there is a creation of continuity" (PR 53), but this is not a metaphysical necessity. Rather, he maintains, "extensive continuity is a special condition arising from the society of creatures which constitute our immediate epoch" (PR 53).

Extensiveness as such is a form of relatedness. Considered in itself it is a potentiality for actualities, not an actuality. It is the most general scheme of potential relatedness. That is, it is the most general scheme or structure exhibited by actualities whereby they stand in relationship to one another. It is the structure of potential standpoints.

Whitehead insists, like Leibniz, that extensiveness *qua* extensiveness must be potential, for extensiveness implies continuity, and continuity pertains to potentiality, not to actuality. Thus this potential scheme is an extensive *continuum*. As Whitehead says, as a "continuum [it] is in itself merely the potentiality for division; an actual entity effects this division" (PR 104).

The doctrine Whitehead has put forward in *Process and Reality* is, therefore, that "the real potentialities relative to all standpoints are coordinated as diverse determinations of one extensive continuum. This extensive continuum is one relational complex in which all potential objectifications find their niche. It underlies the whole world, past, present, and future" (PR 103). Thus "[t]his extensive continuum expresses the solidarity of all possible standpoints throughout the whole process of the world" (PR 103). Whitehead stresses repeatedly that the extensive continuum is not to be regarded as actuality, as some kind of "container": "[i]t is not a fact prior to the world; it is the first determination of order —that is, of real potentiality—arising out of the general character of the world" (PR 103). The extensive continuum is the most general form of order.

It would now be requisite to exhibit how space and time are derivative from this generic form of extensive relatedness as specific forms actualized by some, but not necessarily all, actualities. To do so would, however, extend this paper far beyond the assigned limits. Nor is this necessary for our present purpose, which has been to show that in Whitehead's later period he has developed a theory of extension significantly different from that of his earlier period, a theory which constitutes a major contribution to cosmological thought.

NOTES

[1] Cf. Einstein, *Relativity, the Special and General Theory,* tr. by Robert W. Lawson (New York: Hartsdale House, 1947).

[2] *Leibniz's Philosophical Papers and Letters,* tr. by L. E. Loemker (Chicago: University of Chicago Press, 1956), Letter X, p. 879. Copyright © 1956 by the University of Chicago.

[3] *Ibid.,* p. 1108. My italics.

[4] *Ibid.,* p. 874.

[5] G. Martin, *Kant's Metaphysics and Theory of Science,* tr. by P. G. Lucas (Manchester: University Press, 1955), pp. 38-39.

[6] Loemker, *op. cit.,* p. 980.

[7] Except, of course, for the relations among forms themselves.

The Concept of Experience
in Whitehead's Metaphysics

by Victor Lowe

In a perceptive article, "The Revolt Against Process," [1] Nicholas Rescher recently described and criticized a widespread habit of philosophers now writing in English on metaphysical subjects—the habit (not explicitly defended, except by Strawson) of accepting the thing-and-quality mode of thought and ignoring or thoroughly thingifying process. A kind of companion piece might well be written about the present neglect of the general idea of experience—undoubtedly a related phenomenon. The term had a long history of overgenerous use by philosophers, to be sure. We may nevertheless hope for acknowledgment of the desirability of reaching a satisfactory conception of the individual man's foothold in the universe around him, or at least of carefully formulating whatever concept of experience is prevalent. I believe that Whitehead made the last important contribution to the first-named objective. Those who disagree will still allow that he has a special place of considerable originality among past philosophers of experience. I propose, therefore, to discuss the nature and role of the concept of experience in Whitehead's metaphysics.

This has long been something of a stumbling block for many of his readers. Correct interpretation of it is undoubtedly crucial for that of his entire metaphysics. (That he thought so is suggested by his choice of his conception of experience as the topic for his presidential address to the Eastern Division of the American Philosophical Association in 1931.[2]) In what follows I shall not try to analyze anything in detail, but rather to indicate the perspectives in which (if I rightly understand Whitehead's metaphysics) analysis and judgment of his doctrine of experience should be placed. And no attempt will be made to consider Whitehead's doctrine of prehensions, or other leading aspects of the content of his idea of experience.[3] My concern is with Whitehead's wholesale *use* of 'experi-

"The Concept of Experience in Whitehead's Metaphysics." An earlier version of this paper was read to the Fullerton Club at Bryn Mawr College on October 14, 1961.

ence,' which is one of the things that bother philosophers, today more than ever. Examination of the term's use in any metaphysics naturally divides into two parts—its methodological use, and its contentual use (if any). Both are crucial in Whitehead's case. But the nature of White-head's appeals to experience has been recently discussed.⁴ I shall con-centrate on the fact that Whitehead gives 'experience' a central place when he delineates the content of his metaphysical system.

I

His working hypothesis for the philosophy of organism, Whitehead said, was that "all final individual actualities have the metaphysical character of occasions of experience. . ." (AI 284). To give it the briefest name possible, I call this Whitehead's experientialism. What does it mean?

He explained that he repudiates the idea of a *res vera* devoid of sub-jective immediacy—pure *thing*, a passive object and only an object. To conceive of each and every individual in the pluralistic universe as a throb of *experience* is to conceive it as having an immediate existence in and for itself. Whitehead shares this repudiation and this affirmation with some exponents of the idealistic tradition in metaphysics. But in the philosophy of organism everything is somewhat different from what it was in any earlier position. The unusual element which must receive attention is precisely that which we should expect from a *mathematician* who had turned his sights upon the general theory of existence and be-come convinced of the importance of a substantive conception of ex-perience; or, to turn the situation around, it is the sort of formulation which a Berkeleian could attempt if he had written *A Treatise on Uni-versal Algebra* and the memoir, "On Mathematical Concepts of the Material World." The important notion is that of a special mode of composition of entities: that in which they participate *qua* components in an occasion of experience.

'Composition' must be understood in a wholly temporalistic way, as re-ferring to a synthesizing process. If someone says that Whitehead was evidently not talking about experience as such, but about the process of experien*cing*, the Whiteheadian response must be to agree whole-heartedly with the second half of the remark, while suggesting that some such phrase as "conscious awareness" would be an accurate name for what the other party calls experience, and pointing out that the process of experiencing, though its description must be filled out by scientific and philosophic theory, is sufficiently open to conscious awareness to provide an initial basis for Whitehead's theory of the process. Denial that there is any basis would seem to me egregious; when Whitehead calls experi-ence the "self-enjoyment of being one among many, and of being one arising out of the composition of many" (PR 220), I have no difficulty in finding such self-enjoyment suffusing my moments of consciousness. I have difficulty only in seeing how without some such notion a philosopher can expect to discuss in any large and adequate way either human existence or the general features of the world around him.

The advantage of thinking of Whitehead's attribution of experience to all final individual actualities as first of all the attribution of a peculiar pattern of synthesis to each such actuality (the pattern which he refers to in *Process and Reality* as the "complete formal constitution" of an actual entity) is, that we thereby take the ordinary, conscious-human-experience meanings of some of his terms—notably 'feeling,' 'valuation,' 'appetition,' 'emotion,' 'aim,' 'satisfaction,' 'immediacy,' and 'experience' itself—out of the spotlight in which unwary or hostile readers of the philosophy of organism place them, and remind ourselves that this metaphysician was not dealing with the unity of an experience as Kantians did, nor as panpsychists, absolute idealists, or various psychologists did. This reminder is the more desirable because Whitehead did not call his pluralistic metaphysics a panpsychism, and was not altogether happy when his students—myself, for one—did so. My own conjecture as to why *Process and Reality* (according to Lucien Price's report) [5] was the book he most wanted to write, is that from the 1890's on much of his work had been outside the traditional limitation of mathematical thought to number and quantity;[6] that, as he had a constant, vivid appreciation of the immediacy of value in the passing moment (he did not spend his life going through motions), he had become especially interested in those patterns of relationship—founded upon "the appropriation of the dead by the living"—which constitute our experience of the passing world; and that the possibility of devising a formal scheme of ideas which would express this unique type of composition in a way which applies to all events in nature probably presented itself to him as the last and highest challenge to his theory-creating powers. The result was his construction of that categoreal scheme which, supplemented by a few further notions, is presented in *Process and Reality* as his theory of the nature of things.

It is understood, I trust, that Whitehead's schematic representation of "experiential togetherness" is far from being a precise symbolically stated scheme of the sort that mathematical logicians call a formalization. It is far even from being an English version of a formalized scheme. Some of his categories of explanation seem largely advisory; some are there to help the reader understand others rather than to express further requirements; one of the categoreal obligations states no universal requirement, but a transmutation which "may" occur in the course of a concrescence. But the main purpose of the scheme, after all, was to offer a new network of categories for interpreting the varieties of human experience; to this end, a statement like the thirteenth category of explanation, "There are *many* species of subjective forms, *such as* emotions, valuations, purposes, adversions, aversions, consciousness, *etc.*," in which the words I have italicized especially represent defects from a mathematical logician's point of view, is more useful than I suppose any rigorous symbolic statement could be in the present stage of the history of metaphysics. It must also be doubted whether a faithful rendering of Whitehead's experiential metaphysics of process is possible in the language of set theory, though Dr. Chiaraviglio's work[7] shows how an important, part Whiteheadian, formalization can be thus constructed. However, if Whitehead was right in the prophecy which he made—hypothetically—in "Mathematics and the Good," mankind's development of conceptual tools for the systematic investigation of pattern has barely begun.

There is a prevalent assumption that whatever is defined by a formal scheme of ideas (ideally, by a set of postulates) is *ipso facto* abstract in an invidious sense which removes it from contact with direct, immediate experience. This assumption has been responsible for much mistaken criticism of the method of extensive abstraction which Whitehead used to systematically define points, instants, and the other ideal spatio-temporal entities of mathematical physics in terms of kinds of entities and relations between entities which are observable. In the philosophy of organism, his use of such terms as 'subjective aim' and 'subjective immediacy' *ought* to hinder commission of a similar mistake. But readers still find difficulty; the most common reaction against Whitehead's metaphysics is a protest that it is intolerably abstract. What *is* all this talk, they say, about actual entities and prehensions and nexūs? Yet Whitehead wrote (PR 27) that in framing these three notions he was trying to base philosophical thought upon what is most concrete! Surely—the reaction runs—the concrete things are the identifiable bodies around us, and all our knowledge is knowledge of the behavior of identifiable bodies of one sort or another, got by observing them and framing theories about them. A metaphysics of actual entities, prehensions, and nexūs can only be written by someone who deems himself to have a way of knowing that is superior to the way of science; and the insistent reference to drops of *experience* is his smoke screen.

To maintain this protest one must deny one of Whitehead's cardinal principles about experience—a principle which drew the sympathy of John Dewey. Whitehead expressed it succinctly in the statement, "We experience more than we can analyse," and the explanation, "For we experience the universe, and we analyse in our consciousness a minute selection of its details" (MT 121). (The business of metaphysics is then to recover—by a conscious effort to formulate its character—this totality, the universe, from which the operations of conscious awareness, of naming, of scientific identification and description, have made their selective emphases.) If we fully accept the doctrine that we experience the universe, the terms of any metaphysical scheme constructed in accordance with it will of necessity be intangibles to common sense; and the identifiable bodies of common sense and science will appear as constructs.

The ultimates must be intangibles, because whatever is marked out for us by our hands or eyes, and whatever we are conscious of as an individual object in the external world, is an individual only in the special way in which objects of its kind are individuals (or may at least be taken for individuals) relative to our particular purposes and our perceptive organs. We must then permit *thought* rather than sense, thought not limited to particular purposes, to frame the shapes of the metaphysically ultimate individuals. And this is profitably attempted—we cannot too often remind ourselves—not by demonstrative arguments but only by speculative trial, subject to those requirements of consistency, coherence, and adequacy in (indirect) empirical application, which Whitehead set out so well in the first chapter of *Process and Reality*.

Although the first recommendation for understanding Whitehead's concept of experience is to concentrate upon the *pattern* he ascribes to actual occasions, the subjective term 'self-enjoyment' also names an essential element in this concept. Whitehead does not say that experience consists in being one among many, and arising out of the composition of many; he says that it is the self-enjoyment thereof. Now, if we agree with him that we humans, by the tone of our naïve experience, know directly of the presence of self-enjoyment in our fellows, in our dogs and cats, and perhaps even in the green leaves, still, when we come to the actual occasions in sticks and stones we have, perhaps, none but the most general theoretical reasons for going along with Whitehead. That wholly qualitative kind of fact which we know in ourselves as self-enjoyment, we tend to call not general but special—an emergent at the level of life. Shall we say that the better way to apply the theory of actual occasions at the inorganic level is to suppose there are unities of "subjective form" which provide individuality, and to affirm the presence in principle of self-functioning (i.e., a measure of self-determination), while dropping the terms 'self-enjoyment' and 'experience'—terms which do not, after all, occur in Whitehead's categoreal scheme? The trouble with this proposal is that in Whitehead's system subjective forms are themselves "private matters of fact"; and Whitehead explains that they are qualities, privately enjoyed (PR 32, 443-447). The proposal would be easier to accept if we could simplify the whole discussion of Whitehead's experientialism (and drop the name) in a way which is suggested by a reading of Professor Christian's commentaries. If we distinguish Whitehead's systematic discourse (the terms of which he introduced in the second and third chapters of *Process and Reality*) from his presystematic and postsystematic discourse, and limit the content of Whitehead's metaphysics strictly to his systematic statements and *their* implications, perhaps the term 'experience' and the very notion of a "drop of experience" can be reserved for discussion of certain applications of the system. I do not think this simplification can be admitted as final, for it leaves us with a general theory which in itself gives no indication as to how it is to be applied and how it can be evidenced; the items of the formal pattern stand in certain formal relations to each other but are devoid of empirical meaning. It was natural (and wise) for Whitehead to keep 'experience' out of his technical systematic vocabulary—not only for the reason Professor Christian gives, viz., that Whitehead meant his categories to have possible application beyond the range of our *ordinary* use of 'experience,' [8] but also because the word, as he had just noted in *Symbolism* (p. 16), "is one of the most deceitful in philosophy"; and he did not need to bring this hoary untechnical word explicitly into his categoreal scheme, *provided* no disjunction was set up between the scheme and the idea of occasions of experience.

II

We cannot, then, simplify discussion of Whitehead's experientialism by giving 'experience' the boot. But in considering its contentual meaning we may now return to my first recommendation, and see what questions arise about Whitehead's use of 'experience' in the sense of a mode of composition.

I begin by quoting two passages.

> . . . our whole experience is composed out of our relationships to the rest of things, and of the formation of new relationships constitutive of things to come (MT 43).

> The way in which one actual entity is qualified by other actual entities is the 'experience' of the actual world enjoyed by that actual entity, as subject. The subjectivist principle is that the whole universe consists of elements disclosed in the analysis of the experiences of subjects. Process is the becoming of experience (PR 252).

Whitehead's hypothesis was that this pattern of synthesis is ontologically basic, in the double sense that the "togetherness of the component elements in individual experience . . . is a togetherness of its own kind, explicable by reference to nothing else" (PR 288), and that there is no other mode of composition anywhere in the world that is not derivative from the experiential mode, i.e., not an abstraction from the peculiar togetherness of component elements in individual experience.

To become well satisfied about the meaning of 'derivative,' we should explore all the "discussions and applications" of his metaphysical scheme in Whitehead's books, and any other applications we can think of. A few suggestions are all that I can offer here. To begin with, we easily discover in our experience an indeterminate number of kinds of composition which occur *within* the unity of a total momentary experience. Such are the unity of a momentary visual field, and the unity of the ideas co-present to a consciousness. But other composite unities may be mentioned without making any explicit reference to experience; such are the unity of the nucleus of an atom, the unity of a human body, the unity of a gene, the unity of a living cell, etc., etc. If, when we wish to construct a metaphysical system, one of these is proposed to us as a better model than the unity of an occasion of experience, it will be proper to challenge the proposer to show how the experiential unity can be derived from his alternative. I do not think he will succeed! He will probably not make the attempt, but will instead repudiate the aim at finding or formulating *one* type of unity from which all others are derivative; he will bring in 'contingency,' as the name of an irreducible feature of existence. Now Whitehead—like every metaphysician who consistently rejects that complete necessitarianism of which Spinoza provided the classic example—acknowledged a kind of contingency in existences *qua* existent. But the doctrine of contingency which rejects the conception of a generic mode of unity, constitutive of individuality, cannot admit individuality, in any generic sense, as a generic trait of existence. One who adopts the doctrine has, if you please, a pluralistic metaphysics, but not a pluralistic system.

It will rightly be said, however, that the burden of persuasion concerning the primacy of experiential togetherness falls on Whitehead. Is he claiming—as Dewey once suggested—that he can "derive the matter of experience" from the generic relationships set forth in his categoreal scheme (assuming for the moment that the scheme truthfully states the form of togetherness of entities in occasions of experience)? Certainly not! Whitehead's view is rather that by diverse processes of abstraction from the content of the categoreal scheme it should be possible to arrive at notions which have the characteristic features of our familiar categories; for example, at the notions of enduring material bodies, living organisms, persons, wave-transmission of energy, regions of space-time. And some of this he has done.

What, then, of the proposition that no type of composite entity, not derived from the experiential type, exists anywhere at any time? It would be the height of folly to suppose that this could be proved by any argument. But let us recall the manner in which Whitehead presented his fundamental notions.

> . . . all argument must rest upon premises more fundamental than the conclusions. Discussion of fundamental notions is merely for the purpose of disclosing their coherence, their compatibility, and the specializations which can be derived from their conjunction (AI 379).

This I conceive to be the most that any philosopher can do to show the positive merits of the metaphysics he proposes.

At this point it will be well to notice some of the difficulties in which Whitehead's experientialism is involved. Many philosophers, probably most, cannot begin to consider his hypothesis because of the unusual content of his concept of an experience; I mean his doctrine that external *individuals* are perceived, his objectivist doctrine concerning the datum of experience. That doctrine is outside the announced topic of this paper, and I would in any case have nothing to add to Whitehead's defense of it. It is mentioned here because apart from it we cannot on his own grounds know of a universe of things to which the experientialist hypothesis *might* apply, even in part. The same problem must be faced by anyone who proposes a different metaphysical hypothesis. He must show—from the general character of his experience, I suppose—just how he knows that there is anything to apply his hypothesis to.

If we grant with Whitehead that we do experience the universe and that it is a pluralistic one, we face a double handicap in elaborating a generalized idea of "experiential togetherness." The only model one has is his own experience; and he can consult only those occasions of it which are illumined by consciousness. In making his cosmological generalization, Whitehead dropped consciousness out, along with thought and sense perception. Did he retain some feature—conceptual feeling, perhaps—which might with more reason be assigned to the theory of man than to the theory of the universe? Did he unduly neglect some other feature of experience—spatiality, perhaps? Such questions deserve much more discussion than philosophers have given them. Whitehead did not hesitate to say to his students that if he had leisure for a second go at his metaphysical scheme the result would be somewhat different. My point, however, is that questions of this sort are inevitable and cannot be easily answered; for the term 'experiential togetherness,' used as a name for the pattern which a Whiteheadian theory of actuality sets out to formulate, is an extremely vague one. This latitude can be reduced only by indirect and eventual checks on the ventures that get made.

It is natural but naïve to ask, How shall I recognize an actual occasion? How tell that an A is one of these metaphysical individuals but a B is not? When I asked Whitehead whether the emission of a single quantum of energy by an atom should be considered an actual occasion, he replied, "Probably a whole shower of actual occasions." It would be reckless to discard Whitehead's theory of actuality because, in the present state of human knowledge, we cannot be sure of such applications of it.

Despite the hard questions that can be asked about the idea of experiential togetherness, Whitehead (participating in his own way in the idealistic tradition) argues that it is not open to us to do without it. He defended his experientialism with this argument: the primary datum for philosophical theory is one's self as now experiencing; the relevance of evidence is dictated by the encompassing theoretical framework; on the hypothesis that all actualities are occasions of experience (or societies of such occasions), direct evidence as to the connectedness between one's present and immediately past occasions of experience "can be validly used to suggest categories applying to the connectedness of all occasions in nature" (AI 284); but if you adopt a working hypothesis which separates experiencing individuals (whether these be conceived as substances, events, or what not) from others, you cut yourself off from any reason to suppose that what you discover in the former is true of the latter. "For you cannot prove a theory by evidence which that theory dismisses as irrelevant." So, let us not adopt a dualistic hypothesis. Must we then adopt Whitehead's? It is surely asking too much to demand that we envisage a stone as a society of experiencing individuals before we can have a right to say that directly observed features of our experience, like spatiality, temporality, and causal efficacy, characterize it also. But Whitehead does not make that demand. He does not dictate our modes of envisagement, and we can discuss a stone without attributing any self-enjoyment to any bit of it. Whitehead *does* hold that the only types of *relatedness* which we can observe in nature are those—or are abstracted from those—which we have in our own occasions of experience. This predicament, he conceives, cannot be escaped. "For intuitive judgment is concerned with togetherness in experience, and there is no bridge between togetherness in experience, and togetherness of the non-experiential sort" (PR 289). In our illustration, "the stone as extended" can be taken as a datum only because it is abstracted from the original fact, "my experience of the stone as extended." That this *is* the original fact must be directly seen.

The question arises, How, on Whitehead's grounds, is it possible for anyone to so much as conceive of a type of composition which is neither experiential nor derived from the experiential type? Many conceptions occurring in the history of thought may be set down as mixtures of concepts and verbiage. But the main answer must be that when I have a genuine concept, and it is of a type of composition which I think quite distinct from the experiential type, it is in fact derivative therefrom. It is bound to be so, because my occasion of experience is my present perspective of the whole universe, and this status of individual experience is something which no thinker can escape. The genuine error which remains possible consists in supposing that a derivative type is not derivative but aboriginal, as the simply located bits of matter in the Newtonian world view were thought to be. The error, in short, is an instance of the "fallacy of misplaced concreteness."

I return to the matter of the current neglect of the idea of experience by many philosophers. Certain others strongly urge philosophers to live, or relive, the basic human experience of the *Lebenswelt,* and attempt to describe it. Let us admit that, whatever it is that lies at the heart of human experience, it is desirable for philosophers to know it by consciously living it. But a philosopher's constructive goal is some theory of experience. And no description that focuses upon conscious experience can be a theory of experience. For that, a quite different sort of thing is needed: the idea of composition.

In his earlier publications Whitehead was concerned with the space-time structure of observed nature. He inevitably thought of natural events as composites. Experience was discussed only as sense perception; but (with his doctrine of "significance") a fundamental type of composition was ascribed to that which is given in perception. When Whitehead went beyond the concerns of science he thought of experience as an immediacy of value-enjoyment. But he did not assign the general idea of composition, an idea of scientific cast, to a different world. The fundamental idea in his philosophy became that of "composition attaining worth for itself" (MT 163).

NOTES

[1] *Journal of Philosophy*, 59 (1962), 410-417.

[2] In AI, ch. XI.

[3] I have discussed them in *Understanding Whitehead* (Baltimore: The Johns Hopkins Press, 1962), chs. 2 and 13, and in other passages listed under 'Experience' in the index.

[4] It is a frequent topic in Professor Hartshorne's discussions. I have considered it in *Understanding Whitehead*, especially pp. 285 f., 305-307; and ch. 12 of the book may be read as arguing that a sound conception of empirical method in metaphysics makes "experience" a legitimate candidate for a place in systematic metaphysics.

[5] *Dialogues of Alfred North Whitehead* (Boston: Little, Brown & Co., 1954), pp. 10, 363.

[6] He later wrote (MT 65), "I confess to a larger pleasure in patterns of relationship in which numerical and quantitative relationships are wholly subordinate."

[7] See his paper in this volume, pp. 81-92.

[8] William A. Christian, in *The Relevance of Whitehead*, ed. Ivor Leclerc (London: Allen & Unwin; New York: The Macmillan Co., 1961), p. 83.

The Subjectivist Principle
and the Linguistic Turn

by Richard M. Rorty

I

To understand the needs which *Process and Reality* was intended to satisfy, one must understand Whitehead's diagnosis of the state of modern philosophy: "The difficulties of all schools of modern philosophy lie in the fact that, having accepted the subjectivist principle, they continue to use philosophical categories derived from another point of view" (PR 253). The plausibility of this diagnosis is brought out by the following considerations: The substance-property framework, which philosophical thought has taken over from ordinary language, leads us to think of everything to which we refer as either a substance or a property of a substance. The distinction between a substance and a property is the distinction between what is in principle unrepeatable and what is in principle repeatable, for substances are the referents of proper names, and properties the referents of predicates. Now when we think about knowing, we are led to the conception of the experiencing subject as a substance having, among its properties, mental states. When we ask for the relation of these states to that which is known, it appears natural to say that what we know are other substances. But these mental states are not substances. They must, then, be representations of substances. But our mental states, being properties of a substance, are in principle repeatable. So if they are representations, it seems that they can represent nothing but what is itself repeatable. Thus it seems that our mental states cannot represent other substances, but only the properties of other substances.

This is an unwelcome conclusion. It becomes doubly unwelcome after the Cartesian turn is taken. As Whitehead says:

[Descartes] laid down the principle, that those substances which are the subjects enjoying conscious experiences, provide the primary data for philosophy, namely, themselves as in the enjoyment of such experience. This is the famous subjectivist bias which entered into modern philosophy through Descartes. In this doctrine Descartes undoubtedly made the greatest philosophical discovery since the age of Plato and Aristotle. For his doctrine directly traversed the notion that the proposition, "This stone is grey," expresses a primary form of known fact from which metaphysics can start its generalizations. . . . But . . . Descartes . . . continued to construe the functioning of the subjective enjoyment of experience according to the substance-quality categories. Yet if the enjoyment of experience be the constitutive subjective fact, these categories have lost all claim to any fundamental character in metaphysics (PR 241).

Specifically, the attempt to combine the principle that "the whole universe consists of elements disclosed in the analysis of the experience of subjects" (which Whitehead calls "the subjectivist principle") with the substance-quality framework led straight to Lockeian paradox. For if the experience of substances discloses only repeatables, then substances, since they are unrepeatables, are not disclosed in experience. So, by the subjectivist principle, they do not exist. But if substances do not exist, what does? Not merely properties, one would think, for properties are properties of substances. But then *what?* The history of attempts to answer this question is a history of attempts to fall back on The Unknowable (Locke's "I know not what," Kant's Noumenon, Bradley's Absolute, and the like), and thus to tacitly betray Descartes—alternating with attempts to envisage a world of properties-without-substances (phenomenalism, radical empiricism).

Neither sort of attempt can succeed. The former runs afoul of our conviction that, despite all the inconveniences of subjectivism, the Cartesian quest for clear and distinct ideas, with which to replace the pseudo-explanations of Aristotelianism, was a Good Thing. Aristotelian philosophical explanations depended for their plausibility on the distinction between what is more knowable to us and what is more knowable in itself—a distinction which permits one to shrug off the patent obscurity and indistinctness of such expressions as 'pure actuality' and 'form without matter.' These expressions are obscure and indistinct because they employ contrastive terms in a context in which these terms are prohibited from playing a contrastive role. (We know, e.g., what the difference between a potential house and an actual house is, but we do not know what pure actuality is.) The assumption that in such cases we are nevertheless entitled to postulate the existence of entities described by such expressions, and to use statements about such entities as explanations, is the assumption against which Descartes rebelled. Acceptance of the methodological form of the subjectivist principle—viz., that nothing may be used as a philosophical explanation which is not, in some sense, an object of possible experience—is what binds post-Cartesian philosophers together. (What separates them, as we shall see, is their interpretations of the phrase "object of possible experience.")

But the latter sort of attempt—the attempt to construct a world consisting entirely of repeatables, and thus to treat the substance-property distinction as an eliminable pragmatic convenience—has always run afoul of our conviction that if we once let go of the distinction between the sort of thing which is unrepeatable (the sort of thing, which we ourselves exemplify, of which it is senseless to say that there are two of them) and the repeatable properties of these things, we shall have lost all contact with common sense. In recent years, this conviction has been strengthened by arguments designed to show that the notion of a language which does not contain singular terms is a fake—that such a language cannot serve the purposes which are served by ordinary language.[1] Those arguments suggest that the distinction between unrepeatable and repeatable entities is so firmly built into the structure of our language that proposals to abandon it must necessarily be abortive.

The challenge to modern philosophy, as Whitehead saw it, was to slip between the horns of this dilemma—a dilemma which seems to force us either to betray the Cartesian quest for clarity and distinctness or to betray common sense. His attempt to do so involved a reinterpretation of the notion of "unrepeatable particular." He held that almost everyone since Aristotle had assumed that "this round ball" was a paradigm of such an unrepeatable particular (cf. PR 253). He attempted to find another paradigm—an entity which, though unrepeatable, could nonetheless be experienced, and could be described in terms which would meet the requirements of the subjectivist principle. In other words, he wanted to hold on to the common-sense contrast between the unrepeatable and the repeatable which is embodied in the substance-property categoreal frame (a contrast which his principal rivals—the logical empiricists—were prepared to do away with altogether), while defining "unrepeatable entity" in a way which would conform to "the subjectivist bias of modern philosophy."

The "actual entities" of *Process and Reality* were tailor-made to fit these requirements. To see this, it is helpful to consider the following Lockeian line of argument:

(1) Only the sort of concrete entity which we experience is the sort of concrete entity which we can know about—where 'concrete' has a meaning such that "$K_1, K_2 \ldots K_n$ are the only sorts of concrete entity" entails "all statements containing expressions denoting an entity of any other sort are equivalent to statements which contain only expressions which denote entities of sorts $K_1, K_2 \ldots K_n$."

(2) Substances (defined as unrepeatable entities, uniquely locatable in spatiotemporal regions) and their properties (defined as repeatable entities, locatable in spatiotemporal regions) are the only candidates for the title of *concrete* entities.

(3) All substances are entities which can endure through time and which thus can be substrates of contrary determinations.

(4) Every experience is in principle repeatable—that is, it is (logically)

possible that the same experience be had at different times by the same subject, or be had by two different subjects.

(5) An experience which is repeatable must be the experience of a repeatable entity.

Now (2), taken together with (4) and (5) entails

(6) We do not experience substances, but only their properties.

and (6) and (1) entail

(7) We can only know about properties of substances, never about substances.

This conclusion leads straight to the traditional dilemma: either unrepeatable entities do not exist, or nothing can be known about them. The conclusion may be attacked by attacking any of the premises. Whitehead's challenge is to (4), and takes the form of asserting that only the misleading abstractions built into ordinary language could have persuaded us that the same experience can be had twice. In particular, the assumption that the experiencing subject is a perduring substrate of contrary determinations—premise (3) above—lets us think of experiences as properties of a substance (as colors are properties of a ball). Just as this ball can be now red, now green, and now red again, so I can have the experience A, the experience B, and then the experience A again. But, Whitehead points out, the same facts which impel us to make the experiencing subject a paradigm case of unrepeatability prevent us from thinking of the self as such a perduring substrate—for if we do so think of ourselves, then we shall have to apply the Lockeian argument sketched above to ourselves, and wind up with the conclusion that we never know anything about ourselves—not even, therefore, that we *are* unrepeatable entities. In other words, (4) is plausible only if we adopt a conception of the self which is destroyed by an argument which uses (4) as a premise. So, Whitehead argued, what was needed was a new conception of substance—one which would make it possible to deny (3), and would thus make it possible to deny (4).

Whitehead (and here he was at one with the idealists) thought that the notion that there were unrepeatable and knowable entities could be saved from Lockeian lines of argument only by disentangling the notion of "being unrepeatable" from that of "being a substrate of repeatables," identifying the former notion with that of "being an experience," and conceiving of the latter as an abstraction from the former. But in order to abide (as the idealists did not) by the insistence of common sense that, in every experience, there is a difference between the experience itself and the object of this experience, and that the latter can exist independently of the former, Whitehead had to find a new model of the relation between experience and the object of experience.

For the previous model—which involved the same repeatable entity being attached to two unrepeatable entities—was precisely the model which had brought us to the conclusion that unrepeatables could not, after all, be experienced. To find a new model, he had to find a way in which two unrepeatables could be brought into relation with one another without the mediation of repeatables—"properties" (on the side of the object of experience) and "ideas" (on the side of the subject).

His solution to this problem contained two steps. The first was to model the general relationship *experiencing* on the relationship of "feeling another's feeling of . . ." (cf. PR 216) or *prehending*. The relationship of "prehending" cannot, for Whitehead, be modeled on any relationship which holds among (what his system takes to be) *abstracta;* it therefore cannot be modeled on any familiar relation holding between entities mentioned in ordinary language. For "there is a togetherness of the component elements in individual experience. This 'togetherness' has that special peculiar meaning of 'togetherness in experience.' It is a togetherness of its own kind, explicable by reference to nothing else" (PR 288). Whitehead held that the assumption that there was *another* sort of togetherness (viz., that which united a perduring self with its experiences, or, more generally, a perduring substance with its "accidental" properties) in terms of which "togetherness in experience" needed to be analyzed, created "the insurmountable difficulty for epistemology" (PR 289). He held further that if the Lockeian line of argument was to be gotten around, then it was necessary that *all* other relationships be conceived as abstractions from this fundamental relationship.

In this first step, Whitehead is, of course, quite unoriginal. This step had already been taken by idealists—the only difference being that for metaphors with which to shadow forth the character of this ultimate and irreducible relationship the idealists (other than Bradley) tended to look toward "higher" syntheses (such as scientific theories), whereas Whitehead looked toward "lower" syntheses—examples of "simple feeling." But this difference is of interest only in so far as it is relevant to the *second* step which Whitehead took in order to provide a new model of the subject-object relationship.

This second step consisted in remodeling the *terms* of the relationship which is expressed by the phrase 'togetherness in experience.' This remodeling was dictated by the following requirements: if the realism of common sense is to be maintained, then both the experiencing subject and the object which we experience must be unrepeatable entities (a requirement satisfied by idealism, since the Absolute, which is both the only object and the only subject of experience, is indeed unrepeatable—though not spatiotemporally locatable). But they must be distinct from each other (a requirement which idealism was unable to satisfy, since "distinctness" in this sense is intelligible only as long as spatiotemporality is applicable, and it is therefore impossible to conceive of an unrepeatable entity distinct from the Absolute). Now there is a difficulty in satisfying this second requirement once one adopts "feeling another's feeling of . . ." as the primitive relation which unites subject and object. For "A feeling B's feeling of C" always needs to be expanded into "A's feeling of B's feeling of C's feeling of D's . . ." and so on *ad indefinitum*. We seem to be confronted by the dissolution of every unrepeatable entity into an indefinitely large, seamless web of relationships—the same dissolution which is so familiar a feature of idealism.[2] Given this regress, how are we to find a plurality of distinct entities in it? Whitehead's answer is: "By noticing that 'A feeling the feelings of B' is always an ellipsis for 'A *now* feeling the feelings *felt* by B in the past.' " *The distinction between unrepeatable entities and repeatable entities is simply, for Whitehead, a distinction between present actual entities and past actual entities*—between actual entities (feelings of past feelings bound together in "experienced togetherness") now feeling (i.e., "concrescing") and actual occasions felt.[3] Thus instead of drawing a line between the unrepeatable and the repeatable in such a way that there are two sorts of perduring entities (e.g., unrepeatable balls, and their repeatable colors), Whitehead draws it in such a way that entities switch from one class to the other, simply by ceasing to be. By "taking time seriously," and, specifically, by equating "actuality" with "presentness" (thus entailing that 'actual world' is a token-reflexive term—cf. PR 102 and fn. 4 below), Whitehead tries to make the notion of unrepeatable entity unmysterious and unobjectionable. For it is not mysterious that "time *t*" is unrepeatable, nor that an entity which (logically) can exist only at time *t* should be unrepeatable.

However, it may be objected that to explain the notion of "unrepeatable entity" in this way is hopeless. For to make sense of "entity which *logically* can exist only at time *t*," one needs to give a sense to the notion of an entity whose temporal location is not a mere "accident" of it, but is essential to it—so that the statement "A is at time *t*" is a necessary truth about A. Now it may be thought that this notion is just unintelligible. It does seem that our grammar is such that if we say "A is at time t_i," we may also say "It is a logical possibility that A could have been at time t_j." The contingency of statements about temporal locations seems to be part of the very fabric of temporal discourse. But there *is* one sort of expression which is a necessary truth about the temporal location of a concrete entity: "I am here now" *is* a necessary truth about me. The one sort of statement which can attribute a temporal location to an entity as a necessary feature of that entity is a statement which connects one token-reflexive expression with another token-reflexive expression. More generally, the only referring expressions in ordinary speech which, given a relativistic interpretation of time, can never be used to refer twice to the same entity, are such token-reflexive expressions as 'that . . . now,' 'this . . . now,' 'my . . . now,' 'your . . . now,' and the like.

Now Whitehead's unrepeatable (i.e., present) actual entities, if they are characterizable in terms of ordinary speech at all, must be characterized as entities which can only be referred to by expressions of the form 'my . . . now,' where '. . .' is replaced by expressions of the form 'experienced togetherness of ——, ——, ——, etc.' These latter blanks, it must be noted, are filled in *not* with token-reflexive expressions, but with names of past, and therefore repeatable, actual entities. That is, they are filled in with expressions which stand to 'my . . . now' as "Smith was at spot *s* at time *t*" stands to "I am here now" (uttered by Smith at *s* at *t*).

The difference between entities referred to in the first way and entities referred to in the second way is, for Whitehead, the difference between repeatable and unrepeatable entities. The sense in which it is (timelessly) the "same" entity which once was unrepeatable and is now repeatable is the same sense in which "I am here now" and "Smith was at spot *s* at time *t*" report the "same" occurrence. Whitehead's use of the doctrine of relativity to show that every actual entity has its own space-time scheme—that it atomizes the extensive continuum (cf. PR 104) in a unique way, so that "no two actual entities define the same actual world" (PR 102)—amounts to a claim that present entities can only be referred to by token-reflexive expressions.[4] The difference between Whiteheadian actual entities ('present actual entities'—a phrase which, strictly, is pleonastic for Whitehead) and episodes in the history of persons (or of things, mythically endowed with the ability to say "I") is the difference between entities referable to only in the first way and entities referable to in both ways. (The fact that it is essential to our ordinary ways of speaking that anything referable to in the one way is referable to in the other is the fundamental reason why Whitehead thought ordinary language hopeless for metaphysical purposes, and is the fundamental reason why it is so extraordinarily difficult to translate sentences in Whiteheadian jargon into sentences in ordinary discourse.)

To state this point more formally, let us call "token-reflexive statements" statements in which token-reflexive terms are either the subject of the sentence used to make the statement or in which token-reflexive terms occur essentially in its predicate. We can now say that a basic Whiteheadian thesis is that *the only sort of statement which can describe a nonrepeatable entity is a token-reflexive statement, and that the only entities which non-token-reflexive discourse can describe are repeatable entities.* Now this thesis explains why we naturally make a distinction between repeatable and unrepeatable entities, despite the *prima facie* repeatability of all our experiences, and thus the *prima facie* mysteriousness of the notion of "unrepeatable entity." The root of the notion of "substance" (unrepeatable spatiotemporally locatable entity) is the notion of *self*.[5] We think of some entities as unrepeatable because we think of them as like ourselves—as quasi-people and thus quasi-users of token-reflexive discourse. This thesis also explains why traditional philosophical accounts of the relation between subject and object have never been able to make sense of the notion of "knowledge of an unrepeatable entity." We are unable to make sense of the notion of knowing unrepeatables because when we describe past entities we do not (and cannot) use "their" (token-reflexive) terms, but only our own non-token-reflexive descriptive statements about them. In describing them, as Whitehead says, we objectify them. The principal mark of this objectification is that the "now" of a present actual entity A becomes, for the later actual entities which prehend A, a mere "time *t*." When so objectified, these entities become repeatable entities.[6]

II

I now turn to what seems to me the most fundamental criticism which has been made of Whitehead's attempt to develop a new model of "unrepeatable entity." I have tried to show how, by reinterpreting 'experience' so that it refers not to episodes in the history of a human being but rather to entities describable only in the way outlined above ('my experienced togetherness of ——, ——, ——, etc. now,' where 'now' is pleonastic) Whitehead believes himself to have found a way of denying (4).[7] This reinterpretation is not, Whitehead thought, a mere verbal maneuver. To mediate between the two meanings of 'experience,' he attempts to provide an account of (4)'s plausibility by interpreting the vocabulary used in describing the experiences of human beings as composed of high abstractions from the concrete experiences of the actual entities which are components of the societies which are human beings. Further, he holds that his use of 'experienced togetherness,' and similar terms, in characterizing actual entities is a legitimate metaphorical extension of their ordinary uses.

Now most criticism of the adequacy of Whitehead's system (as opposed to its coherence) consists in questioning his ability to make the connection between his technical meaning of 'experience' (in which 'experience' is synonymous with 'present experienced togetherness' and both are synonymous with 'unrepeatable concrete entity') and the ordinary meaning of the term. Such questioning can be of two different sorts. One may grant to Whitehead that one understands, and can work with, the metaphorically extended meanings of ordinary terms which he uses in formulating his categoreal scheme, but claim that the materials provided are insufficient to construct adequate theories of, e.g., consciousness, personality, language, or moral responsibility. Or one may refuse to grant this, and claim that these meanings are not intelligible and that there is no point in trying to work with them until they are made intelligible.

It is this latter, more radical and more Philistine, criticism of White-head which I wish to discuss (and, in the end, defend) in this paper. This line of criticism bases itself on the view that the Cartesian method-ological requirement that "nothing may be used as a philosophical explanation which is not, in some sense, an object of possible experience" requires a stronger interpretation than Whitehead gives it. Whitehead thinks that this requirement is satisfied if no unknowables are postulated. But he interprets "unknowable" as "vacuous actuality, void of subjective experience" (cf. PR 253). He thinks that if an entity is described as an "experienced togetherness," then, whatever the difficulties of saying any-thing *more* about it, it is absurd to call it an "unknowable." (For "ex-perienced togetherness" is what we know if we know anything.) In other words, he construes "use nothing as a principle of explanation which is not an object of possible experience" in such a way that "being an object of possible experience" does not entail "being describable in a language used for communicating between human beings." If, however, one con-strues the former phrase in such a way that it entails the latter (as "analytic" philosophers do) then one will hold that Whitehead produces mere pseudo-explanations. The "linguistic turn" in philosophy has, in respect to the methodological requirements set for philosophical explana-tion, consisted in adopting the view that the cash value of the rather unclear Cartesian dictum that we should use none but "clear and distinct ideas" is as follows: (a) we should, in offering explanations, use no terms but those which have a nonphilosophical use, and then we should use them in their nonphilosophical senses; or, (b) when we do use other terms (or use terms which have a nonphilosophical use in an abnormal, peculiarly philosophical sense) then we should explicitly endow them with a use (or a new use).

This reformulated dictum will appear weak and platitudinous only until one begins to reflect upon the variations in meaning between apparent near-synonyms in ordinary speech, and upon the complicated presuppositions which are made in quite ordinary and unassuming non-philosophical statements.[8] If one does so reflect, one will see that White-head, no less than Aristotle, is employing terms whose ordinary use presupposes certain standard contrasts—and whose ordinary meaning is determined by the possibility of such contrasts—in new, noncontrastive ways. (Compare the relation between "actual (as contrasted with poten-tial) house" and "pure actuality" with the relation between, e.g., "the form of the argument" and "the subjective form of an actual entity," or between "an efficacious remedy" and "prehension in the mode of causal efficacy.") Every present Whiteheadian actual entity must be thought of as the sort of thing which can only be described *by itself*—in such phrases as 'my . . . now.' But most actual entities, to put it bluntly, can't talk. At best, only the very high-grade ones (the conscious ones) can (and it is not clear whether their use of 'I' or 'my' refers to themselves or rather to the society of which they are a part). In the case of the lower-grade actual entities, we are asked to envisage a sort of entity which (a) it is absurd to think of as talking, but which (b) belongs to a category which is delimited by the condition that entities of this category, if they could talk, would only be able to talk in a certain way.

It is of no real help to be told, as Whitehead tells us, that 'actual entity' is clearer than, e.g., 'pure actuality,' because an actual entity is an experienced togetherness of feeling, and we understand what *that* is. For to understand what 'experienced togetherness' means is to understand how to use this term in discourse about the way in which we ourselves, and other human beings, grasp the features of more or less enduring objects. (It cannot, as Wittgenstein has shown, be thought of as the ability to recognize a peculiar introspectible content.) When the term is used, as Whitehead uses it, as a primitive predicate applying to entities which are not people, and have in common with people only the very fact that they are said to be instances of "experienced togetherness," then it is clear that (as Whitehead himself admits) we are dealing with a "metaphor mutely appealing for an imaginative leap" (PR 6). But the same mute appeal is made (in the form of the "appeal to analogy") by the vocabulary of Aristotelian substantialist metaphysics, and it may well seem that what is being pleaded for is the same in both cases—viz., that we should retain just so much of the ordinary meaning of a term as is required to attribute desirable features (i.e., features which do not raise philosophical problems) to the entities to which the term is applied, while discarding just so much of it as would permit the attribution of undesirable features (i.e., features which raise philosophical problems) to those entities. When confronted with such an appeal, therefore, it seems reasonable to reply that it is the job of the philosopher who transmits it to show that enough of the original meaning of the metaphorical term remains to make its use more than a mere baptism of the problem at hand. In particular, where the terms in question are used to characterize entities, the philosopher needs to show that there is enough meaning left in them so that these entities may actually be *identified* by criteria formulated in these terms. To assert that a theoretical entity is described by certain novel terms, it is not sufficient merely to deduce consequences from the rules governing the use of these novel terms (or the abnormal use of conventional terms). One must also show that hypotheses about the entities so described can be inductively verified by inspection (though, perhaps, indirect inspection) of samples of such entities. If this cannot be done, then the requirements of Cartesian subjectivism remain unfulfilled.

This line of criticism of Whitehead is familiar. It amounts to saying that one cannot satisfy the methodological form of the subjectivist principle simply by borrowing the primitive predicates of the vocabulary in which one will phrase one's philosophical explanations from the ordinary vocabulary of reports of mental states (rather than from the ordinary vocabulary of reports of events in the physical world), unless one can supply criteria for applying these terms, in their extended meanings, to particular cases—instructions which have the same degree of specificity as the criteria which we use in applying these terms to particular cases in their unextended meanings. Now Whitehead admits that nothing approaching this degree of specificity can be obtained. In the first place, the fact that Whiteheadian unrepeatable entities can only be described in token-reflexive statements means that we shall never, ever, be able to describe any such entity other than, perhaps, ourselves. But in fact we shall never even be able to describe *ourselves,* for even the finest discriminations which could conceivably be expressed in symbols used for communication between human beings would be discriminations on a level of abstraction far above the level at which, e.g., the individual entity which is the "I" of this moment prehends another in the mode of causal efficacy. "Language almost exclusively refers to presentational immediacy as interpreted by symbolic reference" (PR 263).

If this criticism is familiar, so is the Whiteheadian answer to it. The answer is that the demand for criteria of such specificity is self-defeating. For, when strictly applied, it would forbid the philosopher to postulate the existence of entities other than those for which criteria of indentification can be provided with the aid of the apparatus available in ordinary language. Now since the philosopher's problems are created precisely by the structure of ordinary language, to subject him to the proposed requirement is to forbid him to solve his problems by transcending the categories built into that structure. Granted that the scientist should be bound by this requirement (roughly, the requirement that there be rules which correlate statements about the existence of particular theoretical entities with statements about the existence of particular observed entities[9]), the philosopher should not be.[10] The attempt to impose "verificationism" on scientists is a natural consequence of conceiving of the aim of scientific inquiry as the discovery of practically useful abstractions, and abstractions are of little practical use unless there is a road back and forth between the abstract and the concrete, and, in particular, unless there are criteria for the identification of theoretical entities. But since philosophical problems are not problems about how to deal with observed phenomena, but about how to find nonparadoxical characterizations of these phenomena, this requirement need not apply.[11] To suggest that we think of our perception of a table on the model of feeling the feelings of another person, rather than on the model of taking pictures of the table and studying them, may be a useful suggestion, even though we may never be able to isolate a single prehension among those which constitute one of the actual occasions which make up the society which **is** the table.

The general Whiteheadian reply to the charge that Whitehead's method betrays the Cartesian quest for clarity and distinctness is, therefore, this: if clarity is defined in terms of fidelity to the basic structures of ordinary language, no "clear" explanation can be given which will dissolve the problems which are built into those structures. For let us suppose that Whitehead is right in saying that the subject-property categoreal frame is the cause of our inability to give a coherent statement of our knowledge of unrepeatable entities. Since so many of the terms of our language have meanings which are determined by the roles which these terms play in asking and answering questions about the possession of qualities by substances, it seems clear that we shall never make any progress if we try to stick to the unextended meanings of this cluster of terms. Further, we shall never extend their meaning far enough unless we can imaginatively leap right out of "the language-game which is their original home." To assume that methodological subjectivism requires us to stay within the language-game in which we find ourselves is to claim, implausibly, that every sort of experience which we have can be expressed in the language currently available to us, and to fail to realize that "a precise language must await a complete metaphysical knowledge" (PR 18). It is an assumption which would make sense only if one held that (a) there is really no "problem of knowledge" to be solved at all, or (b) that the resources of ordinary language are adequate to solve whatever problem there is.

In the preceding paragraphs I have tried to sketch both sides of the somewhat hackneyed quarrel about the value of doing the sort of "speculative philosophy" which *Process and Reality* typifies. This is a quarrel which has never, I think, been satisfactorily resolved. During the reign of phenomenalistically oriented "ideal-language" philosophizing it was fiercely waged; on the whole, the Whiteheadians came out ahead. For they had two very strong *ad hominem* arguments to present. First, the phenomenalistic ideal-language philosophers were failing to do any better at solving traditional epistemological problems than their predecessors. Their phenomenalism drove them to a behavioristic interpretation of mental acts, and such an interpretation proved inadequate for an analysis of intentional statements. Whiteheadians hastened to attribute this failure to the same unwillingness to desert the level of abstraction characteristic of ordinary language which had vitiated previous empiricisms. They took this new failure to be one more demonstration of the need to look beneath this level for the "truly concrete elements in experience." [12] Second, the ideal-language philosophers were in no position to complain about the metaphysicians' habit of postulating entities without being able to supply criteria for picking out instances of such entities. For these philosophers were compelled to admit that the "sense-contents" of their own theory were incapable of being individuated by such criteria, and could only be described in an unspeakable "expressive language." [13]

The triumph of "metaphysics" over "positivism" in which this quarrel seemed to eventuate has made Whiteheadians still more confident that no philosophical explanation which renounces the appeal to "experience too concrete to be expressed in language" can be adequate. Specifically, no such explanation can straighten out the confusions about knowledge which the clash between Cartesian subjectivism and the substance-property framework had made inevitable. This confidence has led to a complacent assurance that the recrudescence of common-sense realism which has marked more recent "linguistic" philosophy is merely a transitory reaction to a transitory delusion. This revived realism has led analytic philosophers to agree with Whiteheadians that Ayer and Russell are just as much "metaphysicians" as the Whiteheadians themselves, and to agree that the metaphysics which they produced was simply "the old Berkeleian, Kantian ontology of the 'sensible manifold' " [14] all over again. But the strategy of postphenomenalistic linguistic philosophy—a return to the realism of common sense, centering on an insistence on the irreducibility of (of all things) the substance-property distinction—strikes Whiteheadians as equally hopeless. "Every new Aristotle," as Hartshorne said in attacking neo-Thomist critics of Whitehead, "can only usher in a new Berkeley." [15] This new sort of linguistic philosophy explicitly adopts the slogan that the resources of ordinary language are adequate to solve every philosophical problem which they are adequate to state—a slogan which provides precisely the dialectical weapon against Whiteheadian appeals to "experiences inexpressible in language" which the phenomenalists had, perforce, abjured. But this slogan strikes Whiteheadians as patently false, and as having been demonstrated to be false by the history of philosophy.

III

In the preceding section of this paper I have been trying to get the following question into focus: Is Whitehead right in saying that an account of knowledge which preserves the realism of common sense must postulate the existence of entities which are describable neither in ordinary language nor in an extension of ordinary language? [16] An answer to this question is a necessary part of the grounds needed for decisions about what is living and what is dead in Whitehead's thought. If he *is* right, and can be shown to be right, then most of contemporary analytic philosophy is heading straight for a dead end—the same dead end in which neo-Thomists have been backing and filling for half a century. But if he is wrong, and can be shown to be wrong, then a step will have been taken toward showing the plausibility of the reinterpretation of Cartesian subjectivism which has been a consequence of the "linguistic turn." For if Whitehead is wrong on this point, then the interlocked claims that to be a clear and distinct idea is to be spoken of in terms which are used in their normal meanings, that to be an "object of possible experience" is to be describable in terms so used, and that no philosophical explanation need go beyond terms so used, are at least not obviously wrong.

I think that Whitehead *is* wrong on this point, and that because he is wrong there is little use in trying to polish up either his theory of actual entities or any other theory which postulates the existence of undescribable unrepeatables as the concrete entities from which the entities describable in ordinary language are "abstractions." However, I cannot here make even a start at *showing* that he was wrong. What I shall do is merely to point to the existence of an alternative way of reconciling the realism of common sense with Cartesian subjectivism, a way which renounces the appeal to undescribable entities and to "experiences inexpressible in ordinary language." If this alternative is successful, then Whitehead is wrong. In my exposition of this alternative, however, I hope to show that it is a development of the same insight which guided Whitehead in his search for the "right" sort of unrepeatable entity. This insight is that each experiencing subject has a perspective upon the world, and that any picture of the world which does not include explicit reference to such a perspective is a picture of an abstraction—an abstraction which, if taken (through a "fallacy of misplaced concreteness") to be the primary sort of picture of the world, will lead to paradox.[17] Whitehead's exploration of the consequences of this insight is an extraordinary intellectual achievement. But if he is wrong in his assumption that there are experiences which may be appealed to in support of philosophical explanations, but which are nonetheless not expressible in ordinary language, then we may have to conclude that his system was the wrong vehicle for the expression of this insight.

The view taken by "ordinary-language" philosophers is that the dilemma sketched at the beginning of this paper—the choice between betraying Descartes by resorting to an Unknowable or betraying common sense by postulating a world of repeatables, devoid of unrepeatable particulars—can be evaded simply by a more careful deployment of our ordinary resources for describing mental acts. Although these philosophers cheerfully agree with Whitehead that the attempt to conceive selves as substances and "mental states" as their properties is, in large measure, responsible for the traditional "problem of knowledge," they deny that ordinary language is committed to such a conception.[18] Whitehead has assumed too quickly that, so to speak, there is really one language-game which is played in ordinary language—that of describing substances by reporting their properties—and that all ordinary uses of language somehow "reduce" to this. He has thus made precisely the same mistake as his idealist and phenomenalist rivals—he has assumed that a person's knowledge about a thing is to be analyzed into relations between the thing, the person, and their respective properties. This assumption is based on the assumption that these are the only concrete entities concerned, an assumption which is made explicit in (2) above.[19]

This latter assumption has caused traditional analyses of knowledge to pass over the principal form in which, in ordinary language, we report and discuss our knowledge: the form "S knows ——," where the blank is filled by the name of a *fact* rather than the name of either a substance or a property of a substance. One standard completion of the form "S knows ——" is a clause made up of the word 'that' and a declarative sentence—e.g., "that X is Y." Let us call a *fact* that which is named by such a that-clause. Now the assumption that facts are "abstract" entities in the sense defined above follows naturally from (2). The cash value of this assumption is that statements containing that-clauses—of which the two principal varieties are epistemic statements ("S knows that . . . ," "S believes that . . . ," "S hopes that . . .") and semantic statements (e.g., " '. . .' means that ——")—must have the same meaning as statements which do *not* contain that-clauses. This assumption entails, in other words, that the relation between, e.g., S and the fact which S knows is analyzable into a relation between S and the entities denoted by the referring expressions contained in the that-clause which names the fact in question.

Now if S's knowing that X is Y is decomposable into relations between S and X, between S and Y, and between S and entities of the same categoreal type(s) as X or Y, and if we assume the truth of (2), then it follows that S's knowing that X is Y must be decomposable into a set of relations whose terms are persons, substances, and their properties. What relations are appropriate? Clearly, only those relations which relate persons *qua* conscious subjects (rather than *qua* bodies) to things and their properties—viz., the relations which are usually lumped together under the heading of *experiencing* and have their paradigm in *sensing*. This chain of reasoning is the source of "intuitionist" theories of knowing—theories which hold that all acts of cognition break down into complex intuitions, and which are dominated by the metaphor of the "mental eye." Such theories find it natural to grant the truth of (1), for on their view we cannot *know about* any concrete entity which we do not *know, simpliciter*—"know," in other words, in the way in which we are said to "know" people to whom we've been introduced.[20] Such theories must insist that entities which are knowable-about without being experienceable are one and all *abstracta*. Such theories, therefore, insist on the truth of (1) above.

We thus see how (1) follows naturally from (2), taken together with some fairly plausible additional premises. The view which I shall now sketch sets itself the problem of showing that relations between a person

and a fact (the sort of relation exemplified by "S knows that X is Y")
are irreducible. If this can be shown, then (2) will have been shown to
be false and the way will be open to denying (1). The view in question
comprises the following claims:

(I) The fundamental flaw in previous attempts to discuss knowing
has been the confusion of *facts* with *objects*.[21] We do not know unrepeatable objects, but we do know facts *about* such objects. Our knowledge of
these facts is grounded upon, but is not identical with, our acquaintance
with the repeatable entities proffered by sensory experience. The world
which is symbolized in true statements, and which is composed of "what
we know," is in Wittgenstein's phrase, "a totality of facts, not of things."
(This is the kernel of truth in the "subjectivist bias" of modern philosophy—and, in particular, in Kant's claim that we do not know "things-
in-themselves" but only entities which are already "infected with subjectivity.")

(II) A fact is not to be thought of as a complex of objects.[22] Rather,
it is to be thought of either (a) as what is named by that-clauses, or
(b) as the sort of thing which we know. There is thus no more sense
to the question "What is the ontological status of facts?" than, for Kant,
there was sense to the question "What is the ontological status of phenomena?" Both questions presuppose that we possess knowledge of non-
facts (or non-phenomena) by reference to which we can allot such a status.

(III) Of the two possible ways of thinking of what a fact is, it is
obvious that only the former ("what is named by that-clauses") can be
of any use to us in *explicating* the knowledge-relation. But thinking of
a fact in this way *does* so help us. For if we can disabuse ourselves of the
notion that because language is an expression of knowledge, it is somehow a mere epiphenomenon which cannot be used to explain that of
which it is the expression, we shall see that "S knows that . . ." can be
explicated in terms of " '. . .' means that ———."

(IV) Metalinguistic (semantical) discourse may be used to analyze discourse about knowledge as follows:

(a) we start by recognizing that, in Sellars' words, " ' ". . ." means
———' is the core of a unique mode of discourse which is as distinct
from the description and explanation of empirical facts as is the
language of prescription and justification." [23]

(b) We confine the term 'thoughts' to matters which are reported in
such expressions as "he believes that . . . ," "he knows that . . . ,"
"he guesses that . . ."; we thus exclude from the category of
thoughts *sensations* (i.e., such "mental states" as pains and tickles
which are not naturally reported in that-clauses, but rather in such
locutions as "I feel a . . ."). This distinction expresses the fact that
we *know* facts but *sense* particulars—and thus that, if "experience" is

construed, as we have been construing it here, as "intuition" (where sensing is the paradigm case of intuiting), it is false that we know the same sort of things which we experience.[24]

(c) We view thoughts as entities which have a relation of "about-ness" to entities which are (normally) not thoughts—a relation which is "intentional" in the sense that it can hold between thoughts and entities which do not exist, and perhaps could not exist. The problem for an analysis of knowing is to provide a satisfactory account of this relation. For if we can find an analysis of this relation which will allow for the fact that thoughts can be about entities which (logically) cannot be experienced (e.g., unrepeatable entities), then we shall be in a position to deny (1) above (see p. 136).

(d) Thoughts may, *prima facie,* be analyzed as dispositions to act, and, in particular, dispositions to utter.[25] But such analyses will work only if the utterances the thinker is disposed to utter are meaningful utterances—that is, if we can say something specific about what they do mean.[26] Now it has usually been thought that to describe the meaning of an utterance, since it is clearly not simply to describe the sign-vehicle, must be to describe the thoughts (and, specifically, the intentions) of the utterer. Specifically, it is usually assumed that the "aboutness" which characterizes thoughts cannot be analyzed in terms of the relation of "meaning" which linguistic entities bear to non-linguistic entities without circularity—for the latter relation is itself unintelligible without understanding the way in which thoughts endow sign-vehicles with a special feature called "meaning"—and thus without understanding the "aboutness" of thoughts.[27]

(e) But this assumption is incorrect. It confuses statements about the meaning of utterances (tokening activities) with statements about the meaning of types of utterances (e.g., words, sentences). (Contrast answers to "What did he mean by saying 'It's cold' [when it was actually sizzling]?" with answers to "What does the English sentence 'It's cold' mean?") The latter sort of statement is confirmable in ordinary, unproblematic, intersubjective ways—by noting "semantical regulari-ties," and reporting them in such formulae as "When '. . .' is uttered, then in general such-and-such is the case." [28]

(f) The analysis of "S is thinking that . . . ," therefore, can be built around "S is disposed to utter '. . .' under appropriate condi-tions, and '. . .' means that——." Such an analysis is able to provide the explication of the intentional "about" demanded in (c) above, for we can now analyze "S is thinking about E" as "S is disposed to utter '. . .' under appropriate conditions and '. . .' is about E" (and analyze

"S has knowledge about E" in a similar way). To ascertain what '. . .' is about we merely invoke the principle that statements in which referring expressions occur essentially are normally *about* the entities to which these expressions refer. The sense of aboutness invoked here is "intentional" in the way required. The suggested analyses amount, therefore, to the claim that (a) there is no mystery to *this* sort of aboutness, and that (b) thoughts are about entities in exactly the way in which statements are.

(g) But once aboutness is analyzed in this way, it is clear that no force remains to (1). For on this analysis to say that

> Only the sort of concrete entity which we can experience is the sort of concrete entity which we can know about.

is to say something obviously false. It is to say that, for example, if the value of X in any true statement of the form "S knows that X is Y" is the name of a concrete entity, then it is the name of an entity which can be the content of an experience. This is just as obviously false as the suggestion that it must be the name of a nonfictional entity, or the name of a present entity. The traditional problems of how one can have knowledge of the past, the fictional, and the (logically) inexperienceable are at bottom the same problem. All forms of the problem are resolved by interpreting knowledge as knowledge of facts, rather than objects, and interpreting "knowledge about" as knowledge about entities referred to in the statements which are the names of the facts known. For such an interpretation permits one to see that although our knowledge about the past, the fictional, and the (logically) inexperienceable may be based entirely on experiences of present nonfictional experienceables, we need not view the former as an abstraction from, a logical construction out of, or in any other way "reducible to" the latter. This interpretation, in other words, disentangles S's relation to what he knows about from his relation to what he experiences—or, in other words, disentangles his relation to the "intentional object" of his knowledge from his relation to the experiences which form the ground of his knowledge.

IV

Given this final claim—IV(g)—we are now in a position to say that the substances of common sense are both unrepeatable entities and are known about, without fear of Lockeian attack. We are thus free of the need either to find a new model of "unrepeatable entity" (like Whitehead) or to eliminate unrepeatable entities from our world view and singular terms from our ideal language (like the phenomenalists). Further, we have remained faithful to the linguistic version of the methodological form of Cartesian subjectivism—the elements which go into our explication of ordinary discourse about knowing are drawn from other regions of ordinary discourse, and no appeal is made to the existence of entities for which no criteria of identification can be supplied. The only entities whose existence is presupposed are utterances—which are as readily describable and identifiable as anything could be.

Such are the advantages of this view—if it comes off. To show that it *does* come off is not the purpose of this paper. I shall conclude, rather, with a brief comparison between this method of defending realism and Whitehead's method. The basic strategy of the view just outlined is to explicate problematic features of knowing by reference to unproblematic features of *talking*. The basic strategy which Whitehead employed was to explicate problematic features of knowing by reference to unproblematic features of *feeling*. As we have seen, Whitehead's construal of intentional aboutness in terms of the feeling of past entities by present entities requires him, in order to save realism, to construct a new category of entities—entities which can only be described in token-reflextive terms. We may now note that the strategy employed in the Sellarsian analysis outlined above leads to a similar result. Here too we are led to give central importance to token-reflexive terms.

The reader will have perceived that the crucial claim made in the previous section is IV(a)—the claim that semantical discourse is distinct from, and irreducible to, empirical discourse. If it were not, there would be no point in the claim that it can supply an analysis of epistemic discourse which empirical (and, specifically, "behavioristic") discourse cannot. Unless " '. . .' means ——" is indeed "the core of a unique mode of discourse," it is implausible that the schema " '. . .' means that——" should be both "intentional" enough for the purposes of IV (d) and "behavioristic" enough for those of IV(e). But what is unique about it? The answer to this question is that the assertion of statements of this form, unlike the assertion of empirical statements, *presupposes* the truth of certain token-reflexive statements. For, as Sellars says, "The basic role of signification statements is to say that two expressions, *at least one of which is in our own vocabulary,* have the same use." [29] Thus although statements of this form do not themselves normally contain token-reflexive terms, they will not be true unless statements of the form "Users of the language in which this statement is phrased use '. . .' under the following circumstances: . . ." are true. The truth of the latter sort of statements is presupposed by the assertion of the former sort. The occurrence of such a token-reflexive term as 'the language in which this statement is phrased' is, furthermore, ineliminable. (If one replaces this term by, e.g., 'English,' one will then have to say that the truth of the original signification statements presupposes the further condition that "this statement is in English" is true—a presupposition which is, once more, formulated in a token-reflexive statement.)[30]

We see, then, that semantical statements are always, when made in fully explicit form, token-reflexive statements—statements which involve explicit reference to the language *we* speak *now*. Let us now recall that a crucial step in the analysis of knowing which we have sketched was to insist that what we know are *facts,* and that the only principle for differentiating among facts is that a distinct fact is named by every that-clause which has a distinct meaning. A fact is, in short, an entity which can only be identified in semantical, as opposed to empirical, discourse.[31] A fact is, therefore, an entity which can only be identified with the aid of criteria which, when made fully explicit, involve explicit reference to the language we are now speaking. But this means that the only entities which we can know are entities which we can describe only with the aid of token-reflexive terms. Let us now recall that the same conclusion was reached, along a very different route, by Whitehead. Is there anything more than coincidence in the fact that these two strategies converge at this point?

I think that there is, and that it consists in the fact that both strategies realize that the "subjectivist bias of modern philosophy" can only be reconciled with realism if we can find a way of reconciling the fact that all knowledge is *perspectival* with the fact that knowledge is about objects distinct from and independent of the experiencing subject. For to show that the objects of knowledge are characterizable only in token-reflexive terms is to show that all knowledge is perspectival, and it is also to show, as Michael Dummet has recently pointed out, that there can be no such thing as "the complete description of reality." [32] ('Reality' here means simply "the totality of what is known about.") Both strategies accept this consequence, and both insist that this consequence—the fact that it is logically impossible that there should be a description of reality which is not a description from a perspective which is one among alternative perspectives—does not involve a surrender to idealism. To grant this consequence is to take the wind out of the idealist's sails; to show that it is compatible with the claim that reality remains distinct from, and independent of, our knowledge about it is to defeat him. This thesis—that our knowledge may be about an independent reality without its being the case that it is even logically possible that this reality should be described independently of the observer's perspective—is the common ground shared by both strategies. The relative over-all success of the two strategies may, I believe, best be judged on the basis of their success in making this thesis explicit and convincing. For I should hold that the presentation and defense of this thesis has been, and continues to be, the central task of contemporary philosophy. Whitehead's attempt to break free from the substance-property framework and thereby show that temporal perspectives are internal to the nature of concrete actualities was the last, and the most important, attempt to perform this task prior to the "linguistic turn." But once this turn is taken, new methods of carrying out this task become available.

NOTES

[1] Cf., for example, Strawson's "Singular Terms, Ontology and Identity," *Mind*, 65 (1956), 433-454.

[2] For the view that Whitehead never satisfactorily escapes from this dissolution, and thus is driven to monism, cf. William Alston, "Internal Relatedness and Pluralism in Whitehead," *Review of Metaphysics*, 5 (1951-52), 535-558.

[3] Strictly, this is the distinction between unrepeatable *concrete* entities and repeatable *concrete* entities. Eternal objects are, of course, repeatable, but they are not *concrete* entities in the sense of 'concrete' given by (2) above.

[4] This point expresses, I believe, the cash value of the claim that Whitehead, by "taking time seriously," substituted "process" for "being" as "the inclusive category." This formulation is misleading in various ways—particularly in that, except for the special case of God, Whitehead held firmly to the truth of (2). The proper way of contrasting Whitehead's "process philosophy" with "philosophies of being" is Hartshorne's: ". . . any word, such as 'reality,' or 'being,' can be used as the inclusive term, the point at issue remaining this: Does the term indicate a unique, final totality that does not become, or else rather, in each case of the employment of the term, a new totality which has just become as it is referred to? The question, as Whitehead suggests, is whether the inclusive term is, or is not, a 'demonstrative pronoun' (a token-reflexive term)" ("Process as Inclusive Category: A Reply," *Journal of Philosophy*, 52 [1955], p. 95). Whitehead's attempt to give an intelligible affirmative answer to this latter question about the totality referred to by the inclusive category leads him to say that some of the concrete particular entities which go to make up this totality must themselves be describable only in token-reflexive terms—namely, the present ones. (The expression 'token-reflexive term,' incidentally, is not used by Whitehead himself; like Hartshorne, however, I find it very useful in giving an account of his doctrines. A definition may be helpful: a term is "token-reflexive" if its essential occurrence in a sentence makes that sentence capable of being used to make statements of different truth values depending upon the circumstances in which the statements are made. 'I,' 'this,' and 'now' are perhaps the most common such terms.)

[5] This is why *persons* were, for Aristotle, the paradigm cases of substances. It was only under the influence of the Cartesian reinterpretation of "matter" as "vacuous actuality" (rather than "potentiality for form") that the question "Is the self a substance?" began to take on the appearance of sense. I have tried to describe the motives for this reinterpretation, and the parallels between Aristotelian and Whiteheadian dissents from Cartesian principles, in "Matter and Event" (in *The Concept of Matter*, ed. E. McMullin, Notre Dame University Press, 1963).

[6] But they are not repeatable *because* they have been objectified; they are objectifiable because they are repeatable—that is, past. It is essential to understanding Whitehead to avoid the assumption that when an actual entity becomes past, and is objectified by its successors, it somehow *changes*. No property is added to or taken away from the unrepeatable actual entity of the present when it becomes past—it simply ceases to be. To raise the question of what property is added to an actual entity when it goes from being present and unrepeatable to being past and repeatable is to ask as meaningless a question as the question of what is added to or subtracted from a human being when he dies. Death is not the addition of a property, any more than it is the subtraction of a property called "life"—it is simply ceasing to be.

[7] It may be objected that Whitehead thought that (4) was false even if "experience" were interpreted in the *normal* way. This may be the case; it is rendered plausible by Whitehead's evident conviction that language was inadequate to express certain features of experience. But if he did think this, he at least recognized the hopelessness of trying to rebut, within the framework of ordinary language, the usual defenses of (4). Proponents of (4)—such as the idealists—ask for an example of an unrepeatable

experience. But this demand cannot be met if (a) it is required that this experience be reported in ordinary language, and (b) the ordinary assumption that any episode reportable in token-reflexive language can also be reported in non-token-reflexive language is granted.

[8] The work of Austin and his followers on such variations, and of Wittgenstein and his followers on such presuppositions, have made the force of the dictum increasingly evident.

[9] Or, at least, correlate statements about the statistical behavior of batches of theoretical entities with statements about the existence of particular observed entities.

[10] There are, however, grounds for holding that this requirement should not even be applied to scientific explanations. Cf., e.g., Feyerabend's defense of the view that "introducing a new [scientific] theory involves changes of outlook both with respect to the observable and with respect to the unobservable features of the world, and corresponding changes in the meaning of even the most 'fundamental' terms of the language employed" ("Explanation, Reduction, and Empiricism," *Minnesota Studies in the Philosophy of Science,* III [1962], p. 29).

[11] "Philosophy is explanatory of abstraction, and not of concreteness" (PR 30).

[12] Intentionality—the reference of every conscious judgment to an entity capable of existing independently of that judgment—is, on a Whiteheadian view, to be thought of as grounded upon, and explicable only in terms of, the "presence" of one actual entity "in" another. "The philosophy of organism is mainly devoted to the task of making clear the notion of 'being present in another entity' " (PR 79-80). For if this notion is not admitted, Whitehead thinks, we shall be driven, like Locke, to some form of the doctrine of representative perception (cf. PR 84-85), and then it will be all up with realism.

[13] Cf. C. I. Lewis, *An Analysis of Knowledge and Valuation* (La Salle, Illinois, 1946), p. 204.

[14] The phrase is taken from Austin's characterization of Ayer (*Sense and Sensibilia* [Oxford, 1962], p. 61).

[15] "The Compound Individual" in *Philosophical Essays for Alfred North Whitehead* (New York, 1936), p. 200. On some parallels between "ordinary-language philosophy" and Aristotelian realism, cf. the present writer's "Realism, Categories, and the Linguistic Turn," *International Philosophical Quarterly,* 2 (1962), 307-322.

[16] By "an extension of ordinary language" I mean a systematic use of ordinary terms in non-normal ways, together with an account of these deviant uses—an account which itself *is* phrased in terms used in normal ways. By 'describable' I mean (as above) not simply "capable of being spoken of" but "capable of being spoken of in such a way that hypotheses about these entities are capable of being confirmed by inspection of individual (or statistical) samples of them."

[17] My phrasing of this point is borrowed from Wilfrid Sellars, who has presented the most comprehensive argument for it with which I am familiar in his "Time and the World Order" (*Minnesota Studies in the Philosophy of Science,* III [1962], 527-616, esp. p. 593.) More will be heard of this article, and of other articles by Sellars, in what follows. The "alternative way of reconciling realism and subjectivism" which I shall be describing is, in its essentials, a vulgarized version of a view which Sellars has presented in a series of articles over the past fifteen years. The heart of this defense, as will become clear, is an analysis of knowledge based on "the doctrine of the mental word" (cf. Sellars' "Being and Being Known," *Proceedings of the American Catholic Philosophical Association,* 1960, p. 30). Sellars' articles give the most complete statement of the presuppositions and ramifications of this doctrine which is available. However, this doctrine and the defense of realism which is made possible thereby are not peculiar to Sellars. Some other exponents of the same approach are Geach (in *Mental Acts*) and Bergmann (cf., particularly *Meaning and Existence* [Madison, 1959], pp. 1-38, especially the claim at pp. 29 f. that the inclusion of "the intentional 'means' and the quoting operator" in the ideal language will render it able "to bear the

burden of the philosophy of mind"). If there is a single point of departure common to the various forms which this approach has taken in the recent literature, it is probably Wittgenstein's *Tractatus.*

[18] Cf., e.g., Ryle, *The Concept of Mind* (London, 1949), p. 120.

[19] If one grants this assumption, then, as long as one holds that the sort of concrete entity which we experience is the only sort of concrete entity which we can know about, and as long as one wants to assert that we actually do know about things, one will be obliged to argue that the macroscopic things of common sense are not really unrepeatable entities. (For if they *were* unrepeatable, they couldn't be experienced—only their properties could.) One is driven to saying either that these things are repeatable congeries of repeatable sense-contents (as the phenomenalists did) or that they are repeatable abstractions from the *really* unrepeatable entities (as Whitehead did). One will thus be driven to "reduce" the unrepeatable perduring bodies of common sense to entities of a quite different sort. But these perduring bodies are, as Strawson has argued, "basic" to our ordinary language, in the sense that if we were not able to make identifying references to such bodies, we should not be able to make identifying references to anything else, and thus should not be able to use the language we do. (Cf. *Individuals* [London, 1959], chap. I, esp. pp. 38-39.) Consequently, it is not surprising that both phenomenalist and Whiteheadian "reductions" of these common-sense "basic particulars" must resort to "experiences inexpressible in (ordinary) language" and to the assurance that if only we were able to speak a different sort of language (one, unfortunately, untranslatable into our own) in which identifying references to entities of novel categoreal types *could* be made, everything would be all right.

(Strawson's line of argument is supplemented and expanded by Sellars in "Time and the World Order." Here Sellars argues that the notion of an "event" whose spatiotemporal location is specified topologically is a notion which is parasitical upon our ordinary notion of "episodes occurring in changeable things." He argues, in other words, that the "event" framework of description is not an alternative to the usual substance-property framework of description, but is conceivable only as an abstraction from the latter. The importance of this claim for an analysis of the Whiteheadian categoreal framework is obvious, but the point cannot be followed up here.)

[20] The cases in which "I know . . ." is not completed by a that-clause but by a name or a description of a non-fact (e.g., "the Ambassador," "Brussels," "the Lombard dialect") require a taxonomic treatment which cannot be attempted here, nor can the question of the reducibility of these cases to "knowing that" be discussed. It suffices to note that intuitionist theories of knowing have traditionally tried to isolate a species of "acquaintance" common to all such cases and have insisted that sentences referring to such "acquaintance" be a part of any analysis of "knowing that." Cf. Sellars, "Empiricism and the Philosophy of Mind," *Minnesota Studies in the Philosophy of Science* I (1956), p. 256.

[21] Cf. Ryle, *op. cit.,* pp. 161 f.

[22] Cf. Sellars, "Truth and 'Correspondence,'" *Journal of Philosophy,* 59 (1962), pp. 44 ff.

[23] "Intentionality and the Mental," *Minnesota Studies in the Philosophy of Science* II (1958), p. 527.

[24] Note that the distinction between the intentional notion "having knowledge about" and the nonintentional notion "being aware of" has, as Sellars says, always been characteristic of Physical Realism, and is basic to the account of knowledge being sketched here. ("Physical Realism," *Philosophy and Phenomenological Research,* 15 (1954-1955), pp. 13-32, esp. p. 20. In this article Sellars explains why the confusion of these two notions was "the root error of the positivistic-phenomenalistic tradition," and sketches the similarities between his own criticisms of this error and those made in the course of R. W. Sellars' exposition of Physical Realism. The broad outlines of the difference between the methods used by both Sellarses in defending realism and

those used by Whitehead are presented in R. W. Sellars' "Philosophy of Organism and Physical Realism," *The Philosophy of A. N. Whitehead,* ed. Schilpp (New York, 1941), pp. 405-433, esp. pp. 416 ff.)

[25] They may also, in a more sophisticated version of the view being presented here, be regarded not as dispositions but as introspectible *episodes.* Cf. "Empiricism and the Philosophy of Mind," pp. 317-321. But this important refinement must be passed over.

[26] Cf. R. Chisholm, *Perceiving* (Ithaca, 1957), chap. 11; also Chisholm, "Sentences About Believing", *Minnesota Studies in the Philosophy of Science* II (1958), pp. 510-519, and W. Sellars, "A Semantical Solution to the Mind-Body Problem," *Methodos,* 5 (1953), pp. 61 ff.

[27] The picture involved is that meaning is a sort of subtle electric current which flows from minds into sound waves or inkspots and makes them "glow."

[28] For this use of the term "semantical regularity," and for a general account of how an empirical inquiry into the meaning of words may be conducted without reference to the "intentions" of utterers, see Paul Ziff's *Semantic Analysis* (Ithaca, 1961).

[29] "Being and Being Known," p. 46. Cf. *ibid.,* p. 45: "There is an obvious difference between

 ' "Mensch" signifies *man*'
and
 ' "Mensch" has the same use as "man" '

This difference is that the former won't achieve its purpose of explaining the word 'Mensch' unless the hearer knows the use of the word 'man,' whereas the latter can be fully appreciated by one who doesn't know this use. Thus these two statements are not equivalent. This, however, can be remedied by interpreting the former statement as presupposing that the word 'man' is in the hearer's vocabulary, and hence as equivalent (roughly) to

 ' "Mensch" (in German) has the same use as *your* word "man." ' "

[30] Note that the truth of these latter statements is presupposed by reports of meanings not simply in the sense that such reports would be *unintelligible* to the auditor if the presuppositions were false, but in the sense that these reports would be *false* if these presuppositions were false. If the user of " 'Der Mond ist blau' means that the moon is blue" does not use "the moon is blue" in the same way in which Germans use "Der Mond ist blau," then the statement is false. Nonsemantical statements, however, including such empirical reports of semantical regularities as "When 'Der Mond ist blau' is uttered, then generally the moon is blue," may be unintelligible if their user does not use terms used in the statements in certain ways—but they will still be true. The truth of the empirical statements which verify reports of meaning are themselves language-independent, in the sense that they may be true even if the expressions *used* in them do not have the same use as any of the expressions *mentioned* in them, but this is not the case for statements of the form " '. . .' means that ——." Such statements are language-dependent, in the sense that if they are true then the semantical-statement-user must use '——' in the way in which '. . .' is used. Cf. Sellars, "A Semantical Solution to the Mind-Body Problem," esp. pp. 64-68, 78-79.

[31] See Sellars' claim that "that-clauses are metalinguistic in character": "Time and the World Order," p. 542; also "Truth and 'Correspondence,' " p. 45.

[32] "A Defense of McTaggart's Proof of the Unreality of Time," *Philosophical Review,* 69 (1960), 497-504, esp. pp. 503-504.

Organic Categories
in Whitehead

by Gregory Vlastos

I. Organic Relatedness and the Dialectic

Two terms are organically, or internally, related whenever the essence of either requires a reference to the essence of the other. If *a* and *b* are organic parts, *a* can neither exist nor be conceived apart from *b; a* is not *a,* and could not exist as *a,* except in relation to *b.* Thus stated, this concept confronts at once a formidable objection. The internality of relations, it is said,[1] is a self-contradictory notion. For if, by hypothesis, to know *a* I must also know *b,* I cannot know *a* alone, nor *b* alone. If so, the relation breaks down. We no longer have two terms which can be related, for either term telescopes into its own nature the relation to the other. We are thus involved in a contradictory situation: *a* must be related to *b,* since without *b* it is not *a;* yet *a* cannot be related to *b,* for it cannot stand as a term in a relation.

The classic solution to this difficulty is the Hegelian dialectic. In Hegel we begin with *a* (thesis). But *a* without *b* is not-*a*: it is incomplete, self-contradictory. We are, therefore, forced to take into account *b* (the antithesis), and state the full nature of both in this relation (synthesis). We have thus moved from the abstract to the concrete. The *a* of the synthesis is concrete; it has overcome the contradiction in *a* which arises out of its abstraction from *b.* The expression *aRb* states the transition from the first stage to the third stage. It is essentially dynamic. It could not be made at the first stage, for at that point we did not yet know *a*'s relation to *b;* and it need not be made at the third stage, for now, knowing the relation to *b,* we need not state it all over again in *aRb.* Neglect the dynamic relation which forces the progress from the thesis to the synthesis, and you will only see with Russell a plain self-contradiction in the doctrine of internal relations.

"Organic Categories in Whitehead." Reprinted from the *Journal of Philosophy,* **34** (1937), 253-263. This paper was originally read before a meeting, attended by Whitehead, of the Eastern Division of the American Philosophical Association at Harvard University on December 29, 1936.

Why is it, then, that Whitehead, building on the cornerstone of internal relatedness, should take no notice of the Hegelian dialectic? My answer to this question forms the thesis of this paper.

The three terms of the Hegelian dialectic are ontologically *homogeneous*. Thesis, antithesis, and synthesis are all of the nature of Idea. The *Logic* begins with Being, which is described at once as "pure thought." [2] The development of this initial term is "the movement of thought." [3] No intrusion of any non-ideal factor is required to produce Nature as the "reflected image" of the Idea.[4]

As against this homogeneous dialectical idealism we have the equally homogeneous dialectical materialism of Marx. Here thesis, antithesis, and synthesis are material factors. The result is an equally vigorous, constructive use of the dialectic, though in a quite different direction from Hegel's *Logic*.

In Whitehead, on the other hand, we meet a *heterogeneous* dialectic. Thesis is material ("physical") and antithesis ideal ("conceptual"). Where such heterogeneity occurs, the second term of the triad cannot be generated from the first term by negation, nor the third from the second. First and second have independent origins. No internal contradiction will convert the thesis into the antithesis, and the antithesis into the synthesis. It follows that the dialectic can no longer be used as a heuristic principle. But it does not follow that it cannot be used at all. Insofar as Whitehead makes use of the concept of internal relatedness, he must conserve a certain part of it: the dynamic fusion of polar opposites, the process from the abstract to the concrete. This is best shown in his basic metaphysical unit, the actual entity. Without the dialectic the actual entity can only appear (like the notion of internal relatedness, which it embodies) self-contradictory.

II. Dialectic of Objects and Events

Whitehead's first philosophical treatise, *The Principles of Natural Knowledge,* asks: "What are the ultimate data of science," and how are they "rooted in experience" (PNK Preface)? The answer is given in terms of two irreducible categories: events and objects. It explains time and space to the author's satisfaction as abstractions from certain qualities of the structure of events which make possible the location of objects. This done, the author still feels that his philosophy of nature is incomplete. For "nature includes life" (PNK 64.1). To describe life he finds it necessary to introduce the concept of "rhythm." The peculiar thing about this concept is that it will not fit into the clear and painstaking differentiation of objects from events. "The essence of rhythm is the fusion of sameness and novelty . . ." (PNK 64.7). But sameness has been assigned to objects, and novelty to events. Rhythm cuts across the separation. Thus "[a] rhythm is too concrete to be truly an object . . . is a unique type of natural element, neither a mere event nor a mere object as object is here defined" (PNK 64.8). The author is trying to express "the specific recognizable liveliness" of living things; and he can only do it by bringing his categories of object and event into dynamic interconnection. Objects are required to be more than objects, and events more than events. This is either nonsense, or else an expression of a type of thinking which requires such dynamic contrasts.

The heir to the "rhythm" of the *Principles* is the actual entity of *Process and Reality*. Its description entails a formidable list of polar opposites: becoming and being, many and one, object and subject, subject and superject, physical pole and mental pole, compulsion and freedom, perpetual perishing and objective immortality. It "combines self-identity with self-diversity." It "is the transformation of incoherence into coherence" (PR 38). The dynamic principle underlying this conception is stated plainly at the opening of *Process and Reality:*

> The ultimate metaphysical principle is the advance from disjunction to conjunction, creating a novel entity other than the entities given in disjunction. . . . These ultimate notions of "production of novelty" and of "concrete togetherness" are inexplicable either in terms of higher universals or in terms of the components participating in the concrescence (PR 32).

They are "inexplicable" for the same reason which makes rhythm inexplicable in terms of mere events or mere objects, and, more generally, makes an organic whole inexplicable in terms of its isolated parts.

Pursuing this mode of thought, Whitehead lays violent hands on the traditional distinction between universals and particulars:

> These terms, . . . both in the suggestiveness of the two words and in their current philosophical use, are somewhat misleading. The ontological principle, and the wider doctrine of universal relativity [i.e., relativity of essence and existence to the constitution of the actual entity] . . . blur the sharp distinction between what is universal and what is particular (PR 76).

It is interesting to note the effect which this produces on a distinguished British logician. Miss Stebbing sees here "the collapse of the ultimate distinction between objects and events." [5] She deplores the "inconsistency" with Whitehead's former position, though she takes no account of the final chapter on "Rhythms" in the *Principles,* where, as I have just pointed out, one finds exactly the same type of "blurring" of objects and events in the description of an organic entity. At the same time, Miss Stebbing notes that, in spite of the "blurring," *Process and Reality* by no means abandons the distinction between objects and events, but reaffirms it in "numerous passages." She can only interpret this as a "vacillation" of which "Whitehead himself is unaware." [6] Had Whitehead explained the dialectical nature of this "blurring" between particulars and universals, he would have obviated all this criticism; or else forced his critics to deal with the notion of organic relatedness from the ground up.

One need only look over the list of dynamic opposites which describes the actual entity to find further examples of this "blurring." From any other viewpoint, save that of organic relatedness, the actual entity seems —like the Hegelian *Begriff*—a metaphysical monster, which overrides all established distinctions. Let us follow some of these further.

III. Teleology and Causality

Let *a* and *b* stand for successive temporal phases of an organic process. Consider the relation from the standpoint of *a*. *b* has not yet occurred, yet it is necessary to *a*. Without *b*, *a* is incomplete; and its incompleteness can be expressed as a definite requirement of a certain sort of successor. This incompleteness qualifies *a* now. It is a present predicate with a future reference. It is potentiality. It expresses a biological teleology; a teleology below the level of conscious foresight. *b* is the "end" of *a*, not in the sense that *a* has a conscious anticipation of *b*, but rather that *a* can only achieve its own nature by moving to its completion in *b*.

This is what Hegel sees in the "living organism," where "the final cause is a moulding principle, an energy immanent in the matter, and every member is in its turn a means as well as an end." [7] Similarly Whitehead can speak of a (self-) creative activity as characterizing life: "It is the process of eliciting into actual being factors in the universe which antecedently to that process exist only in the mode of unrealized potentialities" (MT 206-207). Whitehead's "unrealized potentialities existing in the process" correspond to Hegel's "final cause." Both stress the dynamic sense of this teleology: Hegel's "moulding principle, immanent energy," and Whitehead's "creative activity, eliciting into actual being." Both hold that it can occur below the level of consciousness.

Consider now the relation with respect to necessary connection. The transition from *a* to *b* is no bare succession; *b* requires *a* just as much as *a* requires *b*. *b* is teleologically necessary to *a*; and *a* is causally necessary to *b*. Causality and teleology appear as complementary aspects of the same dynamic process. Neither alone would be sufficient to describe it. The organic process is more than causality, since the necessary consequent is implicit (Hegel) or potential (Whitehead) in the antecedent. It is more (and less) than teleology, since the relation of *a* to *b* is not that of conscious intent to physical result, but of an initial stage to a completed process.

The homogeneous dialectic of Hegel finds no difficulty in applying the two notions with complete symmetry to any phase of a given organic process. He points out that "the cause is not only a cause of something else, but also a cause of itself." [8] "Cause of itself" implies final causation;

"cause of something else" efficient causation. Likewise "the effect is not only an effect of something else [efficient causation], but also an effect of itself [final causation]." [9]

In Whitehead, on the other hand, efficient and final causation are apportioned to different phases of organic process: "efficient causation expresses the transition from actual entity to actual entity; and final causation expresses the internal process whereby the actual entity becomes itself" (PR 228). The first phase of the actual entity is "physical"; the antecedent world confronts the nascent entity with the givenness of settled fact. The obvious analogy is to the physical environment of a living thing at any moment of its existence—an environment which includes its own body. Whatever the organism does will be conditioned by this environment; or, to put it the other way, the environment will enter into the activity of the organism. This is Whitehead's doctrine of "objectification" and "inheritance"; of "objective immortality" of the past in the present, or of the "conformation" of the present to the past. He believes that this is an important contribution to the doctrine of causality. Apart from the conservation of the past in the succeeding occasions, he finds nothing to save us from Hume's predicament.

"Internal freedom," or self-causation, attaches to the second phase of the actual entity, the "mental pole." This is one of the most disconcerting parts of Whitehead's philosophy—unless one grasps the organic nature of "conceptual prehension, subjective aim, and eternal object." Professor Morris, for example, would have found Whitehead's doctrine of mind considerably clearer had he classified it as "process" rather than as "intentional act." What does Whitehead mean when he endows every actual entity with a mental pole? Consider such statements as the following:

> In its essence, mentality is the urge towards some vacuous definiteness, to include it in matter-of-fact which is non-vacuous enjoyment (FR 26).

> The subjective aim is not primarily intellectual; it is the lure for feeling. This lure for feeling is the germ of mind. . . . The "lure for feeling" is the final cause guiding the concrescence of feelings. By this concrescence the multifold [physical] datum of the primary phase is gathered into the unity of the final satisfaction of feeling (PR 130, 281).

> The lowest stages of effective mentality . . . involve the faint direction of emphasis by unconscious ideal aim (MT 230).

From all this it must be evident that Whitehead's doctrine of mind is far removed from Brentano's "intentional inexistence of physical phenomena," or Moore's "diaphanous awareness." We have instead a biological theory of mind; mind described as urge, appetition, agency, direction of emphasis. Eternal objects are "Platonic" in the sense in which the Idea of the Good is Platonic.[10] They enter the experience of the organism through the "lure for feeling," through "the unconscious ideal aim" which shapes the material given in the physical pole. They express the potential wholeness of the entity molding selectively the process of its realization. Professor Morris misunderstands Whitehead when he writes:

> Thus instead of the universal being regarded as a stage of mind, and propositions being taken into the mental process, propositions and universals continue to be enshrined in the realm of subsistence . . . , and mind remains primarily a grasping of such entities.[11]

Surely Whitehead's doctrine is that the universal must be regarded as a stage of mind, and that propositions must be taken into the mental process. ". . . the primary function of theories [propositions] is as a lure for feeling, thereby providing immediacy of enjoyment and purpose" (PR 281). Miss Stebbing criticizes Whitehead for blurring the distinction between events and eternal objects; while Professor Morris thinks it would be a good thing to dispense with eternal objects altogether.[12] In both cases the answer lies in the dialectic of internal relatedness.

IV. Individual and Society

Organic relatedness identifies the individual with the organic whole. The parts of such a whole, as parts, cannot be individuals, for they are manifestly incomplete and dependent. Yet each organic part may be in turn an organic whole of a subordinate kind. Society would then be the relation of a given organic whole to other organic wholes of the same order of complexity or concreteness; individuality would be the relation of an organic whole to its own subordinate parts. It would then follow that every society would be an individual; this is illustrated in the Hegelian doctrine that the family is a "person," and that the state is a "person." It would also follow that ultimately there is one wholly concrete individual, the organic whole which is not a part of a superior organic whole; this would be the Hegelian absolute.

Hegel's homogeneous dialetic has no difficulty in constructing a metaphysics on this model. Each dialectical triad is an organic whole, whose synthesis is an individual organically included in a higher individual. This proceeds until the Absolute Individual is reached. The organic environment of each subordinate individual is "implicit" with him, as the particular is implicit in the universal: the environment is internalized.

> The soul is virtually the totality of nature: as an individual soul it is a monad: it is itself the explicitly put totality of its particular world—that world being included [enclosed—*eingeschlossen*] in it and filling it up; and to that world it stands but as to itself.[13]

To experience an external environment is to experience incompleteness. Individuality is internality. The development of individuality is the process by which otherness is internalized and overcome.[14]

Whitehead agrees with Hegel that the organic whole, the actual entity, is the individual. But his heterogeneous dialectic prevents him from pyramiding actual entities to form individuals of higher orders. Two (or more) actual entities could not join to form a higher type of actual entity. The transition from actual entity to actual entity is a linear transition in time. Any actual entity includes ("prehends") all antecedent actual entities in its "datum" or "physical pole." But it includes them under eliminations provided by the subjective aim of its "mental pole." The result is another actual entity, which internalizes the antecedent world in its own "satisfaction," and then contributes its "objective immortality" to its successors. Thus the actual occasions are the "completely real things," the "subjects," the "centres of experience," apart from which "there is nothing, nothing, bare nothingness" (PR 254).

But these individual occasions are in constant flux. "Society" accounts for the fact of permanence. Events perish, but their polar opposites, objects, endure. Actual entities, combining both dynamically, provide for endurance, by the genetic transmission of the same object. Society is the mutual immanence of actual entities via their common inheritance. Since inheritance is temporal, "a set of mutually contemporary occasions cannot form a complete society" (AI 261). Thus we have the interesting doctrine that social relationship occurs only in temporal strings; contemporaries are jointly related via their several derivations from a common past.

There are three types of societies, worked out on the pattern of the heterogeneous dialectic, according to the dominance of the physical pole, the mental pole, or a fusion of the two in their genetic relationships:

(1) Societies of the type of "crystals, rocks, planets, and suns," marked by a monotonous re-enactment of a basic pattern from occasion to occasion. Here a massive stability irons out the novelty provided by the mental pole, "eliminating the detailed diversities of the various members" (PR 155, 154).

(2) Societies of the type of the lower organisms, marked by originality of response. This is Whitehead's definition of life: "[A] single occasion is alive when the subjective aim which determines its process of concrescence has introduced a novelty of definiteness not to be found in the inherited data of its primary phase" (PR 159).

(3) Societies of the type of the higher organisms, which find means of transmitting the originality of one occasion to succeeding occasions. This is the phenomenon of learning and memory, which "binds originality within bounds, and gains the massiveness due to reiterated character" (PR 163).

In (1) we have the dominance of efficient causation; in (2) of final causation; in (3) a synthesis of the two. Needless to say, the physiological application of this is entirely lacking. Whitehead is obviously interested in the pattern which repeats in cosmic history the phases of the actual occasion: "Thus life is a passage from physical order to pure mental originality, and from pure mental originality to canalized mental originality" (PR 164). He is interested also in "the absolute end" to which this evolution is instrumental: the "evocation of intensities" in each perishing occasion (PR 161). Perhaps the most instructive feature of this concept of society is that the highest stage of the dialectic is common to the higher animals and man. Whitehead does not make clear how rational communication through symbols makes possible a type of community which is at least as far removed from a herd of cattle as that is from loose aggregations of unicellular organisms. The limitation, I believe, is inherent in his organic concepts: something more than merely organic relatedness seems necessary to account for the distinctive features of human association.

Let us not lose sight, however, of the essential consequence within Whitehead's philosophy: that society is a derivative notion. The "completely real things" are the individual occasions, the actual entities. "Society" is merely shorthand for certain features of these. It reminds us that certain types of genetic coordination exist between successive occasions. How account for this coordination, short of invoking a pre-established harmony? The problem can be narrowed down to the mental pole of each actual entity. The mental pole of a given entity is totally underived from any other temporal entity: it is "internally free." Yet it determines the role of that entity in the creative advance. How account for the various types of order which have taken shape in an evolving universe, if the mental poles of successive entities are unrelated? And how can this relationship take place?

Here Whitehead introduces a notion corresponding to the Hegelian Absolute, but constructed on the pattern of the heterogeneous dialectic. God preserves the opposition of physical and mental pole, synthesized in a final "satisfaction." But in his case the mental pole comes first. This constitutes the "primordial appetition," which is a timeless pattern of order pervading the creative process, and determining the mental pole of each successive occasion. The physical pole of God is his "consequent nature," which is "the physical prehension by God of the actualities of the evolving universe" (PR 134). The fusion of the two constitutes "the ultimate unity of the multiplicity of actual fact with the primordial conceptual fact." It is "the reconciliation of permanence and flux" (PR 525, 529) in an everlasting reality, just as Hegel's Absolute provides a reconciliation of universal and particular, subjectivity and objectivity in an Infinite Whole.

VI. Conclusion

If the preceding analysis is correct, we should look for Whitehead's permanent contribution to philosophy in his description of the genuinely organic parts of our experience. His doctrine of mind is a doctrine of the organic foundations of mind. He employs in this analysis a unique variant of the Hegelian dialectic, which interprets all process as an interplay of matter and idea in temporal actualities, and of idea and matter in a nontemporal actuality. This is his most original contribution, and the feature by which the ultimate value of his philosophy must be judged.[15]

NOTES

[1] As, for example, by Bertrand Russell, in *Philosophical Essays* (Longmans, Green, & Co., 1910), pp. 153 ff.

[2] Paragraph 86, translation by Wallace.

[3] Paragraph 87, translation by Wallace.

[4] The *Encyclopedia* Logic closes with these words: "We began with Being, abstract Being: where we now are we also have the Idea as Being: but this Idea which has Being is Nature." (¶244, Zusatz, translation by Wallace.)

[5] *Mind,* **39** (1930), 474.

[6] *Loc. cit.*

[7] *Logic,* ¶57.

[8] *Ibid.,* ¶153, Zusatz.

[9] *Loc. cit.*

[10] *Republic,* 505d, e.

[11] *Six Theories of Mind,* p. 201.

[12] *Ibid.,* p. 202. The first one to raise the question in print is, so far as I know, Professor E. W. Hall, in "Of What Use Are Whitehead's Eternal Objects?" (*Journal of Philosophy,* 27 (1930), 29-44; reprinted in the present volume, pp. 107-116. This paper raises fundamental issues, and deserves close study. Without presuming to deal with it in a footnote, I should like to draw attention to the form in which the writer puts his question: "Why not dispense with eternal objects altogether? Why not say that the only real entities are actual entities? (p. 36; this volume, p. 109). Surely the answer is that actual entities *are* "the only real entities." Whitehead's "ontological principle" tells us this in so many words, as Professor Hall notes. But this does not mean that eternal objects are of no use. We must retain them to express the mental pole of the actual entities. (This, of course, on the assumption that we wish to conserve the main lines of Whitehead's metaphysics.) To the question, "Are not eternal objects simply aspects of actualities, with no status of their own?," I should return an unqualified affirmative. Professor Hall is not satisfied with this "Yes," and maintains that Whitehead has also a "No" to this question: "This answer seems to be explicitly upon his [Whitehead's] lips when he tells us about the original disjunctive multiplicity of eternal objects, which, by means of creativity, passes into the conjunctive unity of particular occasions. Creativity 'is that ultimate principle by which the many, which are the universe disjunctively, become the one actual occasion, which is the universe conjunctively' " (p. 37; this volume, p. 110; quotation from Whitehead, PR 31). I am afraid this rests on a misunderstanding of Whitehead's text. Whitehead has told us nothing about "the original disjunctive multiplicity of eternal objects." Eternal objects are not mentioned in the sentence quoted from Whitehead, or in its context. The obvious interpretation of "universe disjunctively" is, on the contrary, in terms of the many *actual entities* which form the "datum" of a nascent actual entity.

[13] *Philosophy of Mind*, ¶403, translation by Wallace.

[14] *Philosophy of Right*, ¶7, Zusatz, translation by Dyde.

[15] The relevance of the foregoing to contemporary discussions of Whitehead might be suggested in a brief reference to one of the latest comments on this philosophy: Dr. D. Bidney's paper on "The Problem of Substance in Spinoza and Whitehead" (*The Philosophical Review*, **45** (1936), 574-592). Dr. Bidney says:

"Briefly put, the reasons for the inadequacy of Whitehead's system are two. First, he attempts to derive the actual from the potential. This I regard as intrinsically impossible and unintelligible. Secondly, he is trying to combine a monistic metaphysics with a pluralistic theory of physics and biology—a fallacy similar to that of Spinoza" (p. 591).

Both of these criticisms disregard the dialectical rhythm of the philosophy of organism:

1. I do not see how one can say that Whitehead "attempts to derive the actual from the potential." The basic unit from which (i.e., from whose analysis) potentiality and everything else is derived in Whitehead's thought is the actual entity. Potentiality is always an aspect of some actual entity; and a dialectical aspect—i.e., meaningless apart from its dialectical opposite of "settled fact." What, then, can Dr. Bidney mean by saying that Whitehead "derives the actual from the potential"? He must be thinking of the relation of God to each actual occasion: God as "the primordial appetition." Let us recall what this means: God is an actual entity, with a "mental pole" (the primordial appetition), and a "physical pole" (the "consequent nature"); each actual occasion likewise has a "physical pole" and a "mental pole." It is only the "mental pole" of the temporal occasion that is derived from the "mental pole" of God: "But the initial stage of its aim [i.e., the aim of a temporal occasion] is an endowment which the subject inherits from the inevitable ordering of things, conceptually realized in the nature of God" (PR 373). Thus it is not the actuality of the occasion that is derived from the potentiality of God, but the potentiality of the occasion from the potentiality of God. One may ask how one potentiality can be derived from another. This is one of the mysteries of Whitehead's metaphysics whose solution I leave to others. The only point that matters now is that in no case is there derivation of actuality from potentiality.

2. Again, I do not see how the term "monistic" can fairly describe Whitehead's metaphysics in opposition to the "pluralism" of his theory of physics and biology. The whole point of his philosophy is to combine monism and pluralism, the one and the many, in the metaphysical notion of the actual entity, and its associated notions of prehension and concrescence. His particular interpretation of organic relatedness veers in the direction of pluralism; witness his doctrine of society. The difference between Whitehead's monadism and Hegel's monism is the difference between the "heterogeneous" and the "homogeneous" dialectic.

Part IV

Ethics, Aesthetics, and Philosophical Theology

The Vision of Beauty and
the Temporality of Deity
in Whitehead's Philosophy

by *Nathaniel Lawrence*

> Religion will not regain its old power until it can face change in the
> same spirit as does science.
>
> —WHITEHEAD

Whitehead once said that Aristotle's metaphysical deity was hardly
"available for religious purposes" (SMW 249). Seventeen years later
Stephen Ely came to the conclusion that Whitehead's God was defective
in the same respect.[1] The presuppositions of what sort of a God *would*
be available for religious purposes emerge slowly in Ely's essay. Whitehead's God is then shown as having failed to meet the demands imposed
by these presuppositions. It is my theme that Whitehead was attempting
—among other things—to develop a notion of God that might select
the best in religious consciousness, rather than merely conform to prevailing notions of what kind of God might be satisfactory.

To perform such a task in a few pages means simplification of perhaps
the most complex feature of Whitehead's mature philosophy. I sympa-
thize in advance with those whose knowledge of Whitehead may be of-
fended by a skeletonizing of his doctrine of God.

But if we must be simple, we can also be systematic. The first thing
to notice is that at least Whitehead is not blown up by his own petard.

"The Vision of Beauty and the Temporality of Deity in Whitehead's Philosophy."
Reprinted, with minor revisions, from the Whitehead Centennial Issue of the *Journal
of Philosophy,* 58 (1961), 543-553.

Whitehead's statement that Aristotle's God was not available for religious purposes meant only that the Prime Mover appeared simply as a system-completing necessity and that there was about the awareness of the Prime Mover none of that warmth of feeling which characterizes the religious attitude. It should be clear to all critics, friendly or not, that this absence of feeling in the relation between man and God is precisely what White-head proposes to remedy. His task can thus be stated simply as the effort to close the gap between a God of thought and a God of feeling. Such a procedure was not a forced procedure for Whitehead, because feelings, in an extended sense of the word "feeling," are the elementary relations in the world-process. The idea of a felt God, Himself capable of feeling and therefore a God not wholly remote or intellectually defined, is White-head's correction of Aristotle's barren conception of a Prime Mover.

With this initial point out of the way, we may proceed to a direct examination of Ely's criticism, ending with a statement of an important but not commonly remarked feature of Whitehead's philosophy of re-ligion. In this essay I propose to show the following: (1) that Ely im-properly solicits support for his view from Plato, whereas Whitehead actually derives much from Plato; (2) that Ely seems to mean by "re-ligious availability" something that has but little support from religion; (3) that Whitehead's repeated recourse to aesthetic vocabulary is essential in his relating of the temporality of God to the overcoming of evil; (4) that Whitehead's metaphysics is not simply a metaphysics including re-ligious doctrine and thought, but that it is a metaphysics of religious experience as well. (5) Fifthly, I shall try to summarize the problem of "religious availability" in the light of point 4; and, finally, (6) I append some remarks on the usefulness of aesthetic language.

I

We shall begin with a sustained passage from Ely:

All values are then fundamentally aesthetic. This makes it easier to under-stand why God, overwhelmed with an immense vision of cosmic beauty, is not concerned with our finite sufferings, difficulties, and triumphs—except as material for aesthetic delight. God, we must say definitely, is not primarily good. He does not will the good; He wills the beautiful. Suffering humanity might well call this God's attention to the utterance, made near the close of his life, of a deeply religious man. "When a man honours beauty above goodness," said Plato, "this is nothing else than a literal and total dis-honouring of the soul" (Ely 52).

This passage is a tangle of many confusions. Since Whitehead is sub-stantially influenced by Plato and Plato is here so badly represented, we must at the outset unscramble the confusion on Plato.

First, it is hard to explain why Ely uses only a fraction of a sentence from the Bury translation of the *Laws* to make his point. The full sentence reads as follows:

> Again, when a man honours beauty above goodness, this is nothing else than a literal and total dishonouring of the soul; for such a statement asserts that the body is more honourable than the soul,—but falsely, since nothing earth-born is more honourable than the things of heaven, and he that surmises otherwise concerning the soul knows not that in it he possesses, and neglects, a thing most admirable.[2]

Thus Plato is speaking here of sensuous beauty, not the beauty that appeals to soul or spirit. This latter idea of beauty, far from being condemned by Plato, is exalted in the highest terms.

Plato uses two words that are both translated as "beauty": τό κάλλος and τὸ καλόν. The double-lambda word has the sense of adornment or *décor,* sensuous beauty. The single-lambda form has the sense of nobility or worth. Thus, for instance, the word καλοδιδάσκαλος means "a teacher of virtue." In the *Symposium,*[3] where Plato develops the famous figure of the ladder of beauty, near the end of Diotima's oration, he uses the single-lambda form almost exclusively. The double-lambda form is rare enough in the *Republic* to be attributed to the carelessness of a copyist.[4]

Secondly and briefly, the word that Bury translates as "goodness" is ἀρετή, usually translated as "virtue." It is more happily rendered as "excellence," but in no case should it be confused with moral goodness, that is, with ἀγαθόν. Plato's distinction is that between the active striving to excel and the passive enjoyment of the sensuously beautiful. Plato makes no effort to raise the morally good above the spiritually beautiful.

On the contrary and thirdly, if it be important to know what Plato thought of genuine beauty, we may go to the famous passage in the *Symposium.* Here Plato says:

> ". . . so that in the end he comes to know the very essence of beauty. In that state of life above all others, my dear Socrates," said the Mantinean woman, "a man finds it truly worth while to live, as he contemplates essential beauty" (211C-D; p. 207).

Commenting on this passage, F. M. Cornford says of beauty that for Plato it simply *is* the good, considered as an object of desire.[5]

I have labored this point because it bears on Whitehead's approach. Plato says in the passage just quoted that a man finds it worthwhile to live in the contemplation of essential beauty. However, this contemplation is not a passive reverie. Rather, it is a disciplinary vision: discplinary in that it subordinates other values to itself, and a vision in that it is pervasively present as the ultimate in objective worth. The same vision is called by a moral name in the *Republic.*

Let us put aside any support from Plato. There is little else in Ely to show that Whitehead's God is not religiously available. Ely's complaint takes the curious form of arguing that if what I regard as good is not instrumented by God, then such a God is not religiously available. For instance, he says,

> God can work wonders, but I do not think he can merge me and my values into an indefinitely immense system and still claim that I have maintained *my* individuality and my values. Of course, if human values are not fundamentally the same as God's values, they will not be preserved in any case. Then the whole question falls, as there is in that case no possibility of showing that God is good in our sense of the term (Ely 49).

Ely's charge is "guilty of having failed to take account of human values, having failed to preserve individuality, and having failed to be good in our sense of the term." Now this is surely an odd charge to bring into court. For millions of men who certainly have felt that God was religiously available, it is never the case that one postulates the human good as the norm and then asks whether or not God conforms. Quite the opposite. The good was understood by definition to be that which God wills. Job's God was available for religious purposes. The Psalmist sings, "How unsearchable are his judgments and his ways past finding out." A God who punishes all mankind for the sin of the first man, which sin he permitted with foreknowledge, a God who deals out retribution, who exacts penalties, who gets exceeding wroth if his people worship his ethnic first cousins, who crushes whole nations in his anger (what of the nursling child and the frightened, unknowing mother? They are his victims, too)—all these have been available for religious purposes. Having little concern for the human conception of value does not seem to be a serious limitation on God's religious availability. In some cases, it almost seems to be an absolute prerequisite for divine status.

Unless pre-Danielic Israel had no religion, we should not take this line of argument very seriously. In fact, if we begin looking about for Gods that will meet this demand of preserving *my* individuality and *my* values, we find few of the great religions that will supply us. In Hinduism and Buddhism my individuality is metaphysically denied. In Islam and late Judaism my individuality is problematically capable of survival, but *my* conception of value does not have much religious force unless it conforms to God's will. Only in certain strains and aspects of Christianity do we find this demand *both* for a personal God who cares for my values and for a personal immortality for my individuality.

III

We are forced to the conclusion that Ely's complaint is really a normative judgment, not a descriptive one: Whitehead's God is transmoral, a divine artist, some of whose pigments are genuine evil and genuine suffering. Ely deals with two kinds of evil: the evil of suffering (Ely 44-45) and the evil of perishing (Ely 48). In *Process and Reality* Whitehead says,

> . . . the immediacy of sorrow and pain is transformed into an element of triumph. This is the notion of redemption through suffering, which haunts the world. It is the generalization of its very minor exemplification as the aesthetic value of discords in art (PR 531).

Of this view Ely complains that Whitehead supposes that "playing a wider role will make one content with his lot" and that "we can find, at best, only a vicarious joy in our sufferings and our tragedies. The actual experience of joy is God's, and we can rejoice only because God has it" (Ely 49-50). To make matters worse, Whitehead says in *Adventures of Ideas* that "The real world is good when it is beautiful. . . . Thus Beauty is left as the one aim which by its very nature is self-satisfying" (AI 345, 342). This passage leads Ely to the misuse of Plato cited at the outset of the present essay.

Before we can go further we must very briefly review Whitehead's conception of God in the mature period. God is there presented as having two natures, which he calls the Primordial Nature and the Consequent Nature. The Primordial Nature is the repositum of all possible value, but only as possible. In this repositum there lies the entire multiplicity of eternal objects, which are all the qualities, characteristics, or properties that could characterize any event or set of events. There is no single final ordering of these eternal properties, but the possible orderings of them are themselves complex eternal objects (SMW ch. X) and are therefore part of this multiplicity.

God as primordial is mental in that the concepts of all possibilities lie in Him, only ideally, not actually (PR 521-522). This realm of possibility is not merely a celestial parts department or emporium. It is the realm to which the event-in-process-of-formation is drawn as it proceeds from its fixed background of fact. The Primordial Nature of God is like Aristotle's Prime Mover in that it is eternal, complete, and the object of desire toward which all things are drawn. But it is not conscious, for consciousness requires the fusion of conceptual *and* physical feeling. Clearly, this aspect of God is *not* available for religious purposes. The entire issue thus rests with the Consequent Nature of God. Where the Primordial Nature is complete, the Consequent Nature is incomplete. Where the Primordial Nature is nonconscious, the Consequent Nature is conscious. Where the

Primordial Nature proffers possible values, the Consequent Nature conserves actual values. Where the Primordial Nature is eternal, the Consequent Nature is everlasting (PR 521-524).

The everlastingness of God is prefigured by Whitehead in *Religion in the Making*, where he says of God that He is the "nontemporal actual entity," what men "call God—the supreme God of rationalized religion" (RM 90). Two terms stand out: the *non*temporality of God, and *rationalized* religion. The nontemporality of God, as Whitehead abundantly explains in the closing passages of *Process and Reality*, is not His eternality; this is the property of the Primordial Nature. What is eternal is non-actual; i.e., it is not itself time-structured or time-dependent in order to be what it is. The Consequent Nature of God is derived "from the temporal world": it is what is "permanent," in which the temporal world is "perfected" (PR 527). But neither God nor the world reaches "static completion" (PR 529); this static completeness belongs to the Primordial Nature. The incompleteness of the everlasting nature of God rests on the fact that time is real, and the Consequent Nature of God constantly receives the datum of completed actual entities into the unending completion of His Consequent Nature. "The purpose of God is the attainment of value in the temporal world," says Whitehead (RM 100).

However, this "nontemporality" of God needs explication. *Three distinct modes of existence with respect to time are presented:* (1) The Primordial Nature of God and the eternal objects therein are *time-free,* eternal. (2) Actual occasions are *time-structured;* they and all the societies they compose, except the world as a whole, come to completion—i.e., to temporal closure—and thus become a challenge to the Consequent Nature of God, who must both conserve them in their objective immortality and compose them in that harmony which is His constant aim. (3) The third type of existence is not time-structured, but it is *time-concerned,* so to speak, and *time-dependent;* this is the Consequent Nature of God, abiding, everlasting, and in this sense temporal and incomplete.

The objects of God's will are the disparate actualities, which, when complete, slip backward into the stream of time. They replace one another. What does not change is the will to harmonize them. The will is unchanged by time, everlastingly the same, yet always engaged in the struggle with what is temporally delivered to it. What these temporal entities become is in some sense free for them and irrevocable, insofar as they are individual. But their freedom and their completedness pose a problem beyond themselves which, by reason of their completedness, they are impotent to deal with.

With this brief statement of the role of the Consequent Nature of God we must be here content, though it offers many puzzles. What I have tried to show is that Whitehead renders rational a concept from the familiar language of Christianity which might otherwise be challenged as to its rationality—the eternal will of God. Where Christianity writes "eternal," Whitehead writes "everlasting." Where Christianity writes "will," Whitehead writes "aim."

IV

The will of God to produce harmony from what is partly evil, while granting each creature its freedom to fail and to suffer, is more commonly explained in aesthetic language. But since it is a will and since it proposes to mitigate what is evil and since Whitehead repeatedly says that God "saves" the world (e.g., PR 525, 526) through this harmonizing, we can hardly say that Whitehead's God has no moral stature nor any moral goal. Moreover, Whitehead says, "Morality of outlook is inseparably conjoined with generality of outlook" (PR 23). He also says, in an infrequently remarked passage which links morality with art, "The canons of art are merely the expression, in specialized forms, of the requisites for depth of experience. The principles of morality are allied to the canons of art, in that they also express, in another connection, the same requisites" (PR 483). To the question of why the language of morality occasionally suffers in Whitehead's hands, the answer seems clear: it is the complacency and self-interestedness of much of what is called moral that he wishes to avoid. Thus he says, "Of course it is true that the defence of morals is the battle-cry which best rallies stupidity against change. Perhaps countless ages ago respectable amoebae refused to migrate from ocean to dry land—refusing in defence of morals" (AI 345-346).

The temporality of God leads us to a highly significant phrase: "the Supreme God of rationalized religion." Notice that Whitehead does not say "rational religion." What is it that is *rationalized,* that is, placed in rational coherence with the rest of experience? The answer is: religious experience. It is false to think that some kinds of experience come with special warrants of acceptability that other experience does not have. But disparate elements of experience must be rendered coherent. The organization of Whitehead's work makes this abundantly clear.

1. The section from which this phrase is taken is called "A metaphysical description." Whitehead says of it, "The following description is set out for immediate comparison with the deliverances of religious experience" (RM 89).

2. The section before this one begins with the sentence, "In the previous lectures religious experience was considered as a fact" (RM 86).

3. The previous lecture is nothing less than a review of "The Religious Consciousness in History," "The Description of Religious Experience," "God," and "The Quest of God." These are not my titles; they are Whitehead's. Whitehead thus takes up where William James's Gifford lectures leave off. James was concerned with the phenomenology of religious experience. Whitehead explains the metaphysical accommodation of

religious experience, which is a factor within the whole of experience. The religious availability of Whitehead's God thus appears in a quite different light.

Let us now skeletonize the complaints about this availability and reinforce them. My purposes and my conception of the morally or naturally good are not met in the world about me. They fail in many ways. I am faced with "the evil of perishing." Not only do I perish, but, before my time, those whom I love perish. Whitehead's son Eric was shot down in the First World War. Whitehead dedicated his first work in the philosophy of science to his dead son. I reproduce the dedication, not for its sentiment but for its doctrinal content.

> To Eric Alfred Whitehead, Royal Flying Corps, November 27, 1898, to March 13, 1918. Killed in action over the Forêt de Gobain giving himself that the city of his vision may not perish. The music of his life was without discord, perfect in its beauty (PNK iv).

The key terms here are 'vision,' 'not perish,' 'beauty.' The compact thought is existentially significant. Beyond the horror of that death and his own sorrow Whitehead conceived his son's vision in the language of beauty. So much for what philosophers call natural evil. "Your character," Whitehead says, "is developed according to your faith" (RM 15).

Again, my moral vision is constantly abused. The wicked prosper. The good suffer, and my assuagement for these facts is the aesthetic vision of the Consequent Nature of God, forever completing His own existence by a harmony that rescinds the objective evil but gives me, as finite, no mercy. Cold comfort, Ely says. "It is not likely to give anyone much comfort to know that no matter what happens in this world, God can see it in an ideal setting that makes it an enjoyable sight" (Ely 41).

Whitehead is not unaware of this issue. He says, in one of the most stinging passages in the entire corpus,

> Good people of narrow sympathies are apt to be unfeeling and unprogressive, enjoying their egotistical goodness. Their case, on a higher level, is analogous to that of the man completely degraded to a hog. They have reached a state of stable goodness, so far as their own interior life is concerned. This type of moral correctitude is, on a larger view, so like evil that the distinction is trivial.
>
> Thus if God be an actual entity which enters into every creative phase and yet is above change, He must be exempt from internal inconsistency which is the note of evil. Since God is actual, He must include in himself a synthesis of the total universe. There is, therefore, in God's nature the aspect of the realm of forms as qualified by the world, and the aspect of the world as qualified by the forms (RM 98).

So much, then, for moral evil as well as natural evil.

Whitehead's intention is not primarily to render the idea of God palatable to anyone's idea of religious need and to accomplish this on metaphysical grounds. This is not a buyer's market, where the metaphysics must either put up an acceptable product or withdraw it when it is found not to be religiously available. The whole project is of an entirely different sort: to explain the relation of religious experience to experience generally. What is true of experience generally is true of experience in its religious aspect, Whitehead says.

> The moment of religious consciousness starts from self-valuation, but it broadens into the concept of the world as a realm of adjusted values, mutually intensifying or mutually destructive. The intuition into the actual world gives a particular definite content to the bare notion of a principle determining the grading of values. It also exhibits emotions, purposes, and physical conditions, as subservient factors in the emergence of value (RM 59-60).

A metaphysics of religious experience is confronted with certain *facts*. These facts are the ability of the subjective purposes in consciousness to rise above their common limits, transpersonally or even transmorally— a point heavily emphasized by Kierkegaard, incidentally—to a grasp of value that erases temporal losses. Nor will it do to attribute this transcending ability and the religious experience that fulfills it to pathology, for it carries with it not only private authenticity but publicly noticeable beatification. We may play such idle games as are commonly played by David Hume and Bertrand Russell, in which skeptical theory is pursued with endless diligence, but then practical success becomes a mystery, a kind of secular miracle. There is, on the one hand, the subjective persuasion of religious experience, which stretches beyond standard conceptions of value. On the other hand, there is the worth of lives so guided. The correlation of these facts is badly in need of understanding. To use Whitehead's term, they need to be *rationalized*. Some men do have such vision beyond average values, and it has publicly noticeable consequences. Any metaphysic worthy of the name must accommodate these facts. The primary role of a metaphysic is to describe what is, systematically and rationally. Derivatively it may lead men to deeper insight.

We may say, then, of the question of the religious availability of Whitehead's God that it is improper, provided some ill-defined standard of availability is pursued at the outset. "O God . . . ," says W. H. Auden in a mocking poem, "Leave Thy heavens and come down to our earth of waterclocks and hedges. Become our uncle. Look after Baby, amuse Grandfather, escort Madam to the Opera, help Willy with his homework, introduce Muriel to a handsome naval officer." [6] Some men have got beyond such a conception of God and found him to be religiously available. As things now stand, the availability is admittedly not widespread. For that matter, neither is the knowledge of the fact that the sun doesn't move through the heavens, although this is much easier to demonstrate. We are not yet done with the Ptolemaic period, when man and his earth were at the center of things.

V

One final point remains. Aside from the misleading character of moral language, why should the aesthetic metaphor be used? Or better, if some vocabulary must be given an extended meaning, why the aesthetic vocabulary?

No doubt every kind of value terminology is somewhat limited when it comes to the problems of religion. Perhaps the language of religious value should be distinct from all other forms. Yet religious value and the language of religious value are extremely sophisticated. But by what means shall the secular mind be brought into religious sensitivity? Or by what series of steps, starting where, does a young mind, aesthetically alive but perhaps quite unresponsive to the language of morals or the language of mysticism, come to any religious understanding? It is a failure of much religious practice that it confines itself to the language and thought of morality, which tends to be restrictive, and the language and thought of mysticism, which is supernatural. The total confinement of religious insight to what is on the one hand antinatural or on the other hand supernatural does not seem like a very promising procedure for either engendering or developing religious sensibility. If organized religion finds itself limited in its capacity to appeal to people of intellect or sensibility, it is not man who has rejected God, but rather peddlers of the image of God who have rejected man. Aesthetic sensibility is the most natural of all types of value sensibility. It begins with the delight of the child in the world of the senses. It is often the substitute for moral self-restraint in adolescents who may have come privately to the conviction that moral restriction and moral taboo have no claim upon their own decisions. Commitments to taste, discrimination, and personal fastidiousness may step forward and produce a behavior masking as moral but actually based upon aesthetic self-respect. At the highest level of religious achievement, that of mystical insight or mystical commitment, the common literary representation is always in terms of beauty. From beginning to end it would seem that, if some metaphor must be chosen for religious insight and for the relation of God to the world, the aesthetic metaphor is not only as good as any but perhaps better than any. I have tried to show briefly that it displays a deep and *continuous* current of value sensibility. In addition, where morality is restrictive, aesthetic sensibility and the aesthetic metaphor are creative. Where mere morality obtains, only the forbidden and the forbidding or else the compulsive and barren sense of duty operate. Over against this, the aesthetic metaphor and the aesthetic mode offer excitement, allurement, inspiration.

NOTES

¹ Stephen Ely, *The Religious Availability of Whitehead's God* (Madison: University of Wisconsin Press, 1942).

² Plato, *Laws*, translated by R. G. Bury (London: Heinemann, 1926; Loeb Classical library), 727 D-E, vol. I, p. 325.

³ Plato, *Symposium*, translated by W. R. M. Lamb (London: Heinemann, 1939; Loeb Classical Library).

⁴ The most troublesome dialogue in this respect is the *Philebus,* in which both forms appear commonly. To attribute the apparent randomness to either ironic or dialectic intent would require very imaginative scholarship.

⁵ F. M. Cornford, *The Republic of Plato* (Oxford: Clarendon Press, 1941), p. 216.

⁶ W. H. Auden, "The Massacre of the Innocents," in *For the Time Being* (New York: Random House, 1944), p. 122. Copyright 1944 by W. H. Auden. Reprinted from *The Collected Poetry of W. H. Auden,* by permission of Random House, Inc.

Responsibility, Punishment, and Whitehead's Theory of the Self

by Donald W. Sherburne

I

Paul Weiss has continually needled the supporters of Whitehead on various aspects of the philosophical system they explicate and defend, and the Whiteheadians have indeed been fortunate in obtaining the services of such an acute and vigorous gadfly. The concept of the self in Whitehead's philosophy has been one of Weiss' favorite targets. Writing as a contributor to *The Relevance of Whitehead*,[1] a volume of essays commemorating the centenary of the birth of Whitehead, Weiss admonishes: "Held to too tenaciously the view [that actual occasions perish when and as they become] would prevent Whitehead from affirming that there were any beings, other than God, which actually persist. As a consequence he would not be able to explain how a man could be self-identical over the course of an individual life, how any man could ever be guilty for something done by *him* years ago, how there could be an ethics of obligation, political action, artistic production, or an historical process." [2] It is quite proper to reply to Weiss as George Kline did reply in reviewing the commemorative volume: "Weiss himself seems quite insensitive to the difficulties which Whitehead has exposed in the Aristotelian alternative." [3] Yet though it is true that the Whiteheadians can raise formidable objections to Weiss' account of the self, as well as vice versa, in all likelihood the final philosophical significance of both parties will be determined by the success of the sustained effort of constructive thought which each puts into its own system and not by the acerbity of their attacks on each other. Therefore, it certainly will not do *simply* to point out Weiss' own difficulties by way of retaliation against his attacks; rather, Whiteheadians must also get down to the much more difficult business of explicating, reformulating, and extending their own position. The present paper is an experiment in this direction. The mode of procedure will be as follows: Whitehead's theory of the self will be retained in all its starkness, in precisely the form Weiss finds objectionable. It will then be shown that this theory of the self has the interesting consequence that it can be combined in a novel manner with the views on responsibility and punishment held by such as Hume, Ayer, and Schlick. This simple exercise does not pretend to solve all the problems in this area, but it may resolve a few and perhaps it will open up new lines of thought that might bear further examination.

II

To begin with, two basic world views must be presented. The first is the Block Universe view described thus by Russell:

> There are such invariable relations between different events at the same or different times that, given the state of the whole universe throughout any finite time, however short, every previous and subsequent event can theoretically be determined as a function of the given events during that time.[4]

The second is the Real Possibilities view described thus by William James:

> . . . the parts have a certain amount of loose play on one another, so that the laying down of one of them does not necessarily determine what the others shall be. . . . [A]ctualities seem to float in a wider sea of possibilities from out of which they are chosen. . . .[5]

Relating respectively to these two world views are the following two traditional attitudes toward punishment described thus by Raphael Demos:

> Moralists have raised the question as to how punishment may be justified, and their answers to the question generally have been of two sorts: they have appealed to the principle either of retributive justice or to that of beneficial consequences.[6]

The Block Universe view has tended toward beneficial consequences and the Real Possibilities view toward retributive justice. Speaking of punishment from the Block Universe point of view, Moritz Schlick writes:

> What is punishment, actually? The view still often expressed, that it is a natural *retaliation* for past wrong, ought no longer to be defended in cultivated society; for the opinion that an increase in sorrow can be "made good again" by further sorrow is altogether barbarous. . . . Punishment is an educative measure, and as such is a means to the formation of motives, which are in part to prevent the wrongdoer from repeating the act (reformation) and in part to prevent others from committing a similar act (intimidation).[7]

Exhibiting the grounds for punishment from the point of view of one camp within the Real Possibilities position, Edwyn Bevan writes:

> [I]f anyone goes to hell, in the Catholic view, it is his own fault, because he has freely and voluntarily chosen evil. . . . The wrongdoer suffers the pain of hell, in their view . . . because he deserves it—although there is no possibility of the pain making him better.[8]

Whitehead, of course, belongs to the Real Possibilities tradition. This tradition has a powerful appeal, particularly in the light of the success of Whitehead's philosophy in interpreting the basic principles of modern science and of such telling arguments as William James' "The Dilemma of Determinism." Heisenberg's Indeterminacy Principle is also interpreted by some as support for this view. On the other hand, in the area of punishment an emphasis on control and direction as over against retribution also has a powerful appeal to the modern mind. Schlick's assertion that punishment conceived as retaliation is a barbarous notion is convincing to readers steeped in current sociology and psychology. The thesis of this paper is that Whitehead's concept of the self permits a marriage of the Real Possibilities view and a theory of punishment grounded on reformation and deterrence. Far from being a liability, as Weiss argues, Whitehead's theory of the self leads, when explicitly joined to the Real Possibilities view, to a position which incorporates the best aspects of the Hume-Ayer-Schlick attitude toward punishment while rejecting an atavistic emphasis on retribution.

III

It is necessary to adumbrate Whitehead's theory of the self. Whitehead's is an atomistic, pluralistic system. Each of the concrete, fully real entities of the system is termed an "actual entity," or, alternatively, "actual occasion." Actual entities are *micro*cosmic. Each of these actual entities is energetic—i.e., it acts, it is a process of becoming—and each actual entity is self-situated—i.e., it is non-adjectival.[9] In William James' terminology, it is a drop of experience. Actual entities do not change position, nor do they endure through time; as Weiss noted in the passage quoted at the beginning of this paper, their being is their becoming, but they perish when and as they become. Like Aristotle's outer heavens, they are not in time, but rather time is in them; i.e., time is an abstraction from the ongoingness whereby generation after generation of actual entities succeed one another in the creative ongoingness of the universe.

The trees, houses, automobiles, and people which we encounter in our *macro*cosmic world are not single actual entities, but rather societies, or nexūs, of actual entities. In any such society there are untold numbers of actual entities. The nexūs which are trees, houses, automobiles, and people are four-dimensional nexūs. A slice of a nexus at a given instant is a three-dimensional, geometrical pattern composed of myriad actual entities. A full, temporally extended nexus consists of generation after generation of actual entities linked into roughly the same geometrical pattern as a result of the prehensive bonds which bind the generations together into strands of inherited features. These strands of inheritance spanning generations of actual entities are frequently referred to as "enduring objects."

In terms of this general scheme Whitehead reformulates and attempts to resolve the traditional mind-body problem. The nexus which is a stone is a comparatively homogeneous nexus, but the nexus which is a human being is a very complex society which is, in fact, a society of societies, or what Whitehead terms a structured society. Within this structured society stretches a regnant society, a society which is spatially thin, a society which is a temporally extended strand that wanders in its temporal unfolding from part to part of the brain, inheriting the vivid experiences of the many subordinate societies over which it ranges and refreshing and modifying those subordinate societies with its novel re-actions to its environment. The mind, as distinct from the brain, must be associated with the regnant nexus which wanders from part to part of the brain. This regnant nexus can be likened to a string of beads ex-tended in the dimension of time, except that there is no string, no substantial substratum, enduring through the succession of entities.

This is the scheme of ideas in terms of which a Whiteheadian must frame his theory of the self. Whitehead's position emerges clearly in a striking passage.

> In the quotation from the second *Meditation:* " 'I am, I exist,' is necessarily true each time that I pronounce it, or that I mentally conceive it," Descartes adopts the position that an act of experience is the primary type of actual occasion. But in his subsequent developments he assumes that his mental substances endure change. Here he goes beyond his argument. For each time he pronounces "I am, I exist," the actual occasion, which is the ego, is different. . . . (PR 116).

The notion of a substance enduring through change is unacceptable to Whitehead. "Actual entities perish, but do not change; they are what they are" (PR 52). Again, "The fundamental meaning of the notion of 'change' is 'the difference between [successive] actual occasions comprised in some determinate event' " (PR 114).[10]

Now, what are the consequences of this Whiteheadian position for a theory of punishment and for the notion of responsibility? They seem to raise the question: why execute a murderer or pin a medal on a military hero? In each case, given the Whiteheadian position, the actual entities whose free decisions were responsible for the deeds have perished. There is no concrete, actual element present in the *post facto* person which was actual at the time of the deed. It seems impossible to find a resting place for the responsibility usually regarded as correlative to free decision; in short, responsibility seems to be incompatible with this Whiteheadian theory of the self, and consequently any attempt by a Whiteheadian to ground punishment upon retribution seems doomed.

It is now clear why Weiss and other substance philosophers find Whitehead's theory objectionable on moral grounds. They note his great emphasis on the internal freedom possessed by each actual entity in molding the character of its own being, and then can find no place in the system for the correlative guilt and responsibility which, they argue, this freedom entails; for, since actual entities perish immediately upon becoming, nothing endures which could assume the responsibility or guilt.

IV

Turning now to the positive aspect of this paper, the attempt to exonerate Whitehead from these charges of inadequacy, I wish to eliminate at the start one possible line of rejoinder. It is *not* possible, in my opinion (though some may want to disagree with me), to save Whitehead by joining the concept of responsibility to the notion of a nexus, or enduring object. My reasons for rejecting this possibility are as follows. A nexus is an abstraction; it has being only as a function of the actual entities constitutive of it. To seek the locus of responsibility is to seek a reason, and the ontological principle, the most fundamental principle of Whitehead's system, asserts: ". . . to search for a *reason* is to search for one or more actual entities; . . . actual entities are the only *reasons*" (PR 37). ". . . every *decision* is referable to one or more actual entities, because in separation from actual entities there is nothing, merely nonentity. . ." (PR 68). (Italics added.) To lodge responsibility in a nexus is to commit the Fallacy of Misplaced Concreteness. To appeal to a nexus as the locus of responsibility is, as Whitehead remarks in a different context, ". . . exactly analogous to an appeal to an imaginary terrier to kill a real rat" (PR 348). Denying in this way the possibility of joining the concept of responsibility to the notion of a nexus undermines the last possibility of grounding punishment on retribution within the framework of Whitehead's system, because (1) since the actual entities to which any given decision can be traced have perished, they are beyond punishment and (2) the argument of this paragraph has shown that there is no other candidate for punishment if punishment is to be grounded on retribution.

But this conclusion does not entail that responsibility and punishment thereby become concepts impossible for the Whiteheadians to preserve within their system. To obviate this eventuality I offer a straightforward suggestion: abandon the effort to ground punishment on retribution. Certainly there is sound moral intuition in Schlick's view that the doctrine of retribution "is altogether barbarous." I wish to argue that if Schlick's reasonable and persuasive argument be accepted,[11] then it is precisely Whitehead's theory of the self which enables one to incorporate Schlick's insight into Whitehead's Real Possibilities cosmology.

Only a few of the directions in which this basic suggestion might be developed and defended can be adumbrated here, but it is hoped that the following remarks may increase the plausibility of the proposal.

First, consider responsibility. The responsibility correlative to freedom is not obviated by the suggested solution. It is true that actual entities responsible for certain decisions can be traced, but not recovered, for they have perished. A remark of Whitehead's reported by William Ernest Hocking is relevant: "You can't catch a moment by the scruff of the neck—*it's gone*, you know."[12] Nevertheless, the fact that you can't catch an actual entity by the scruff of the neck and deal with it at leisure does not mean that it is not both responsible and judged. Each actual entity is (a) responsible to God and (b) judged by God as God's consequent nature evolves. (a) An actual entity is responsible to God as a result of entertaining in its initial phase a conceptual aim, derived from God, which points toward the manner of becoming on the part of that actual entity which would result in maximizing intensity and harmony of feeling in the evolving universe. The actual entity can "turn its back," so to speak, on this divine lure as it makes its own autonomous decisions by which it becomes actual, but it is responsible for its decisions,[13] and (b) its decisions are judged. What each actual entity decides to make of itself has its impact as datum for the consequent nature of God, and what God makes of that actual entity as it is absorbed into his consequent nature is God's judgment of the subjective decision of that actual entity. As Whitehead writes, there is a ". . . judge arising out of the very nature of things. . ." (PR 533). The Whiteheadian cosmology is such that responsibility and judgment are built into the system at the microcosmic level; they are not eliminated by the suggestions of this paper. In fact, the Whiteheadian cosmology pushes one to the sound moral view "judge not, that ye be not judged"; it provides for final judgment while recognizing ultimate judgment to be not human, but divine.

Secondly, it must be shown that Whitehead's theory of the self is such as to encourage, even demand, that Schlick's insights into the justification of punishment be incorporated into Whitehead's cosmology. It is the superjective aspect of concrescing actual entities which creates this demand, so the superjective character of an actual entity must now be examined.

Whitehead writes: "An actual entity is to be conceived both as a subject presiding over its own immediacy of becoming, and a superject which is the atomic creature exercising its function of objective immortality" (PR 71). It seems odd to speak of an actual entity *exercising* its function of objective immortality precisely because, when objectively immortal, a creature has perished and can *do* nothing. Whitehead could be interpreted as meaning here that even as a "subject presiding over its own immediacy of becoming," an actual entity is concerned with what impact it will have in the future when it will be objectively immortal, when it will be a datum for other concrescences. It is concerned right now with what its impact on them will be in the future, and in as far as it has this concern it is superject. The crucial point for the argument which follows is this: as concrescing subject the actual entity is already superject; that is, how it will have its impact on future occasions can be, depending upon the degree of sophistication of the entity, an important factor already, "right now," as it is becoming. In this sense an actual entity can be said to *exercise* its function of objective immortality; i.e., it anticipates the effect of its present decisions on the future and modifies present decisions in the light of this effect.

This discussion of the superjective character of an actual entity, particularly the last sentence, deepens the meaning of two passages from Whitehead: "The effect of the present on the future is the business of morals" and "The greater part of morality hinges on the determination of relevance in the future" (AI 346; PR 41). These statements are not only illuminated by the discussion of superject above, they also fairly beg for some mode of *rapprochement* with the position of Schlick concerning the justification of punishment. This *rapprochement* must now be provided.

Schlick, it will be recalled, grounds punishment on both deterrence and reformation. The deterministic aspect of Schlick's Block Universe view makes it plausible for him to emphasize deterrence, but deterrence cannot be the primary justification for punishment within a Real Possibilities cosmology. There is considerable disillusionment with punishment as a deterrent force in any case. Richard B. Brandt opines that

> . . . it is doubtful whether threats of punishment have as much deterrent value as is often supposed. Threats of punishment will have little effect on morons, or on persons to whom normal living offers few prospects of an interesting existence. Moreover, persons from better economic or social circumstances will be deterred sufficiently by the prospect of conviction in a public trial and being at the disposal of a board for a period of years.[14]

The positive emphasis on reformation as the justification for punishment which is presupposed by my own argument is presented in broad outline by Brandt as follows:

Some thinkers today believe that criminal justice in Great Britain and the United States is in need of substantial revision. If we agree with their proposals, we have even less reason for favoring the retributive principle; but we must also question the traditional utilitarian emphasis on deterrence as the primary function of the institution of criminal justice.

Their proposal, roughly, is that we should extend, to all criminal justice, the practices of juvenile courts and institutions for the reform of juvenile offenders. Here, retributive concepts have been largely discarded at least in theory, and psychiatric treatment and programs for the prevention of crime by means of slum clearance, the organization of boys' clubs, and so forth, have replaced even deterrence as guiding ideas for social action.[15]

It remains now to discover how this general position, emphasizing reformation, works out when interpreted in terms of the particular categories of Whitehead's system.

Not all Whiteheadian actual entities have the same degree of sophistication. "They differ among themselves: God is an actual entity, and so is the most trivial puff of existence in far-off empty space" (PR 28). The difference is a function of the degree of sophistication of the mental poles of the entities. Insofar as an entity is of a primitive sort with little power of originality in its mental pole, the superjective aspect of that entity approaches the vanishing point, efficient causation reigns supreme, and it and other similar entities become ". . . vehicles for receiving, for storing in a napkin, and for restoring without loss or gain" (PR 269). This is the level of the inorganic. As entities become located at sensitive points within the progressively more specialized societies constituting the more highly evolved organisms, the more organized environment on which they draw enables them to become less totally dominated by efficient causation and progressively more sensitive to final causation; i.e., the extent to which they *"exercise* their function of objective immortality," in the precise sense given to this phrase above, becomes more marked. They become superjectively oriented; they anticipate the effects of their present decisions on the future and modify their present decisions accordingly; they operate telically in the light of goals, purposes and ideals. To operate telically in the light of goals, purposes, and ideals is to be human and is to face the demands of morality: ". . . the actual entity, in a state of process during which it is not fully definite, determines its own ultimate definiteness. This is the whole point of moral responsibility" (PR 390).

Punishment must be moral; a theory of punishment cannot flout moral intuitions—this assumption underlies all current discussions of punishment, as, for example, when utilitarians are attacked on the grounds that their theory must lead to the position that one ought to punish innocent people and is hence unacceptable for the reason that this practice is obviously morally reprehensible.[16] Morality within the Whiteheadian scheme demands that creative decision "always be used toward the actualization of the wider, more complete creative order of good" where increase of value is understood as "the enlargement of the scope and depth of community of actualities." [17] The implications for a theory of punishment are clear: punishment, to be justified, must be goal-creating; it must literally be creative punishment in that it seeks to reveal possibilities leading to depth and harmony of experience. A juvenile delinquent or a perennial lawbreaker is, except in pathological cases, an individual who either has no goals at all and simply drifts in bitter helplessness and frustration, or else has antisocial goals, goals which are incompatible with the maximum harmonization of the goals of the other members of society. Punishment in these cases can be justified only if it is humane, only if it creates the conditions under which superjective—i.e., goal-seeking—activity is possible. The incarceration of an offender is morally justifiable only to the extent that the offender is taught a trade, or otherwise educated to assume a constructive role in society, at the same time that he is led to project his own future activity into a harmonious pattern of social relationships. An indispensable aspect of all rehabilitation is the elimination of chronic unemployment, discrimination in all its forms, and other social ailments which tend to frustrate irrationally the goal-oriented activity engendered by rehabilitation.

J. D. Mabbott argues against punishment justified by an appeal to deterrence and reformation, as this theory is held by Schlick, Nowell-Smith, Ebersole and others, on the grounds that "to be punished for reform reasons is to be treated like a dog." [18] His argument is reminiscent of Joseph Wood Krutch's polemic in *The Measure of Man* against B. F. Skinner's *Walden Two*. In both instances the argument against deterrence and reform is an argument against the deterministic presuppositions of the protagonists, Schlick and Skinner, and the argument is based on the deep, and sound, moral conviction that these men lose sight of the very essence of what it is to be a human being. The position of this paper, based as it is on the libertarian cosmology of Whitehead, preserves the moral insight of Mabbott and Krutch that a theory of punishment must not rob man of his humanity—indeed, it links punishment closely to the most human of attributes, namely goal-seeking, telic activity. On the other hand, it has escaped the disadvantages of what has often seemed to be the only alternative to the dehumanization of man, namely, the retributive principle.

In summary, preserving Whitehead's theory of the self in all its starkness enables one (a) to reject the atavistic appeal to retribution as the basis for punishment; (b) to incorporate the reformation aspect of the theory of Schlick into the Whiteheadian scheme; (c) to accept (a) and (b) while retaining the notions of freedom and creativity; and (d) to retain in cosmology the notions of responsibility and judgment, each properly grounded in a direct relationship with the divine element in the world.

NOTES

[1] Edited by Ivor Leclerc (London: George Allen & Unwin Ltd.; New York: The Macmillan Co., 1961).

[2] *Op. cit.*, p. 331. Nathan Rotenstreich has urged the same general criticism in "The Superject and Moral Responsibility," *Review of Metaphysics*, 10 (1956-57), 201. He writes, p. 203, "[Moral responsibility] presupposes the fact of consciousness which bridges over the different stages of the personal existence . . ."

[3] *Journal of Philosophy*, 58 (1961), 824.

[4] *Our Knowledge of the External World* (London: George Allen & Unwin Ltd., 1949 edition), p. 224.

[5] "The Dilemma of Determinism," in *The Will to Believe* (London: Longmans, Green & Co., 1897), pp. 150-151.

[6] "Some Reflections on Threats and Punishments," *Review of Metaphysics*, 11 (1957-58), 224. In fairness to Professor Demos it should be noted that he goes on to argue that the question itself is illegitimate.

[7] *Problems of Ethics* (New York: Prentice-Hall, 1939), p. 152.

[8] *Symbolism and Belief* (Boston: Beacon Press, 1957), pp. 237 n.1, 237.

[9] The terms used in this sentence are borrowed from Ellen S. Haring, "The Ontological Principle," *Review of Metaphysics*, 16 (1962-63), 7.

[10] In this context Whitehead is using the term 'event' synonymously with the phrase 'temporally extended nexus of actual occasions.'

[11] The emphasis of this paper is not on a detailed study of punishment, but rather on the examination of Whitehead's metaphysics with the aim of seeing if that metaphysics is compatible with the theory of punishment espoused by Schlick. If the reader wishes detailed arguments as to why Schlick's attitude toward the retributive principle appears to me to be sound, I refer him to the lucid and detailed discussion of this principle in Richard B. Brandt, *Ethical Theory* (Englewood Cliffs: Prentice-Hall, 1959), ch. 19, and in particular to the five specific arguments on pp. 500-501 which lead Brandt, quite correctly in my opinion, to reject the retributive principle.

[12] "Whitehead as I Knew Him," this volume, p. 8.

[13] This same point is made in the language of moral obligation by Daniel D. Williams in his article "Moral Obligation in Process Philosophy," especially Sec. II, this volume, pp. 190-191.

[14] Brandt, *op. cit.*, p. 504. He goes on to cite the well-known story of how picking pockets was once a capital offense in England and how for a time hangings for this crime were public in order to maximize the deterrent effects of this harsh punishment. But it seems, so the story goes, that hangings in public had to be abolished because such crimes as picking pockets were so frequent during the spectacle!

[15] *Ibid.*, p. 503.

[16] This example is designed simply to illustrate the relationship between morality and punishment; the utilitarian, of course, has an oft-repeated, and to my mind convincing, reply to this charge. See Brandt, *op. cit.*, pp. 494-495 for an indication of his line of defense.

[17] Williams, *op. cit.*, this volume, p. 190.

[18] J. D. Mabbott, "Freewill and Punishment" in *Contemporary British Philosophy* (Third Series), H. D. Lewis, editor (London: George Allen & Unwin Ltd., 1956), p. 303. See also pp. 308-309.

Moral Obligation in
Process Philosophy

by Daniel D. Williams

The purpose of this paper is to examine the nature of moral obligation from the perspective of process philosophy by showing how this philosophy may deal with two specific problems in the moral life: first, the problem of choices which involve the doing of evil; and second, the aspect of temporal spread in the situations which require moral decision. It is an implicit concern of the paper to show that ethics is inseparable from metaphysics. One way a metaphysical perspective may justify itself is to show that it can illuminate problems of moral decision.

I

My presuppositions are the following:

1. Everything actual is a concrete process. That is, every moment of its being involves reference to a past from which there is a route of inheritance, and a future which involves possibilities. Everything actual has a structure which relates it to the past, to other entities, and to the future.

2. God is the supreme actuality by virtue of which there is a world of finite concrete actualities held together in a societal relationship exhibiting order, relatedness, and definiteness.

3. God's essential nature, here called his primordial nature, is the realm of ordered possibilities. It is abstract, and therefore never exhaustive of any achieved actuality or state of God's own being.

4. God's primordial nature involves the integrity of his vision of the good; that is, it involves an order and gradation of value. God is that function in the world by virtue of which every occasion is either positively or negatively related to the possibility of increase of value.

5. Increase of value is the enlargement of the scope and depth of

"Moral Obligation in Process Philosophy." Reprinted from the *Journal of Philosophy*, **56** (1959), 263-270.

community of actualities. It involves depth of feeling-awareness including qualitative richness, ordered harmony, appreciative communion, and creative advance. Creative advance is the bringing of new structures of value to the enrichment of established orders. It may involve displacement of the old.

6. Some creatures have freedom to make decisions which take into account alternative possibilities for future actualization of value, or which involve destruction of value.

II

From the standpoint of these assumptions the following statements follow with respect to the nature of moral obligation:

1. Moral obligation is the claim of possible good upon the free decision of any creature who is able to consider the effect of his action in relation to that good.

2. God is the source of moral obligation since God is the sole reality by virtue of which there is a unified structure of possible good in any situation.

3. There is a double aspect of moral obligation derived from the two aspects of God's being:

(a) There is the absolute obligation derived from the integrity of God's aim for the creatures. This means that freedom should always be used toward the actualization of the wider, more complete creative order of good. This obligation is absolute, eternal, and in its essential nature does not change. It is implied in every moral choice; and it means that principles of moral action cannot be derived from the analysis of particular historical processes alone. Beyond the definable possibilities of any specific historical situation there stretches the inexhaustible possibility of completion in a wider frame of reference, and that frame of reference ultimately lies in the vision of God.

This position agrees with Immanuel Kant that there are absolute moral requirements implied in human freedom, and with the platonists that the Form of the Good gives the final law to all being.

But there is also a radical difference from these philosophies. The structure of the absolute good is abstract. It is an order of possibilities which does not exhaust the nature of its exemplification in any concrete actuality, not even in the being of God.

Therefore, the second aspect (b) of moral obligation is the requirement for the concrete appraisal of the historical situation in which decisions are taken. What we ought to do here and now can never be derived solely from the statement of principles, whether ultimate principles or derivative ones. Moral decision is a response to the concrete working of God in a situation riddled with the ambiguities of historical good and evil, and with the mysteries of as yet unapprehended qualities and possibilities.

Therefore, the nature of moral obligation has to be stated in a somewhat more complex way. It includes the obligation to participate in the present situation by making such decisions as will reflect both basic integrity of aim, and relationship to the concretely given. Thus there is an absolute moral obligation to do more than acknowledge and obey moral principles, though that is never set aside. There is the absolute obligation to make decisions which bring the good into actuality in those present processes within which one stands.

It follows that there is in every moral decision an aspect which transcends all prediction of what, concretely, will be required. Ethical behavior is genuinely creative in that the very act of decision brings into being a concrete good which cannot be wholly predicted or recognized on the basis of any vision of abstract possibilities, not even the divine vision itself, though nothing the creatures can do can affect the ultimate unity and integrity of the divine vision. In the strange words of the book of Genesis: it is after the world is created that God declares it good.

III

There are endless problems in elaborating a moral doctrine (including the relation of "moral" value to other kinds of values). I shall try to show that this position can cope with the problems involved in two special aspects of the moral life. Any moral theory must prove itself by showing its relevance to specific choices. Indeed, one advantage which may be claimed for the present position is that it anticipates an infinite series of situations involving moral choices which have their unpredictable aspects. Moral theorists will always have new problems to solve.

The first problem dealt with here is that which concerns the choices in which acceptance of the doing of positive evil seems necessary in order to preserve any good. The problem is so clearly stated by Dr. Henry N. Wieman from a perspective closely related to the one here developed that I refer to his analysis in *The Source of Human Good*. In discussing types of evil, Dr. Wieman analyzes the role of "protective hierarchies" in human society.

Hierarchical structures in government, economic life, and systems of status and privilege, including those which make possible the intellectual life, represent an "ordering of life [which] is a hard necessity, but it is evil" (pp. 117-118). "It is necessary to enable the creative event to produce the richest fulfillment of value with those most capable of engaging in that kind of communication. It is evil because it imposes upon many an undue protection from pain and discomfort; upon some an undue fatigue from hard labor. . ." and so on (pp. 119-120).

The moral problem here is a difficult one; but I do not see how it can be left just where Dr. Wieman leaves it. For he holds that the absolute obligation is to give oneself to the transforming power of the creative event or process (p. 124). Yet the maintenance of the hierarchies is essential to the working of the event itself. How can anything be necessary to the working of the creative process which is not ingredient in that process itself? The obligation which God lays upon the world is the fulfillment of all the conditions necessary to the achievement of his creative aim. If one of those necessities is the device of the protective hierarchy, then surely in a concrete situation there is an obligation to respect that element of value in the hierarchy. It cannot be simply evil. It is certainly ambiguous in relation to good and evil, but not sheer evil. I am not sure but what my conclusion here coincides with Dr. Wieman's regarding the practical obligation to respect the function of the hierarchies; but once this obligation is recognized it seems to me to have implications for the doctrine of how God works in the world. This cannot be restricted to that "high peak of creative transformation [which] will continue to soar far above the mass of people with only a very few finding a place there" (p. 124). God is also involved in more humdrum tasks. Whatever constitutes a necessity for man constitutes in some way a necessity for God also insofar as God is involved in promoting human good.

This position does not in any way relieve us of the problem of dealing with moral choices in ambiguous situations. That there are such ambiguities in which, so far as we can see, any choice involves at least the risk of evil and perhaps the certainty of it, is certainly recognized by Dr. Wieman. Some way must be found to assert the absolute element in moral obligation and yet to take account of such ambiguity. Otherwise moral obligation is split up among the conflicting claims of alternative values. Love is torn apart into sacrificial and mutual love; justice and brotherhood are made mutually exclusive opposites.

The doctrine of process philosophy that the absolute obligation to participate in the integrity of God's aim toward the fuller good also involves the obligation to reckon with the concrete possibilities in actual processes, throws some light on the moral problem here.

It may be that actualization is always involved in the ambiguities of good and evil. For one consideration, every advance includes a possible risk of new evil. The most honest moral intention can create a new situation riddled with evil. But we need not point only to cases where the purity of our motives might be assumed. We have to recognize the possibility that every choice we make is tainted with an interest either in self-satisfaction or self-destruction which cannot stand before the claim of God upon us. But if this be the case, then it is our moral obligation to recognize our actual state, to allow for it, and to make our moral choices in the light of our self-knowledge with its confession of the evil that we do. Since our self-knowledge is not complete, our confession of it can never be. But there are degrees. When one who wields power submits his judgments to a wider criticism, he may be acknowledging that his own bias needs such a corrective. We have no moral obligation to act as if we were morally incorruptible. Quite the contrary, we have an absolute obligation to make decisions which take account of our own fallibility.

This is not to deny but rather to underline the tragic problem of the necessities of our existence such as those imposed by decisions concerning the development of weapons which potentially can destroy the whole human race. But it is to hold that moral obligation is not set aside by these necessities; rather it is a service of the creative event to make decisions in the light of whatever wisdom we can muster about the concrete factors, and to do with them what expresses, however obliquely, the affirmation of the wider and deeper good which God is creating.

IV

A second aspect of the problem of moral obligation has to do with the fact that what we decide about is, in every case, not a static situation, but a process. This becomes clear in the analysis of the dilemmas just discussed; for part of the problem of the "necessities" has to do with questions of the outcome of a historic process. Necessary for what end? for how long? with what result? All these are questions which are pertinent to moral choice.

In the view of process philosophy every moral decision is itself a process and involves a relationship to the "becoming" of other actualities. Here some of the deepest perplexity of moral choice arises, for we cannot see the end of our actions; and we are dealing with realities which do not disclose their full being to us except through the spread of time. Since there are no discernible limits to the future in which our actions may have some relevance, we are obligated to ask about the effects of our acts "in the long run"; but how long is this?

I suggest that we begin the analysis here with some aspects of the effect of the time dimension on specific moral choices where we can within limits take account of the historic route along which our choices lie. A concrete example is at hand in the recent decision of the Supreme Court bearing upon the desegregation of public schools. Professor Edmond Cahn has pointed out the significance of the method of handling the case and its decision. Having made its decision, the court allowed time for consideration of means of implementing it. In its second decision, after hearing arguments concerning implementation, the Court revealed a preference for "an effective gradual adjustment," and took account of possible differences of timing in local situations. It is in this decision that the District Courts are ordered to proceed toward the abolition of racial discrimination in the schools "with all deliberate speed." The qualifying word, 'deliberate,' surely contains a moral injunction to hold to the goal; but also to move with a certain caution toward the taking of specific steps.

Professor Cahn's comments on the principle involved here are highly pertinent to the analysis of moral problems in the perspective of process philosophy. He points out the important difference between "time when" something is to be done and "time during which." And he says: "the duration or 'time during which' a transaction occurs is one of the critical dimensions of the transaction itself. Frequently its inmost nature is determined by how long it lasts. . . . Duration is a moral dimension." Thus the Supreme Court found that duration could be inserted as a wedge between "either and or." [1]

There are, of course, factors involved in every legal decision which go beyond the range of any moral theory. What "deliberate speed" means in the language of the Supreme Court will have to be argued and determined by lawyers and courts within their frame of reference. But the moral problem here is clear. It is the question of the way in which the timing of any action is related to our obligation to perform it. That moral theory has had so little to say about this problem is a puzzling fact. It is John Dewey pre-eminently in contemporary philosophy who has pointed out how sterile and irrelevant much traditional discussion of the means-ends relationship has been, precisely because the continuum of concrete process in which means and ends function has been overlooked.

In the perspective of process philosophy the fact that moral principles are guides to action within processes is a fundamental aspect of the whole viewpoint. To insist on decision according to principle without reference to the historic routes of becoming in the lives of those affected is irresponsible. "Insistence on birth at the wrong season is the trick of evil," says Whitehead (PR 341). In a sense this doctrine lends itself to a certain conservatism in personal and social ethics; "take your time," "don't rush me," "let it work itself out" are homely moral maxims with a wisdom greater than much arbitrary moralizing.

But the principle is equally valid that the concrete nature of process requires action "before it is too late." Historic processes which lead to monstrous evil can be arrested at a certain point, beyond which there is no return. To fail to act at the point where arrest is possible may be the great moral error, no matter how heroic the too late attack may be. It also is clear that there are times and seasons for the beginning of relationships, in individual and social histories, when to fail to seize the right time means to lose all hope for that future good.

There is a further reply to be made to the criticism that this view can become a rationale for an indefinite postponement of deliberate social change. One hears it said: "in another generation we will have public school integration; but not now." But in the view here being defended there is always a question of the integrity of the fundamental aim. Moral obligation means present identification with a line of creative advance, or resistance to an evil tendency. The fundamental decision, made in the core of the personality, may not be observable in overt action at once; but the decision is there. To refuse the basic decision by postponing to some future generation or situation the actual crisis is morally self-destructive.

There will always be some consequences of decision, even if they affect only the inner structure of the personality. In a social universe they also begin to affect the network of relationships in which one stands. It should be pointed out that the view here taken does not exclude the possibility of a situation where nothing whatever can be done except the expression of the integrity of an absolute aim. There are situations created in which it is too late for anyone to do anything to arrest the historic developments which lead to catastrophe. The only moral requirement may be simply recognition of the realities and personal acknowledgment of the absolute will to the good which resides in God.

The recognition of such situations underlies much of the existentialist ethics. The alternatives often seem to be either sheer witness to integrity when no significant moral choice is possible, or reliance on the creativity of the personal decision beyond all rules and norms. We need not deny such situations; but the decisions taken within them are still taken within the context of the historic life of a community and they have their consequences for the new orders of existence as yet unknown.

V

Process philosophy offers a metaphysics and theory of value which holds together absoluteness of moral obligation with acknowledgment of the creative and the tragic factors which attend ethical decision in an unfinished world.

NOTE

[1] Edmond Cahn, *The Moral Decision* (Bloomington: Indiana University Press, 1955), pp. 274-277.

Part V
Documents and Materials

Unpublished Letter from
Whitehead to Hartshorne
(January 2, 1936)

Whitehead wrote very few letters and almost none on philosophic subjects. Bertrand Russell, in his reminiscences of Whitehead, throws interesting light on this fact and the reasons for it.

> I once wrote a letter to him [Russell recalls] on a mathematical point, as to which I urgently needed an answer for an article I was writing against Poincaré. He did not answer, so I wrote again. He still did not answer, so I telegraphed. As he was still silent, I sent a reply-paid telegram. But in the end, I had to travel down to Broadstairs to get the answer. His friends gradually got to know this peculiarity, and on the rare occasions when any of them got a letter from him they would all assemble to congratulate the recipient. He justified himself by saying that if he answered letters, he would have no time for original work. I think the justification was complete and unanswerable.[1]

The letter which follows may well be unique as an epistolary clarification of, and commentary on, key points in Whitehead's philosophy. It is published here for the first time, through the kindness of Professor Charles Hartshorne and of Whitehead's son, Dr. North Whitehead. Except for two brief omissions—indicated by asterisks—the text of the letter is reproduced without change; the abbreviations are Whitehead's.

504 Radnor Hall
984 Memorial Drive
Cambridge - Mass. Jan 2nd - 1936

Dear Hartshorne

First, I want to tell you how touched and pleased Evelyn and I have been by the presentation of the volume of Philosophical Essays, in anticipation of my 75th Birthday. It was a wonderful experience.

Of course I have glanced through the contents, and now I am slowly studying the individual essays, before expressing myself to the contributors. I have just finished a second careful perusal of your essay.

My general impression of the whole book, together with my knowledge of the individual contributors, confirms my long standing belief that in the oncoming generation America will be the centre of worthwhile philosophy—

NOTE

[1] *Portraits from Memory* (New York: Simon and Schuster, 1956), p. 104. Copyright 1951, 1952, 1953, 1956 by Bertrand Russell; by permission of Simon and Schuster, Inc.

504 Radnor Hall
784 Memorial Drive
Cambridge, Mass.
Jan. 2nd, 1936

Dear Hartshorne

First, I want to tell you how touched and pleased Evelyn and I have been by the presentation of the volume of Philosophical Essays, in anticipation of my 75th Birthday. It was a wonderful experience.

Of course I have glanced through the contents, and now I am slowly studying the individual essays, before expressing myself to the contributors. I have just finished a second careful perusal of your essay.

My general impression of the whole book, together with my knowledge of the individual contributors, confirms my longstanding belief that in the oncoming generation America will be the centre of worthwhile philosophy.* * *

My belief is that the effective founders of the American Renaissance are Charles Peirce and William James. Of these men, W.J. is the analogue to Plato, and C.P. to Aristotle, though the time-order does not correspond, and the analogy must not be pressed too far. Have you read Ralph Perry's new book (2 vols.) on James? It is a wonderful disclosure of the living repercussions of late 19th century thought on a sensitive genius.* * * But I admit W.J. was weak on Rationalization. Also, he expressed himself by the dangerous method of over-statement.

Now as to your recent work. Very naturally I have been immensely interested in it. Your article in the Philosophical Review (July, 1935) gets to the heart of what I have been endeavouring to say, in the most masterly manner. Of course a short article omits whole topics which require elaboration. But you do get hold of the principles of approach, apart from which all my recent writings since 1924 are a mere mass of confusion. Of course, I fully realize that in the development of these principles there is room for grave divergence and much discussion.

Your essay in 'Philosophical Essays' on 'The Compound Individual' is most important, both in its explanation of relationships to the Philosophical Tradition and in its development of the new approach as it has gradually emerged in the last 50 years.

Finally there is your book 'The Philosophy and Psychology of Sensation'. It entranced me by its development of the result of a novelty of approach to questions buried under the faulty presuppositions of traditional thought.

I do hope that you have more work on hand.

There is one point as to which you—and everyone—misconstrue me—obviously my usual faults of exposition are to blame. I mean my doctrine of *eternal objects*. It is a first endeavor to get beyond the absurd simple-mindedness of the traditional treatment of Universals.

As to the *loci* where I have treated the doctrine, cf. the chapter on *'Abstraction'* in Science and the Modern World, and in 'Process and Reality', indexed under the headings *'Eternal Object'*, *'Form'*, *'Sensum'*, *'Pattern'*.

The points to notice are (i) that 'Et. Obj.' are the carriers of potentiality into realization;

and (ii) that they thereby carry mentality into matter of fact;

and (iii) that no eternal object in any finite realization can exhibit the full potentialities of its nature. It has an individual essence—whereby it is the same eternal object on diverse occasions, and it has a relational essence whereby it has an infinitude of modes of entry into realization. But realization introduces finitude (in Spinoza's sense), with the extension of the infinitude of incompatibles in the relational essence.

(iv) The relational essence of each 'Etern. Obj.' involves its (potential) interconnections with all other eternal objects. The traditional doctrine of the absolute isolation of universals is as great a (tacit) error, as the isolation of primary substances. The realization of the 'compound individual' involves a finite realization of a complete pattern of eternal objects. The *absolute* abstraction of eternal objects from each other is an analogous error to their abstraction from some mode of realization, and to the abstraction of *res verae* from each other.

(v) The simple-minded way in which traditional philosophy—e.g. Hume, Bradley, etc.—has treated universals is the root of all evils. This is the great merit of the *'Gestalt'* people.

I am afraid I have bored you—But this letter is a measure of my interest in your work.

Sincerely yrs
Alfred North Whitehead

Contributors

GEORGE L. KLINE, the editor, was educated at Boston University, Columbia College, and Columbia University. He has taught at Columbia, the University of Chicago, and Swarthmore College and is at present Associate Professor of Philosophy and Russian at Bryn Mawr College. He is the author of *Spinoza in Soviet Philosophy* (1952) and translator of Zenkovsky's *History of Russian Philosophy* (1953). He has contributed an essay, "Whitehead in the Non-English-Speaking World," to the *Festschrift* for Charles Hartshorne (ed. Reese and Freeman, 1963).

V. C. CHAPPELL was educated at Yale and Heidelberg. He has taught at Yale and is at present Assistant Professor of Philosophy at the University of Chicago. He is the author of various articles on metaphysics and philosophy of mind and has edited *The Philosophy of Mind* (1962) as well as the Modern Library edition of Hume (1963). His doctoral dissertation (1958) was on "The Philosophy of Process."

LUCIO CHIARAVIGLIO was educated (in mathematics and theology as well as philosophy) at the University of Buenos Aires, the University of Chicago, and Emory University. He is at present Assistant Professor of Philosophy at Emory. He is the author of papers on Whitehead and has contributed an essay, "Extension and Abstraction," to the *Festschrift* for Charles Hartshorne (ed. Reese and Freeman, 1963).

WILLIAM A. CHRISTIAN was educated at Davidson College, Union Theological Seminary (Va.), Edinburgh, Oxford, the Chicago Theological Seminary, and Yale. He has taught at Smith and Swarthmore and is at present Professor of Religion at Yale. He is the author of several articles on Whitehead and of *An Interpretation of Whitehead's Metaphysics* (1959). He contributed an essay, "Some Uses of Reason," to *The Relevance of Whitehead* (ed. Leclerc, 1961) and an essay, "The Concept of God as a Derivative Notion in Whitehead's Metaphysics," to the *Festschrift* for Charles Hartshorne (ed. Reese and Freeman, 1963).

MASON W. GROSS was educated at Cambridge University and Harvard, where he studied with Whitehead. He has taught at Harvard, Columbia, and Rutgers and was an instructor in Philosophy at Columbia in 1941 when his article

Contributors 201

"Whitehead's Answer to Hume" was published. He is at present President and Professor of Philosophy, Rutgers University. He is co-editor (with F. S. C. Northrop) of *Alfred North Whitehead: An Anthology* (1953; paperback edition 1962).

EVERETT W. HALL (1901-1960) was educated at Lawrence College and Cornell. In 1930, when his article "Of What Use Are Professor Whitehead's Eternal Objects?" was published, he was teaching at the University of Chicago. At the time of his death he was Professor of Philosophy and Chairman of the Department at the University of North Carolina. His books include *What Is Value?* (1952) and *Philosophical Systems: A Categorial Analysis* (1960).

CHARLES HARTSHORNE was educated at Haverford College and Harvard and Freiburg Universities. He was Whitehead's assistant for one semester at Harvard. He has taught at Harvard, the University of Chicago, Stanford University, Melbourne University, Kyoto University, the University of Washington, and Emory University. He is now Professor of Philosophy at the University of Texas. He is the author of many books, including *The Divine Relativity* (1948; paperback edition 1962), *Reality as Social Process* (1953), and *The Logic of Perfection and Other Essays in Neo-Classical Metaphysics* (1961); co-author of *Whitehead and the Modern World* (1950); and a co-editor of the forthcoming German edition of Whitehead's works. He contributed an essay, "The Compound Individual," to *Philosophical Essays for Alfred North Whitehead* (1936), an essay, "Whitehead's Idea of God," to the Whitehead volume of the *Library of Living Philosophers* (ed. Schilpp, 1941, 2nd ed. 1951), and two essays, "Whitehead and Contemporary Philosophy" and "Metaphysics and the Modality of Existential Judgments," to *The Relevance of Whitehead* (ed. Leclerc, 1961).

WILLIAM ERNEST HOCKING was educated at Harvard, Göttingen, Berlin, and Heidelberg. He taught at the University of California, Yale, and Harvard, and is at present Alford Professor of Philosophy Emeritus of Harvard University. He makes his home in Madison, New Hampshire. Among his many books are *The Meaning of God in Human Experience* (1912; paperback edition, 1963) and *Lasting Elements of Individualism* (1937). He contributed an essay, "Whitehead on Mind and Nature," to the Whitehead volume of the *Library of Living Philosophers* (ed. Schilpp, 1941, 2nd ed. 1951). He was Gifford Lecturer at the University of Glasgow in 1937-1939.

NATHANIEL LAWRENCE was educated at Stanford University and Harvard. He has taught at Harvard, Wellesley College, the Universities of Illinois, California, and Louisiana, and at Yale; he is at present Professor of Philosophy and Chairman of the Department at Williams College. He is the author of *Whitehead's Philosophical Development* (1956) and of journal articles on Whitehead; he contributed an essay, "Time, Value, and the Self," to *The Relevance of Whitehead* (ed. Leclerc, 1961) and a chapter on Whitehead to Brumbaugh and Lawrence, *Philosophers on Education: Six Essays on the Foundation of Western Thought* (1963).

HUGUES LEBLANC was educated at St. Hyacinthe College (Quebec), The University of Montreal, and Harvard. He has taught at Columbia, Haverford College, Swarthmore College, and the University of Pennsylvania. He is at present Professor of Philosophy at Bryn Mawr College. He is the author of

An Introduction to Deductive Logic (1955) and *Statistical and Inductive Probabilities* (1962), and of many articles in the field of logic and philosophy of science.

IVOR LECLERC was educated at the University of Capetown and the University of London. He has taught at the University of Bonn, and is at present Senior Lecturer in Logic and Metaphysics at the University of Glasgow. He is the author of numerous articles on Whitehead's philosophy and of the book *Whitehead's Metaphysics: An Introductory Exposition* (1958). He edited *The Relevance of Whitehead* (1961) and contributed an essay, "Whitehead and the Theory of Form," to the *Festschrift* for Charles Hartshorne (ed. Reese and Freeman, 1963). He is also a co-editor of the forthcoming German edition of Whitehead's works.

VICTOR LOWE was educated at Case Institute and at Harvard, where he studied with Whitehead. He has taught at Syracuse University and Ohio State, and is now Professor of Philosophy at Johns Hopkins. He is the author of *Understanding Whitehead* (1962). In the Whitehead volume of the *Library of Living Philosophers* (ed. Schilpp, 1941, 2nd ed. 1951) he wrote "The Development of Whitehead's Philosophy" and was co-compiler of the Bibliography of Whitehead's Writings. He is the author of various articles on Whitehead, on William James, and on C. I. Lewis, and has contributed essays on Whitehead to *Classic American Philosophers* (ed. M. H. Fisch, 1951), *Whitehead and the Modern World* (1950), and *The Relevance of Whitehead* (ed. Leclerc, 1961).

RALPH V. NORMAN, JR., was educated at the Universities of Tennessee and Tübingen, and at Yale. He has taught at Yale and is at present Assistant Professor of Religion and Philosophy at Miami University in Oxford, Ohio. His doctoral dissertation (1961) was concerned with a problem in the philosophical theology of Royce and Whitehead.

ROBERT M. PALTER was educated at Columbia and the University of Chicago. He has taught at Northwestern University and is at present Associate Professor of Philosophy and Physical Sciences at Chicago. He is the author of *Whitehead's Philosophy of Science* (1960) and the editor of *Toward Modern Science* (1961). He has contributed an essay, "Science and Its History in the Philosophy of Whitehead," to the *Festschrift* for Charles Hartshorne (ed. Reese and Freeman, 1963).

JAMES WESLEY ROBSON was educated at the University of Washington and at Harvard. He has taught at Columbia, the University of Washington, and Lawrence College. In 1941 when his article, "Whitehead's Answer to Hume," was published, he was teaching at the University of California at Los Angeles. He is now at UCLA, as Admissions Officer and Professor of Philosophy.

RICHARD M. RORTY was educated at the University of Chicago and at Yale. He has taught at Yale and at Wellesley College and is at present Assistant Professor of Philosophy at Princeton. He has published a number of articles, including "Matter and Event" (1962), a comparative study in the metaphysics of Aristotle and Whitehead.

DONALD W. SHERBURNE was educated at Middlebury College, Oxford, and Yale. He has taught at Yale and is at present Assistant Professor of Philosophy at Vanderbilt University. He is the author of *A Whiteheadian Aesthetic:*

Some Implications of Whitehead's Metaphysical Speculation (1961) and *A Key to Whitehead's Process and Reality* (1963).

GREGORY VLASTOS was educated at Roberts College in Istanbul, Turkey, the Chicago Theological Seminary, and Harvard, where he wrote his doctoral dissertation under Whitehead's supervision. In 1937, when his paper, "Organic Categories in Whitehead," was published, he was teaching at Queen's University, Kingston, Ontario. He has also taught at Cornell, and is at present Professor of Philosophy at Princeton. He has published many papers on ancient philosophy. He was at the Institute for Advanced Study (Princeton) in 1954-1955 and was John Locke lecturer at Oxford in 1960.

DANIEL D. WILLIAMS was educated at the Universities of Denver and Chicago, at Chicago Theological Seminary, and at Columbia University. He has taught at Chicago and is at present Roosevelt Professor of Systematic Theology at Union Theological Seminary in New York. He is the author of *God's Grace and Man's Hope* (1949) and *What Present Day Theologians Are Thinking* (1952; revised edition 1959). He contributed an essay, "Deity, Monarchy, and Metaphysics: Whitehead's Critique of the Theological Tradition," to *The Relevance of Whitehead* (ed. Leclerc, 1961) and an essay, "How Does God Act?: An Essay in Whitehead's Metaphysics," for the *Festschrift* for Charles Hartshorne (ed. Reese and Freeman, 1963).

INDEX

"Abstractness," 3, 23
"Actual entities," 19, 69, 81-84, 87, 89, 91, 95-96, 102, 126, 142-143, 160, 181
  (*See* "Actual occasions")
"Actual occasions," 45, 71, 78, 130
  (*See* "Actual entities")
Alexander, Samuel, 5
Alston, William, 154n2
Anderson, A. R., 32n9
Anselm, 21
Anticipation, 59, 60
"Apostles, The" (student group at Cambridge University), 9, 17n1
Aquinas, Thomas, 24
Aristotle, 25, 72, 120, 135, 136, 146, 198; on God, 168, 169, 172
Auden, W. H., 176
Austin, J. L., 155n8
Ayer, A. J., 146, 180

Bergmann, Gustav, 155n17
Bergson, Henri, 8, 18, 19
Berkeley, George, 146
Bevan, Edwyn, 181
Bidney, David, 167n15
Bohr, Niels, 11
Boolean algebra, 27
Bradley, F. H., 2, 13, 19, 135, 138, 199
Brandt, Richard B., 185, 188n11
Brentano, Franz, 162
Bryn Mawr College, 11
Buddhism, 25, 26

Cartesian cosmology, 63, 64, 69
"Cartesian subjectivism," 146, 147, 150
Chappell, V. C., 1, 5, 19
Chiaraviglio, Lucio, 4, 127
Chisholm, R., 157n26
Christian, William A., 2, 5, 22, 23, 26n2, 128, 129
"Concrescence," 71, 73, 94, 95, 98
"Concreteness," 3, 136
Cornford, F. M., 170
"Corpuscular societies," 45
"Cosmic epochs," 64, 96, 106

Demos, Raphael, 180, 188n6
Descartes, René, 10, 35, 118, 119, 121, 134, 135, 147, 182

Dewey, John, 11, 127, 130, 194
Dummett, Michael, 153

Einstein, Albert, 11, 118
Ely, Stephen, 168, 169, 171, 172
"Enduring objects," 44, 88, 94, 106
"Epochal theory of time" 71, 73, 77
"Eternal objects," 20, 21, 45, 81, 82, 85-87, 89-92, 100, 102-116, 120, 162, 199
"Extensive abstraction," 49, 83, 84
"Extensive continuum," 50, 87, 94, 108, 121, 122, 140

"Fallacy of misplaced concreteness," 87, 147, 183
Fechner, G. T., 18, 24
"Feelings":
  conceptual, 82
  physical, 82, 85, 86
"Flat loci," 82, 83, 86

Geach, Peter, 155n17
Geometry, non-Euclidean, 49
God:
  Consequent Nature of, 20-21, 23, 24, 88, 112, 172, 173
  Primordial Nature of, 23, 24, 88, 111, 112, 172, 173
Gross, Mason W., 2, 5

Hall, Everett W., 1, 4, 166n12
Haring, Ellen S., 188n9
Hartshorne, Charles, 4, 5, 11, 133n4, 146, 154n4, 196, 198
Harvard University, 7, 10, 16
Hegel, G. W. F., 2, 3, 4, 11, 13, 116n2, 158, 159, 161, 164, 165
"Heterogeneous dialectic," 159, 164, 165, 167n15
Hiż, H., 32n9
Hocking, W. E., 24, 184
Hume, David, 2, 19, 35, 36, 39, 54-55, 57, 61-62, 63-69, 176, 180, 199

Induction, justification of, 53, 58, 63-65
"Internal relations," 60, 63, 65, 68, 158

James, William, 9, 11, 180, 181, 198

204